THE EUCHARIST IN ECUMENICAL DIALOGUE

Edited by Leonard Swidler

Kenan B. Osborne – Leonard Swidler
Maximos Aghiorgoussis – Edward J. Kilmartin
David A. Scott – Herbert J. Ryan
George A. Lindbeck – Avery Dulles
Ross Mackenzie – Christopher Kiesling
J. Robert Nelson – Gerard S. Sloyan
Arthur B. Crabtree – John A. Hardon
Eric Werner – Monika K. Hellwig

Preface by William W. Cardinal Baum

PAULIST PRESS
New York, N.Y./Paramus, N.J.

JOURNAL OF ECUMENICAL STUDIES

ISBN: 0-8091-1953-6

Published by:

Paulist Press
Editorial Office: 1865 Broadway, N.Y., N.Y. 10023
Business Office: 400 Sette Drive, Paramus, N.J. 07652

Journal of Ecumenical Studies
Temple University, Philadelphia, PA 19122

Since this book is being co-published by the *Journal of Ecumenical Studies* and Paulist Press, there is double pagination. The numbers in brackets are the running pagination for the Spring, 1976 (Volume 13, Number 2), issue of the *Journal.*

CONTENTS

PREFACE

The purpose of ecumenical dialogue is to contribute to the restoration of that full organic unity of Christians for which the Lord prayed on the night before He died for us. In my opinion, this special issue of the *Journal of Ecumenical Studies* is a significant contribution to the common theological reflection which is an indispensable preparation for the reception of this divine gift.

This issue has been prompted by the 1976 celebration of the International Eucharistic Congress in Philadelphia. The purpose of this Congress is to praise God, our Father, for the gift of His Son to us, and especially, for the continuing presence of His Risen Humanity in the Eucharist. The Eucharist is the source of divine life for the pilgrim Church. It is the anticipation of that heavenly banquet to which the teaching of the gospel invites us.

Through the celebration of the Eucharist, the Church is caught up in the movement of the Lord's sacrificial offering and there is thus established that unbreakable communion of spirit which is the fruit of the paschal mystery.

The Eucharist is thus the sacrament of unity. For this reason, we cannot approach the Eucharist without a deep yearning for the unity of all Christians. The articles in this special issue express the views of particular Christian and Jewish scholars. Still, the insights contained in these pages, and the fruitful dialogue to which they witness, will be a great joy to us who will be ardently praying for this unity during the celebration of the Eucharistic Congress.

William W. Cardinal Baum
Archbishop of Washington, DC

EUCHARIST IN THEOLOGICAL PERSPECTIVE

Kenan B. Osborne

PRECIS

Contemporary Roman Catholic eucharistic theology is not monolithic, but open-ended, having moved from the scholastic-Tridentine framework that dominated for 300 years to the present.

Three influences have led to a rethinking of Roman Catholic eucharistic theology: science and its understanding of substance, phenomenology and its concern with meaning, and the ecumenical dialogue. The areas around which change in thinking is taking place are: the expanded notion of the sacrament, the meaning of presence, and the social and cultural dimension of the Roman Catholic Church's sacramental life.

The result is a considerable expansion of areas of ecumenical discussion on topics interrelated with the Eucharist.

Kenan B. Osborne, O.F.M. (Roman Catholic), A.B., San Luis Rey (CA) College, S.T.B., Old Mission Theological Seminary (Santa Barbara), S.T.L., Catholic University of America, Dr. Theol., Ludwig-Maximilians-Universität (Munich), is Professor of Systematic Theology at the Graduate Theological Union and President and Dean of the Franciscan School of Theology in Berkeley. An associate editor of the *Journal of Ecumenical Studies*, his publications include several articles and the books, *New Being* and *Christ Today*.

CONTEMPORARY UNDERSTANDINGS OF THE EUCHARIST
A Survey of Catholic Thinking

Kenan B. Osborne

All the articles in this issue of the *Journal of Ecumenical Studies* focus on some ecumenical aspect of contemporary eucharistic theology, as this is found within the author's own tradition. Such a presentation is then picked up in dialogical fashion by a Roman Catholic theologian, who explores further ramifications of its ecumenical possibilities. As a result, this introductory article centers more simply on the general trends in contemporary Roman Catholic eucharistic theology which have emerged within the last few decades. What follows, then, can only be a brief survey, not an in-depth discussion, and it is hoped that the readers will see that on this matter contemporary Roman Catholic theology is not monolithically structured according to a scholastic-Tridentine blueprint, but rather has seriously moved to a much more open-ended framework. It is also hoped that the readers of this survey will come to understand, at least in a general sort of way, those precise areas around which Catholic theologians are attempting to rethink the theology of the Eucharist.

At the outset, however, it seems wise to indicate certain themes which will not be treated. The first of these themes is the renewal within Catholic eucharistic liturgy. Undoubtedly, major changes have taken place during the last decades as regards the Catholic celebration of the Eucharist, for example, the change from Latin to the vernacular, the deemphasis on private celebration and the emphasis on communal concelebration, the development of a variety of eucharistic prayers, etc. Committees of theologians and other experts worked long and hard at each state of this renewal. They formulated their own criteria, out of which they evaluated each of the proposed liturgical changes. Indeed, it is fair to say that such committees were working out of a presupposed eucharistic theology, but it would be far beyond the scope of this introductory essay to enter into the liturgical renewal as such. Nonetheless, the silence of this essay on the matter of liturgy in no way intends to indicate that a theology of the Eucharist can be understood apart from its concrete, existential liturgical celebration.

The second theme which will not be treated in this survey is the theme of priestly ministry. Clearly, the theology of priestly ministry is deeply interconnected with one's theology of Eucharist, and this interconnection was highlighted in the development of the many conferences held between Lutheran and Catholic scholars during the years 1965-1974. The topic discussed at the very first Lutheran-Catholic dialogue was simply the Nicene Creed. This topic was selected "because it is a basic statement of faith for both traditions, arises out of the post-Apostolic period, and affords some clues to an understanding of the development of dogma in the life of the church."[1] This initial conference

---

[1] *The Status of the Nicene Creed as Dogma of the Church,* published jointly by

worked so well that a second conference was held in 1966 focusing on one selected item out of that same creed, namely "one Baptism for the remission of sins."[2] However, this topic of baptism brought the question of the relationship between baptism and Eucharist into high relief, since baptism as an initiation rite is intended to welcome the newly baptized into the full life of the Christian community. Hans Otto Wolber, a German Protestant bishop, expresses the situation with great clarity: "Through baptism Christians are basically invited to the table of the Lord."[3] One wonders, accordingly, what grounds there might be for Christian communities, including Roman Catholicism, to recognize on the one hand the validity of the baptism in another tradition, but on the other hand refuse such baptized Christians access to the Eucharist. This is surely one of the underlying reasons why the third conference of Lutheran and Catholic scholars, held between 1966 and 1967, tackled the more difficult question, ecumenically speaking, on the Eucharist.[4] These discussions, though more thorny than the other two, led the participants to consider as the subsequent theme the question of intercommunion, but a weekend conference on the matter clearly indicated that the question of ministry had to be confronted, with the result that the conferences throughout 1968 and 1969 dealt with the theme "Eucharist and Ministry."[5] This concrete example indicates that a theology of Eucharist and a theology of priestly ministry are intimately interwoven. Nonetheless, this introductory essay will not address the theme of contemporary Catholic thought on priestly ministry, but once more such a silence should in no way indicate that a satisfactory eucharistic theology can be developed apart from its relationship to a theology of the ministerial priesthood.

These, then, are the two areas which unfortunately will not be treated in this introductory essay. Let us turn now to the changes in contemporary eucharistic theology within Catholicism, indicating first of all the reasons why a change of thinking began to occur. Secondly, we will consider the major areas around which contemporary Catholic eucharistic theology revolves.

The Reasons for Change

It is well known that in the period of scholasticism, roughly the twelfth and

representatives of the U.S.A. National Committee of the Lutheran World Federation and the Bishops' Commission for Ecumenical Affairs (Washington: NCWC, 1965), p. 1.

[2] Paul C. Empie and William W. Baum, eds., *One Baptism for the Remission of Sins: Lutherans and Catholics in Dialogue*, vol. 2 (Washington: NCWC, 1966).

[3] "Jahresbericht 1971/1972 des Leitenden Bischofs der Vereinigten Evangelisch-Lutherischen Kirche in Deutschland," in R. Mumm and M. Lienhard, eds., *Eucharistische Gastfreundschaft* (Kassel: Johannes Stauda Verlag, 1974), p. 60.

[4] *The Eucharist as Sacrifice: Lutherans and Catholics in Dialogue*, vol. 3 (Washington: NCWC, 1968).

[5] *Eucharist and Ministry: Lutherans and Catholics in Dialogue*, vol. 4 (Washington: NCWC, 1970).

thirteenth centuries, and most significantly in the writings of St. Thomas Aquinas, St. Bonaventure, and John Duns Scotus, sacramental theology, including that of the Eucharist, received a fairly systematic format, and terms such as matter, form, cause, effect, and transubstantiation received acceptability and eventually became quite standard in Roman Catholic thought. In the sixteenth century the Council of Trent overlayed this kind of thinking with a quite official endorsement. In the centuries following this council Catholic theology on the Eucharist operated generally within this scholastic-Tridentine framework. Burkhard Neunheuser, in his historical study on the Eucharist within Roman Catholic thought from the middle ages to the present, *Eucharistie in Mittelalter und Neuzeit,*[6] surveys the situation from the end of the sixteenth century down to the beginning of the twentieth century in a single page. As pioneers of some change he cites the distinguished work of such theologians as L. Billot, S.J. (d. 1931); M. de la Taille, S.J. (d. 1933); Odo Casels, O.S.B. (d. 1948); and A. Vonier (d. 1938).[7] This indicates that for a good three hundred years no clearly significant change took place within Roman Catholicism regarding eucharistic theology. What work was done in those centuries, important as it might have been, operated totally within the scholastic-Tridentine framework. It must also be said that even the scholars Neunheuser cites did not really approach the Eucharist from a position outside of that same framework.

Actually, it was a non-theological area that forced other theologians than those mentioned above to reconsider the Catholic teaching on the Eucharist. This non-theological source was science, more particularly, physics. Contemporary physics, with its molecular, atomic, and subatomic structures, with Heisenberg's theory of quantum mechanics and Einstein's theory of relativity, raised some fundamental questions regarding the meaning of the term "substance." A few Catholic theologians such as J. Ternus, A. Maltha, and F. Unterkircher,[8] addressed themselves to this issue in the years just preceding the Second World War. Not much really developed from this initial consideration. After the Second World War the issue was raised again, particularly in the exchange of articles between F. Selvaggi, S.J., and C. Colombo. The fundamental issue raised in all these discussions is certainly not trivial, and this issue has two aspects: first of all there is the question whether or not the theologian is so autonomous in his or her work that he or she need not enter into dialogue with contemporary scientific modes of thought. The second question is equally important: is or is not the presence of Christ in the Eucharist related in some way to our physical reality, and, if not, then are we free to describe this presence purely within metaphysical or symbolical terms?[9]

---

[6]*Eucharistie in Mittelalter und Neuzeit* (Freiburg: Herder, 1963).

[7]Ibid., pp. 64-65. Johannes Betz says practically the same thing in his article "Eucharistie" in *Lexikon für Theologie und Kirche,* vol. 3, pp. 1150-1151.

[8]For a detailed bibliography of this entire question, cf. E. Schillebeeckx, *The Eucharist* (New York: Sheed and Ward, 1968), pp. 95-96.

[9]Cf. Richard G. Cipolla, "Selvaggi Revisited: Transubstantiation and Contemporary Science," *Theological Studies* 35 (December, 1974): 667-691.

The positions which both Selvaggi and Colombo took on this matter appear to us today somewhat ridiculous, but they do highlight the division of thinking on the fundamental issues mentioned above. For his part, Selvaggi affirmed the necessity of theologians entering into straightforward dialogue with contemporary science and equally affirmed that the presence of Christ in the Eucharist relates to the physical reality of our world in some way or another. However, when he went on further to specify the mode of eucharistic presence, based on these affirmations, he became ridiculous. He argued that since the basic substance within bread or wine consists of thousands of molecular structures, there are correspondingly the same number of transubstantiations.

Colombo, on his part, took an opposite stand and in his reply to Selvaggi stated that theologians are really dealing with a metaphysical reality quite beyond the parameters of contemporary physics. This position is affirming both that the theologian does not have to engage in serious dialogue with contemporary physics, and that the eucharistic presence can adequately be described in purely metaphysical terms. Such a position tends equally to become ludicrous.

Of itself, this Selvaggi-Colombo debate, that was joined, of course, by other theologians of that day, led nowhere. Nonetheless, the issue that it raised influenced in no small degree a number of other theologians who eventually became associated with the term "transsignification." We will come back to these men momentarily.

A second major influence for a change of approach to eucharistic theology within Roman Catholicism is the philosophical movement called phenomenology. Phenomenology is more a method and a movement than a system of philosophy, and its primary concern is that of meaning, particularly meaning within a human context. More important than the question of what a thing is in itself or substantially is the question of what it means within its relationship to human existence and the way in which we from our human standpoint can unlock this meaning. The question of meaning was posted most strongly by the French philosopher Maurice Merleau-Ponty,[10] and the question of interpretation or hermeneutics most pointedly by Paul Ricoeur.[11] This philosophical style, phenomenology, finds its echo in the efforts of some Catholic theologians in their discussions on the Eucharist, particularly in their efforts to situate the Eucharist not in a physical or metaphysical framework but within the framework of human existence. This will be more evident when we discuss the major areas of thought around which such contemporary thinking revolves.

A third causative factor for a change in thinking derives directly from ecumenical dialogue. Such dialogue has forced theologians to be more cautious in

---

[10]Cf. Maurice Merleau-Ponty, *Phenomenology of Perception,* trans. by Colin Smith (New York: Humanities Press, 1962); idem, *Signs,* trans. by Richard C. McCleary (Evanston: Northwestern University Press, 1964); and idem, *The Visible and the Invisible,* ed. by Claude Lefort and trans. by Alphonso Lingis (Evanston: Northwestern University Press, 1968).

[11]Cf. among the many works by Paul Ricoeur, *The Conflict of Interpretations: Essays in Hermeneutics,* ed. by Don Ihde (Evanston: Northwestern University Press, 1974).

the use of terms such as transubstantiation, to be more open to the insights of other traditions, and to rethink the presuppositions out of which one theologizes.

Other causative factors, such as the rise of historical consciousness, the development of philosophical pluralism, the confrontation of the church with the third world, could likewise be enumerated. In fact all of the causative factors which gave rise to the change of theological thinking within the total gamut of Catholic theology and which were so dramatically highlighted by the Second Vatican Council could be enumerated, but the three instances above undoubtedly played the most significant role as regards Catholic Eucharist theology specifically.

The Major Areas of Change

In my opinion there are three major areas around which the change in Catholic thinking on the Eucharist revolves: first, there is the healthy expansion of the very concept of sacrament; secondly, there is the studied discussion on the very meaning of presence, particularly interpersonal human presence; and thirdly, there is the social and cultural dimension involved in the church's sacramental life. Let us consider these three points individually.

1. The Expanded Notion of Sacrament

One of the important and truly exciting gains of contemporary eucharistic theology is the expanded notion of sacrament, which focuses sharply on the interrelationship among Christ, the church, and the Eucharist, i.e., among Christology, ecclesiology, and eucharistic, or for that matter sacramental, theology. In this turn of events, Karl Rahner, S.J.,[12] and Edward Schillebeeckx, O.P.,[13] led the way. In their view, to understand the meaning of the Eucharist as sacrament one must first understand to some degree that Jesus Christ himself, in his humanness, is a sacrament, indeed, the original sacrament, and that the church as well is a sacrament. Since Christ in his humanness is the original sacrament, one must first appreciate how his humanness is a concrete historical sacrament or sign of God's loving and forgiving stance toward all men and women. Schillebeeckx puts it in these words: "The man Jesus, as the personal visible realization of divine grace of redemption, is *the* sacrament, the primordial sacrament, because this man, the Son of God himself, is intended by the Father to be in his humanity the only way to the actuality of redemption."[14] This humanness of Jesus is the fundamental visible sign to all of us that God forgives and loves, which in general terms is what Christianity has understood by redemption.

---

[12]Cf. Karl Rahner, *The Church and the Sacraments* (New York: Herder and Herder, 1963).

[13]Cf. E. Schillebeeckx, *Christ the Sacrament of the Encounter with God* (New York: Sheed and Ward, 1963).

[14]Ibid., p. 15.

Secondly, the church itself must be seen as a sign or sacrament. It is, under this aspect, the sign or sacrament of the Christ-event itself and all that it involves for all men and women, both within the Christian community and without. As a sacrament the church is saying something to all the world: what this same world, now redeemed by the Christ-event, fundamentally means.

It is against this expanded notion of sacrament, expanded in the sense that the term sacrament is no longer restricted to the seven sacramental rites of the Catholic Church, that these same rites take on an added dimension and are given a broader context. Of note is the fact that several documents on various sacraments, which were issued by the Vatican, have followed this procedure, thus officially endorsing such an approach. For instance, in the document on priestly ministry, *Presbyterorum Ordines,* which was promulgated by the Second Vatican Council, the first section (n. 2) addresses itself to the priesthood of Christ, and then to the priesthood of all believers, and only after this to the ministerial priest. A similar progression can be seen in the document issued in 1972 on the renewal of the sacrament of penance, *Ordo Paenitentiae.* In the introductory section, called the *Praenotanda,* the Christ-event itself is first treated as a reconciliation-event; next the church-event is described as a reconciliation-event; and only then is the sacrament of penance considered in its role as a reconciliation-event.

This progression—Christ, church, sacrament—tends to give a richer and deeper context to the entire question of individual sacraments, including the Eucharist. It also stresses the point that only on the basis of a theology of Christ is a theology of the church meaningful, and likewise that only on the basis of a theology of Christ *and* a theology of the church is a theology of the Eucharist meaningful. Moreover, it reminds us that what one says within the context of eucharistic theology has presuppositions deriving from the theologies on Christ and the church. This is a boon for both the methodology and the content of eucharistic thinking,[15] and it has placed the Eucharist within a framework which is less narrow than that of scholastic-Tridentine theology.

2. The Studied Discussion on the Meaning of Presence

The renewed interest and research on the phenomenon of human interpersonal presence which plays such a centralizing role in the thinking of those theologians who eventually came to be associated in some degree or another with the term "transsignification" is, likewise, an area of major theological discussion. This discussion is important not merely to a few Catholic theologians, but is found in the works of theologians throughout continental Europe, England, and the United States: J. de Baciocchi, S.M.; A. Vanneste; L. Scheffczyk; B. Welte; P. Schoonenberg, S.J.; E. Schillebeeckx, O.P.; L. Smits,

---

[15]Cf. K. B. Osborne, "Methodology and the Christian Sacraments," *Worship* 48 (November, 1974): 536-549.

O.F.M.; C. Davis; and J. Powers, S.J., to mention only a few.[16]

The point of departure in this approach is to articulate eucharistic theology within the framework of human meaning and not within the framework of physical structures. The Eucharist is indeed a meal and involves food and drink, bread and wine. However, it is not simply the physical structures of bread and wine which provide the basis for the sacrament, but rather the total complex of the meal itself. Even to say, however, that the meal is the sacrament and not simply the elements of bread and wine is insufficient. The phenomenon of "meal" must be further described, for a meal is people-eating-together. Perhaps a small example will help illustrate the thrust of this approach. In the German language there are two words for eating: *fressen* and *essen*. *Fressen*, however, is used only for animals, while *essen* is used only in the context of human eating. "Der Hund frisst, aber der Mensch isst." The dog eats (*fressen*) but the human eats (*essen*). In the genius of this language there is a distinction and difference between animal ingestion of food and human ingestion of food, and it is along this distinction between the truly human or anthropological and the physical or biological that these theologians begin their approach. Sacraments involve essentially *human* action.

Even with this distinction, the approach is not clarified enough, for one must proceed to unpack the dynamics of human eating together even further, indicating the progression between some sort of automat or quick-food eating through ordinary family meals to those special meals which as we experience humanly at Thanksgiving, Christmas, or Easter. Not all human eating together is an equally meaningful or personal experience, and one must seek to discover those factors which make a festive meal with close relatives and friends so significant. Such factors far exceed the mere quality of food or the time of preparation; they involve, more fundamentally, the factors of personal interrelation which enter into this highly significant situation of people-eating-together.

This, of course, raises the second aspect of such an approach, an aspect which deals not with human eating but with human presence. Once again this phenomenon must be unpacked as far as its dynamism is concerned, and the entire gamut of interpersonal human presence must be considered, progressing from the autonomous juxtaposition of strangers on a subway, to the presence people open themselves to when they are with casual friends and business associates, down to the intimate presence of two people such as husband and wife. In this view, presence is not an either-or, but a more-or-less situation. In this regard, presence must be seen as involving two moments: first, there is the depth of presence which one is willing to offer to another; secondly, there is the depth of acceptance by the other of this presence which is being offered. Only when personal presence is offered and accepted does one have a genuine situation of

---

[16]For a partial bibliography of these theologians, cf. J. M. Powers, *Eucharistic Theology* (New York: Herder and Herder, 1967), pp. 180-183; also, Schillebeeckx, *The Eucharist*, pp. 107-121.

interpersonal presence. Should it be offered but not accepted it would be an incomplete situation.

The next stage in the development of this approach has to do with the *manner* in which this offer of human presence is made. This generally occurs through some sign or symbol: a handshake, a smile, a word of greeting, or, as the presence becomes more intense and more intimate, through a kiss, an embrace, or sexual union. All of these actions, in some degree or another, attempt to indicate one's relative closeness to another. A kiss might signify no more than a courteous greeting, as is the case in some cultures; in quite other circumstances, the kiss can signify deep intimacy and personal involvement. A ring can signify a marketable value as it lies in the window of a jeweler; the same ring when used in a marriage ceremony can signify something far deeper than a given price. Such actions and things, when brought into the structures of human communication, can take on new meanings, or better they pass from one set of meanings to another set of meanings, and this is what is meant fundamentally by "transsignification."

In many of the writings of the authors mentioned above stress is placed on the fact that the ultimate meaning of something or some action depends on the will of God. It is God who says what something really means. The meaning God intends for it constitutes its own ultimate meaning. In the Eucharist God has transferred the meaning from mere food, mere communal eating, mere table fellowship to the giving of God's very self in and through the sacramental presence of the divine Word incarnate.

Unfortunately, the above could only be a rough sketch of the main outlines of this contemporary approach to the Eucharist by Catholic theologians. The sketch needs to be fleshed out much more, but hopefully it indicates that Catholic scholars have not approached the Eucharist from the standpoint of matter and form, metaphysical substance and physical accidents, but from an entirely different framework.

3. The Social and Cultural Dimension

Finally, an area of change that has attracted the thinking of a number of contemporary scholars is the social and cultural dimension involved in the church's sacramental life. For the English-speaking public, the book, *The Sacraments Today*, by Juan Segundo, S.J., comes readily to mind.[17] This book is one in a series of five volumes put together by Segundo in collaboration with the staff of the Peter Faber Center in Montevideo, Uruguay. Their approach to theology, evidenced in this series, is rooted in the contemporary faith-in-crisis situation, struggles to make the message of the church meaningful within a social and cultural context that is characterized basically as dehumanizing, and essentially takes account of the world, not just the church, in which our contemporary generation lives.

---

[17] Juan L. Segundo, S.J., *The Sacraments Today* (New York: Orbis, 1974).

Segundo, of course, is allied to some degree to the entire movement described as "liberation theology." In this connection both the church and its sacraments are meant to be liberating elements, basically elements which liberate men and women from any and all dehumanizing factors. Segundo, in his book, does not address himself, except by way of example here and there, to the question of the Eucharist; his focus is on the whole scope of sacramentality within the church's life, and accordingly his statements are often quite general in nature.

In the World Council of Churches between 1967 and the present a document on the Eucharist has gone through many stages of revision, but from the very start one of the sections of this document considers the Eucharist in its relationship to the church's mission to the world.[18] The thrust of Segundo's approach and the vistas that are intimated by this document of the World Council of Churches coincide very nicely. The document states: "Reconciled in the eucharist, the members of the body of Christ are called to be servants of reconciliation amongst men and witnesses of the joy of resurrection" (n. 25). Segundo struggles to point out in more detail precisely how the sacraments, and in this instance the Eucharist, bring about this servanthood of reconciliation and this witnessing to the joy of resurrection particularly to people who find the death-forces stronger in their lives than the life-forces, who find themselves in a socio-cultural situation which tends to deny them life rather than enrich their lives.

This movement of liberation theology, particularly as it is expressed in the volumes from the Peter Faber Center, is still within the first stages of its growth, but little by little within Catholic circles it is causing scholars to address the sacraments against the background of contemporary dehumanization.

Such, then, are the major areas around which the change of thinking on the Eucharist among Catholic scholars is now revolving. The above, of course, is merely a sketch of those areas which, in my opinion, have been most causative for the change and have focused the lion's share of research and discussion. It would be foolish to say that contemporary Catholic scholarship on the Eucharist has reached final answers of any kind; however, it would be justified to say that these same Catholic scholars have forwarded contemporary eucharistic theology in no small measure. If one considers the expanded parameters within which these scholars are now working, one can see that the areas for true ecumenical discussion have also been expanded, and hopefully through the collaboration of scholars of sundry dimensions our total Christian theology of the Eucharist will more and more give evidence that we do have one Lord, one faith, and one Eucharist.

---

[18]Cf. *One Baptism, One Eucharist and a Mutually Recognized Ministry* (La Concorde, Lausanne: World Council of Churches, 1975), p. 23.

Study and Discussion Questions

1. How does Osborne characterize the 300-year period from the scholastic-Tridentine period to the beginnings of modern Roman Catholic eucharistic theology? Discuss.
2. What influence did contemporary physics have on Roman Catholic teaching on the Eucharist?
' 3. Do you agree with Osborne's assessment of the Selvaggi-Colombo debate? Discuss.
4. What effect did the philosophical movement of phenomenology have on contemporary Roman Catholic eucharistic theology?
5. What does Osborne mean by "the expanded notion of sacrament" and what is the bearing of this notion on current Roman Catholic eucharistic theology?
6. According to the author, in what way is the "social and cultural dimension" of the sacraments of importance in contemporary Roman Catholic eucharistic theology? Discuss.
7. What links do you find between the aspirations of third-world peoples and a theology of the Eucharist? Discuss.
8. The author mentions the ecumenical dialogue as having greatly influenced Roman Catholic eucharistic theology. Discuss this point with specific reference to the dialogue with the Eastern Orthodox, Episcopalian, and Lutheran churches.

ORTHODOX-CATHOLIC DIALOGUE

Maximos Aghiorgoussis—Edward J. Kilmartin

PRECIS

The Orthodox approach to intercommunion rests upon the ecclesiological implications of the Eucharist. The acceptance or rejection of the sacraments of another church, including its Eucharist, depends on the acceptance or rejection of the true ecclesiality of that church. No official act of the Eastern Orthodox Church has affirmed such "ecclesial status" of other Christian churches.

The author reviews the practice of the ancient church and of the church in the Byzantine period and in modern times. Among contemporary Orthodox views on intercommunion, ranging from the more liberal to the more restrictive, the author holds a "middle view." Officially, the Roman Catholic Church has recognized the ecclesiality of the Orthodox Church and offers communion to the Orthodox. The Orthodox Church has not yet officially granted permission to its members to accept the Roman Catholic offer.

There are obstacles still preventing a full and visible communion among Christians of East and West, among them the need to work out differences in Trinitarian and ecclesiological doctrines. The author hopes for a reassessment by the Roman Catholic Church of its theology of the Holy Spirit and its understanding of the meaning and functioning of the papacy.

Kilmartin summarizes the way in which the Orthodox-Roman Catholic consultations have dealt with the Eucharist since 1965. The 1969 "Agreed Statement on the Eucharist" recognized the present impossibility of eucharistic sharing. Kilmartin finds this Statement important for what it omits as well as for what it contains: it omits mention of the need of an explicit *epiclesis* and mention of the function of the eucharistic narration, and contains no use of the term "transubstantiation," thus, according to Kilmartin, making a needed distinction between dogmas of faith and theologies.

The fundamental question is the "ecclesial context" of the Eucharist, i.e., the willingness of each church to recognize the full ecclesiality of the other and the consequent existence of the sacraments (including the Eucharist) in the other church. The Orthodox have found this more difficult to acknowledge with respect to Roman Catholicism than vice versa.

Several theological issues provide the context of current discussions, including papal jurisdiction as related to Orthodox pastoral office, and the meaning of the priesthood in its representative role. The possibility of Roman Catholics looking favorably on the ordination of women is creating some uneasiness in Eastern Orthodoxy.

Maximos E. Aghiorgoussis (Greek Orthodox), Bacc. Phil., Higher Institute of Philosophy (Louvain), S.Th.D., School of Theology, University of Louvain, is Associate Professor of Systematic Theology at Holy Cross Greek Orthodox Theological School in Brookline, MA, following several years as a pastor. His publications include numerous articles on ecumenical theology, most recently in *The Greek Orthodox Theological Review* (1976, No. 1 and 2).

Edward J. Kilmartin, S.J. (Roman Catholic), holds advanced degrees in philosophy and physical chemistry, and has done doctoral studies at the Gregorian University (Rome). He is Professor of Theology at Weston College, Cambridge, MA, and presently Visiting Professor at the University of Notre Dame. Executive Secretary of the National Bishops' Committee for Dialogue with Orthodox and Other Eastern Churches, his recent articles have appeared in *Theological Studies* (1974 and 1975).

THE HOLY EUCHARIST IN ECUMENICAL DIALOGUE: AN ORTHODOX VIEW

Maximos Aghiorgoussis

With a few rare exceptions, Orthodox theologians uphold the age-old practice of the Eastern Orthodox Church of rejecting any form of the so-called "intercommunion," or better, "sharing of communion" among Christian churches and communities. In the light of the acceptance and practice of sacramental sharing in the West and because of their unfamiliarity with the doctrine and theology of the Eastern Orthodox Church, many Western Christians ask the question: Why does the Christian East so staunchly oppose "intercommunion"? To answer this question, it seems to me that the following items should be considered: (1) the ecclesiological implications of the Holy Eucharist; (2) the way the Orthodox view the Eucharist of the other Christians; and, finally, (3) the obstacles which still remain in the way of full and visible communion among Christians.

I

The Orthodox-Roman Catholic Consultation in the United States states the following in an agreed statement on the church:

> The independent existence of the local church is expressed best in its eucharistic celebration. The sacramental celebration of the Lord's presence in the midst of his people through the working of the Spirit both proclaims the most profound realization of the church and realizes what it proclaims in the measure that the community opens itself to the Spirit.[1]

This statement reflects a doctrine which is central in Orthodox ecclesiology: the Holy Eucharist makes the church, presupposes fullness of ecclesiality, and is the manifestation of this fullness.[2] A given local church is a concrete, complete, and unique manifestation of the one church of Christ, only when the following conditions are fulfilled:

(1) The particular church celebrates in continuity with the apostolic church, with which it shares in the same faith and doctrine the one Eucharist of Christ and of the church.

---

[1] Orthodox-Roman Catholic Consultation, "Agreed Statement on the Church," in *Diakonia* 5 (1970): 72.

[2] See Nicholas Afanassieff, "The Church which Presides in Love," in *The Primacy of Peter in the Orthodox Church,* trans. by Katharine Farrer (London, 1963), pp. 73-76. See also idem, "L'Eucharistie, principal lien entre les Catholiques et les Orthodoxes," *Irénikon* 38 (1965): 338-339.

(2) The regional church celebrates the one Eucharist of the church in an ecclesial context. What is required here is not only the fullness of apostolic faith, but also the direct apostolic succession of this Christian community with regard to the whole range of church life, including uninterrupted succession of ordained priesthood.

(3) In celebrating the one Eucharist of Christ in continuity with the one church, a regional church manifests the fullness of ecclesiality and witnesses to it together with all the other local churches, which share in that same fullness.

The question arises for the Orthodox: In what measure do the churches and ecclesial communities not in communion with the Eastern Orthodox Church fulfill the above requirements? If they do fulfill these requirements, is it at the same level with the Eastern Orthodox Church? The Orthodox feel that both of these questions have to be answered in a positive way before they can envisage communion with any given church.

II

The acceptance or the rejection of the sacraments of a given church depends upon the acceptance or the rejection of its "ecclesiality." However, there is no official act proclaimed by the Eastern Orthodox Church which affirms the "ecclesial status" of other Christian churches and communities.

In the meantime, a general practice has been established within all Eastern Orthodox churches, though the details of this practice vary. We will examine in this study the facts of this practice, first in the ancient church, and then in the Byzantine and modern periods. We will consider the different interpretations of these facts. Finally, we will examine recent developments in the practice of the Eastern Orthodox Church.

(1) A constant rejection of the sacraments and especially of the Eucharist of those who are "outside the church," both schismatics and heretics, can be seen in the practice of the ancient church.

The *Apostolic Canons* (beginning of the fourth century) use very strong terms in condemning the sacraments of heretics: "If a bishop, priest, or deacon worships together with heretics, let him be excommunicated; if he accepts their orders, let him be unfrocked (canon 45). . . . If a bishop or a priest accepts the baptism or the eucharist of heretics, let him be unfrocked. For what agreement is there between Christ and the Devil? Or what is there to share between a faithful person and an unbeliever?" (canon 46).[3]

The Council of Laodicea (360) prohibits heretics from worshipping in Orthodox churches (canon 6). It accepts heretics back into the church and allows them Holy Communion after they anathematize their heresy and are

---

[3] See the Greek text of these canons in Ioannis Karmiris, *Ta Dogmatika kai Symbolika Mnemeia tēs Orthodoxou Katholikēs Ekklēsias,* vol. 1 (Athens, 1960), p. 253.

chrismated again. Also, the council prohibits common worship with schismatics and heretics (canon 33).[4]

Saint Basil (+379) totally rejects the baptism of heretics. They do not have the Spirit. They cannot give what they do not have. Heretics are to be treated as pagans. As for the baptism of schismatics, Saint Basil accepts it because they still belong to the church (*ek tēs Ekklēsias*; canon 1).[5]

The Second Ecumenical Council (381) is very lenient in receiving back the heretics to the church. A confession of faith and an anathema against all heresies is enough for their full acceptance into the church's communion through chrismation. Only those heretics are to be rebaptized who have erroneous practices and doctrines concerning the Christian baptism(canon 7).[6]

Timothy of Alexandria (+385) prohibits the acceptance of Arians and other heretics into the Holy Communion of the church, unless they repent and repudiate their heresy (Question 9 and Answer).[7]

Theophilos of Alexandria (+412) is lenient towards those who received the communion of Arians in good faith, but reprimands those who received that communion knowingly (canon 2).[8]

Finally, the Council *In Trullo* (Quinisext, 691-692) stipulates the way of receiving back into the church's communion several categories of heretics, going from a simple confession of faith to rebaptizing (canon 95).[9]

On the basis of the above facts, we reach the following conclusions: (a) In principle, heretics are not in any way members of the church. Their sacraments are vehemently rejected. (b) Also in principle, schismatics may be considered as members of the church. Their baptism and priesthood are accepted, especially when they return to the church. Their Eucharist is not accepted unless they join the Catholic Church. (c) Leniency (*oikonomia*) may be applied according to the specific needs of certain groups of people, in order to facilitate their return to the church.[10]

(2) As far as both the Byzantine and the modern periods are concerned, we see principles similar to those of the ancient church applied to the Christian West by the Eastern Orthodox Church. Yet, there is one difference with the practice of the ancient church: the Western brothers and sisters never were officially

---

[4]Ibid., pp. 256-258.

[5]Ibid., pp. 275-276.

[6]Ibid., pp. 133.

[7]Ibid., p. 279.

[8]Ibid., p. 282.

[9]Ibid., p. 235.

[10]See more on this in my paper, "Membership of Schismatics and Heretics in the Ancient Church," submitted to the Orthodox-Roman Catholic Consultation, New York, May 19, 1970.

qualified as schismatics or heretics by a general council.[11]

It is the general practice of the church in the East not to condemn the Latin West, in spite of increasing diversification as a result of the "estrangement" between Eastern and Western Christianity. This kind of attitude, which finally prevails in the East, is expressed in two documents provided by an Orthodox prelate at the beginning of the thirteenth century.

Demetrios Chomatenos, Archbishop of Bulgaria, writes to Konstantinos Kabasilas, Archbishop of Dyrrachion, that we can forgive the cultural differences of the Latins. What we cannot forgive is the falsification of the dogma of the Fathers with the addition of the *Filioque* clause to the creed. "Whoever forgives this, is unforgivable" (*ho synchōrōn, asynchōrētos*). Concerning the Latin Eucharist, he continues, we cannot consider it common bread, in spite of the unleavened bread they use. However, the fact that their communion is true (valid), does not mean that we can receive their communion. We cannot abandon our respective customs and reestablish communion with Latins. "But, as they consider our gifts as holy gifts, we also consider their gifts to be holy."[12]

Another text from the same author indicates an even more lenient position current in the East at that time together with that of rejection of the Latin communion. Demetrios speaks of the position (which today we would qualify as liberal) taken by "intellectual people" in the East concerning the giving of Orthodox communion to Latin soldiers who were asking for it. According to them, communion should be given to these Latin soldiers: their church has never been condemned as heretical by a general council. The principle of leniency (*oikonomia*) can be applied here, to "gain the brother for whom our common Lord and Savior shed His blood."[13] This kind of attitude was not only that of *Latinophrones* (friends of the Latins), but also reflects a genuine Orthodox concern toward the West, in applying the old principle of *oikonomia* for the purpose of gaining the brothers and sisters for whom Christ died.

(3) Three interpretations of the practice of the Eastern Orthodox Church concerning the sharing of communion with other churches are given recently by three prominent canonists. They represent three tendencies within Orthodoxy concerning this same subject.

The late Hamilcar Alivizatos, Professor of Canon Law at the University of Athens, is the representative of the liberal view. The sacraments of the other churches, he says, are valid *per se* and not because the Orthodox Church vali-

[11]The local synod of Constantinople in 1976, which declared the Roman Catholic, Lutheran, Anglican, and Calvinistic baptism to be null and void, does not have the authority of a general council. The reasons for this condemnation were pastoral, not theological. This act was practically forgotten as soon as it accomplished its purpose, although it was never formally annulled. See Ieronymos Kotsonis, *Problēmata tēs Ekklēsiastikēs Oikonomias* (Athens, 1957), pp. 189-192.

[12]See G. Rallis and M. Potlis, *Syntagma tōn theiōn kai ierōn kanonōn,* vol. 5 (Athens, 1855), pp. 430-434.

[13]Ibid., vol. 5, pp. 435-436.

dates them. They are the work of the Holy Spirit, present in the other churches, as in the Orthodox Church. In the case of an earnest need, as far and as much as the church involved has a valid priesthood and has the same doctrine concerning the Eucharist as the Orthodox Church, "intercommunion" can be practiced in both senses: Orthodox can receive the communion of others, and they can give their communion to others.[14] I would agree with the late well-respected professor and ecumenist with regard to the application of *oikonomia* to the sacraments of non-Orthodox *per se*. But I would disagree with him concerning "intercommunion." In his love for the brother and sister for whom Christ shed His blood, Professor Alivizatos failed to consider communion in its aspect as manifestation of ecclesial fullness and commitment to the Lord as the Truth of God. If there are doubts about the presence of the total truth of Christ in a given church, it would be an act of disobedience to the Lord (the Truth) to participate in the Eucharist of this church.

Ieronymos Kotsonis, former Professor of Canon Law at the University of Thessalonike and former Archbishop of Athens, is the representative of the ultra-conservative view. The former Primate of Greece applies the ancient canons regarding schismatics and heretics to contemporary Christians. The latter, not being in communion with Orthodoxy, do not have the Spirit, who works exclusively within the canonical boundaries of the Orthodox Church. Both from the point of view of leniency (*oikonomia*) and strictness (*akribeia*), the sacraments of the others, including the Eucharist, are null and void. The only instance where *oikonomia* (or even *akribeia*) can be applied is the case of a "return" to Orthodoxy.[15] With all due respect to the prelate, I feel that this kind of position is very difficult to sustain. It is almost a blasphemy against the Holy Spirit not to acknowledge its workings among other Christians. To apply old categories to contemporary Christians is an anachronism. It was already an anachronism for the Byzantines.[16] It is even more so today.

The late Father Nicholas Afanassieff, another Professor of Canon Law, who taught at the Saint Sergius Russian Orthodox Institute in Paris, France, is the exponent of the realistic position with regard to the Eucharist of the other Christians. Father Afanassieff feels that the same Eucharist is celebrated on the Orthodox and the Roman Catholic altar. It is the one Eucharist of the church. Thus, the Eucharist is the unbroken link which unites profoundly and in an invisible way the Eastern Orthodox and Roman Catholics in spite of the apparent visible separation between their two churches. Father Afanassieff does not suggest "intercommunion." He is aware of the doctrinal and canonical problems which first have to be resolved before the profound communion existing between the two churches becomes a visible and manifest reality.[17] I fully agree

---

[14]Hamilcar Alivizatos, *Ē Oikonomia kata to Kanonikon Dhikaion tēs Orthodoxou Ekklēsias* (Athens, 1949), pp. 83-88.

[15]Kotsonis, *Problēmata*, pp. 184-206.

[16]See Chomatenos quoted above in Rallis and Potlis, *Syntagma*, p. 435.

[17]Afanassieff, *L'Eucharistie*, pp. 337-339.

with the position of Father Afanassieff. Moreover, I would like to extend his views to include all Christians who share in the one Eucharist of Christ along with the Eastern Orthodox Church. I feel that this position is in conformity with the best canonical tradition of Eastern Orthodoxy as described above.

(4) Among other recent prophetic acts which show the continuity of church practice in dealing with the Christian West is the lifting of the anathemas of 1054 between Rome and Constantinople. The idea behind this lifting, as described in the common statement published on December 7, 1965, in both Rome and Constantinople, is not to abolish the schism, but to put an end to whatever is the cause of that schism: mutual hatred and misunderstandings.[18] However, what this act implies is an official mutual recognition of each other's ecclesiality by the two most venerable churches of Christianity, Rome and Constantinople.

Other prophetic events which take place in today's ecumenical movement are the visits exchanged by prelates of different churches and Christian communities, such as those between Pope Paul VI and the great, late Patriarch Athenagoras of Constantinople. Also, other such events are the exchange of holy objects, such as chalices, episcopal insignia (crosses and *enkolpia*), and relics of saints. All these events may signify a *de facto* recognition of each other's hierarchy and ecclesiality. Yet, no official response is given as yet by the Christian East to an important prophetic act exhibited by the Roman Catholic Church at the Second Vatican Council: the *Decree on Ecumenism*. The latter recognizes the ecclesiality of the Eastern Orthodox Church and offers the Roman Catholic communion to the Orthodox.[19] The answer expected is an official recognition by the Eastern Orthodox Church of the ecclesiality of the Roman Catholic Church. However, the problems connected with the reestablishment of full communion between Eastern Orthodoxy and Roman Catholicism are not yet resolved. This is why the authorities of the Eastern Orthodox Church have not granted permission to the Orthodox faithful to accept the offer of Roman Catholic communion.[20]

III

The agreed statement on the Eucharist published by the Orthodox and Roman Catholic theologians in the United States concludes thus:

---

[18]See the whole text in Karmiris, *Ta Dogmatika,* vol. 2 (Athens, 1968), pp. 1026 [1106] -1030 [1110].

[19]See Walter Abbott, S.J., *The Documents of Vatican II,* trans. by Msgr. Joseph Gallagher (New York, 1966), pp. 357-361.

[20]See "The Discipline of Holy Communion" (a statement unanimously approved by the Standing Conference of Orthodox Bishops in America at its meeting on January 22, 1965, at the Greek Orthodox Archdiocese, New York City), in *Guidelines for Orthodox Christians in Ecumenical Relations* (New York, 1973), pp. 52-53.

> Recognizing the importance of this consensus we are aware that serious differences exist in our understanding of the Church, eucharistic discipline, and pastoral practice, which now prevent us from communicating in one another's churches. Our task should consist in further exploring how these differences are related to the agreement stated above and how they can be resolved.[21]

As far as Orthodox and Roman Catholics are concerned, this statement assigns to us the task before us: to eliminate difficulties toward reestablishing full communion between our two churches. I hope that this task undertaken here between Orthodox and Catholic theologians will be taken up by the entirety of the two churches they represent.

It is my hope that, as far as the Orthodox Church is concerned, an official act will be issued by it reflecting its realistic evaluation of the other churches and ecclesial communities. The drafts and introductory reports of the Preparatory Commission of the Great Synod to come make this hope realistic. We read in the report on "Economy in the Orthodox Church":

> A further goal is . . . to lead all to the one Lord, the one faith, the one baptism, the one breaking of bread, the one God and Father of all (Eph. 4:5-6).

> Acting in this way, our Orthodox Church aims at the following positive results . . .

> To assess accurately the positive aspects in the faith and doctrine professed by those outside of her, in their ecclesiological structure, sacramental grace, and eschatological hope, faithful to God's word and the Gospel of salvation . . .

> To assess in all fairness the situations created in centuries past, but also in more recent times, within Orthodoxy and outside it, involving the reception by economy of the sacraments of other believers on the basis of the Church's canonical practice.[22]

With regard to the Western church, I hope that it will undertake an in-depth study of the procession of the Holy Spirit and that eventually it will return to a pre-Augustinian theology and doctrine on the Holy Trinity. Moreover, I anticipate that the West will balance its ecclesiology with regard to the interplay of primacy and true collegiality with real interdependence between the two. I look forward to seeing the primacy in the West being considered not in terms of "universal jurisdiction," but in terms of "universal service" (*diakonia*). Then the way will be paved for full communion between Eastern Orthodox and Roman Catholic Churches.

---

[21] Orthodox-Roman Catholic Consultation, "An Agreed Statement on the Eucharist," in *Diakonia* 5 (1970): 72.

[22] See Interorthodox Commission in preparation for the next Great and Holy Council of the Orthodox Church, *Towards the Great Council*, trans. by S.P.C.K. (London, 1972), pp. 50-51.

Conclusion

What was true during the life of the ancient and Byzantine Church continues to be true and normative for the church of today: ecclesial fullness is a requirement for sharing in each other's Eucharist. Thus, regarding the Eastern Orthodox and the Roman Catholic Churches, full harmony between their two traditions is a prerequisite for visible sacramental communion between them. It is true that

> our two traditions are not easily harmonized. Yet we believe that the Spirit is ever active to show us the way by which we can live together as one and many. We have the hope that we will be open to his promptings wherever they may lead. "For so will harmony reign, in order that God through the Lord and in the Holy Spirit may be glorified, the Father and the Son and the Holy Spirit" (Apostolic Canons, cn. 34).[23]

CATHOLIC RESPONSE BY EDWARD J. KILMARTIN

In his essay the esteemed professor of theology at Holy Cross Orthodox School of Theology shows that he is in agreement with the more common position of Orthodox theologians concerning the ecclesial reality of the Roman Catholic Church. He founds his position, in part, on the way the Orthodox Church has traditionally dealt with the Roman Catholic Church. The recent gesture of the Patriarch of Constantinople, lifting the anathema of 1054, is viewed as another instance of the implicit recognition of the ecclesiality of the Roman Catholic Church.

This consideration leads the author to affirm the truth of the Roman Catholic Eucharist and to make the further observation that the celebration of the one Eucharist unites the two churches in "an invisible way." Still this fact does not warrant eucharistic sharing because it is, by its nature, a manifestation of communion in the fullness of ecclesiality found only in the Orthodox Church.

Through these reflections on the profound unity which already exists between the Orthodox and Roman Catholic Churches, the author brings out the urgency of working toward the realization of visible communion. In the present state, which approximates that of *akoinonisia* (absence of canonical and sacramental communion), these churches have the duty to proceed to recover communion on all levels.

Among the actual obstacles to full communion, the author finds major

---

[23]Orthodox-Roman Catholic Consultation, "An Agreed Statement on the Church," in *Diakonia* 10 (1975): 184.

problems in the area of the doctrine of the Trinity and ecclesiology. He expresses the hope that the Western church will change its theology of the Trinity and balance its ecclesiology with regard to the relation of primacy to collegiality.

In the matter of Trinitarian doctrine the need for Orthodox and Roman Catholic theologians to cooperate in a serious study of the divergent perspectives and legitimate concerns of each tradition is surely great. They must be continually corrected by one another in the effort to define the boundary line between dogma and further theologizing which cannot command the assent of faith. However, this writer does not believe that the differences between the two traditions in the matter of the Trinity are such that they represent a real obstacle to reunion. This can be seen from the increasingly tolerant attitude of Orthodox and Catholic scholars toward the different Trinitarian theologies which characterize the East and West.[1]

The recent dialogue between Oriental Orthodox and Roman Catholic theologians held in Vienna, September 7-11, 1971, is a good example of what can be done through scholarly cooperation. This session closed with a joint statement on belief in Jesus Christ, truly God and truly human, and at the same time with the recognition "of differences in theological interpretation of the mystery of Christ because of our different ecclesiastical and theological traditions."[2]

In the matter of ecclesiology likewise both churches need to study together the notion of jurisdiction and its christological dimension in relation to the theology of the local church. In the East, stress on the independence of the local church has led to the isolation of certain churches. Hence the problem remains for them of realizing the catholicity of the one church. Serious study of the question of primacy is needed in this context. On the other hand, in the West the problem of the extent of the primacy of the pope needs attention. The experience of both churches shows that the communion of local churches of Christ is always threatened through centralization or congregational federation.

The official dialogue between Orthodox and Roman Catholic theologians in the U.S.A. is committed to a cooperative study of the issues raised by Fr. Maximos. Given the fraternal spirit which has characterized this consultation in the past, there is every reason to hope that this study will be done with the enthusiasm which should mark those who eat from the one table of the Lord and so confess their unity in Christ.

---

[1]Cf., for example, the issue of *Istina* vol. 17, nos. 3-4 (1972), which is dedicated to the *Filioque* controversy.

[2]"Nonofficial Consultation between Theologians of the Oriental Orthodox and the Roman Catholic Churches," *Diakonia* 7 (1972): 291. A similar joint statement was issued by Paul VI and the Syrian Orthodox Patriarch Mar Ignatius Jacob III on October 27, 1971 (*Acta Apostolicae Sedis* 63 [1971] : 814).

THE ORTHODOX-ROMAN CATHOLIC DIALOGUE
ON THE EUCHARIST

Edward J. Kilmartin

In 1965 the National Catholic Conference of Bishops Committee for Ecumenical and Interreligious Affairs, in cooperation with the Standing Conference of Canonical Orthodox Bishops of America, established the Orthodox-Roman Catholic Consultation for the purpose of investigating theological issues and pastoral problems of common concern. This consultation, representing Orthodox and Roman Catholic episcopal conferences, has no similar counterpart elsewhere. Since the preliminary meeting at Worcester, Massachusetts, September 9, 1965, it has convened eleven times. Two sessions are planned for 1976. The consultation is chaired jointly by Archbishop Iakovos, Greek Orthodox Archbishop of North and South America, and Archbishop William Baum of the Archdiocese of Washington, DC, who succeeded Bishop Bernard Flanagan of the Diocese of Worcester, Massachusetts, in 1973.

The discussions of this consultation on the subject of the Eucharist is the theme of this essay. A factual report will be given of these discussions, followed by a consideration of their significance. Then attention will be called to some theological problems related to the Eucharist which are a current concern of the consultation. Finally some personal observations will be made on the theological context in which these problems will have to be discussed.[1]

I

In this consultation the subject of the Eucharist was introduced in connection with the following themes: the nature of the church and ways of realization of local church;[2] sacramental sharing between Orthodox and Roman Catholic Churches;[3] theology of pastoral office;[4] and the new changes in the Roman Mass.[5] Moreover, a lengthy discussion of the meaning of the eucharistic celebra-

---

[1]This writer has been executive secretary of the Catholic Bishops Committee for Dialogue with the Orthodox and Other Eastern Churches since 1969, and a member of this consultation since 1967.

[2]IV Meeting, Maryknoll, NY, December 6-7, 1968 (Theme: Eucharist and Church); V Meering, Worcester, MA, December 12-13, 1969 (Theme: Eucharist: Sacrament of the Church); XII Meeting, Washington, DC, May 19-20, 1975 (Theme: The Concept of Church).

[3]II Meeting, New York, NY, September 29, 1966 (Theme: Sacramental Sharing); III Meeting, Worcester, MA, May 5-6, 1967 (Theme: Eucharistic Sharing); VI Meeting, New York, NY, May 19-20, 1970 (Theme: Canonical Orthodox and Roman Catholic Legislation concerning Common Worship).

[4]XII Meeting, Washington, DC, May 19-20, 1975 (Theme: Theology of Priesthood).

[5]VI Meeting, New York, NY, May 19-20, 1970 (Theme: The New Order of the Roman Mass).

tion itself took place at the fifth meeting held at Worcester, December 12-13, 1969. At this session the consultation found no major difficulty about formulating a common statement which was made public under the title, "An Agreed Statement on the Holy Eucharist."[6]

This document is a compendium of traditional eucharistic doctrine in the form of six propositions. The eucharistic celebration is described as a memorial of the history of salvation in which the Holy Spirit comes, according to the promise of Christ, to consecrate the elements to be the Body and Blood of Christ and to sanctify the faithful. The eucharistic worship of the church is understood to take place in union with the saving worship of Christ and so to be a source of blessings for the living and dead for whom intercession is made. Eucharistic communion is explained as nourishment for the faithful with a view to making them temples of the Holy Spirit and to building up the Body of Christ. The anticipated transformation of the whole cosmos which takes place in the believer through the Eucharist is linked to the duty of announcing this to the whole world. Finally the mission of service of the gospel to the world in all its ramifications is viewed as a necessary consequence of the eucharistic celebration in which believers profess unity with one another in Christ who came to mediate salvation to the world through both word and loving actions. The conclusion of this statement refers to the question of eucharistic sharing between the churches. Reflecting the two previous discussions of this theme,[7] it affirms that such sharing is not possible at present because of "serious differences ... in our understanding of Church, eucharistic discipline and pastoral practice."

Apart from this document only one other of the three agreed statements published by the consultation has a reference to the Eucharist. The fourth thesis of "An Agreed Statement on the Church," issued at the eleventh meeting, New York City, December 9-10, 1974, reads in part as follows:

> The independent existence of the local church is expressed best in its eucharistic celebration. The sacramental celebration of the Lord's presence in the midst of his people through the work of the Spirit both proclaims the most profound realization of the Church and realizes what it proclaims in the measure that the community gives itself to the Spirit.[8]

II

These discussions about the Eucharist, as well as the few published state-

---

[6]The full text, published in many newspapers and journals, can be found in *Diakonia* 5 (1970): 72. A comparison between this statement and those of other bilateral consultations dealing with the same subject is made in "The Bilateral Consultations between the Roman Catholic Church in the United States and other Christian Communities," *Proceedings of the Catholic Theological Society of America* 27 (1972): 207-215.

[7]Cf. note 3.

[8]The full text is found in *Diakonia* 10 (1975): 184.

ments, confirm what is generally recognized: There is no fundamental disagreement between Orthodox and Roman Catholic understanding of the meaning of the eucharistic celebration, the requirement of ministry ordained in apostolic succession for the realization of the Eucharist, the essential rite necessary to express the meaning of the Eucharist, and the relation of Eucharist to church.[9]

The "Agreed Statement on the Holy Eucharist" took for granted the requirement of ministry in apostolic succession and the basic conformity of both liturgical traditions to the meaning of the Eucharist. Hence it concluded that on these levels of belief and practice the necessary conditions for eucharistic sharing between the churches exist. The fact that eucharistic sharing is not possible at present was based on other grounds, as the conclusion of the consensus report indicates.

The objective content of this agreed statement is based on the liturgical witness and theological understanding of the meaning of the Eucharist which has always been recognized as essentially the same in both traditions. Such an agreed statement should surprise no one. Still the statement is significant for certain omissions.

No reference is made to the necessity of an explicit *epiclesis* (prayer to God to send the Holy Spirit who will transform the elements into the body and blood of Jesus) of the Holy Spirit or the precise function of this *epiclesis* and the narrative of institution of the Eucharist in relation to the consecration of the bread and wine. Noticeable also is the absence of any reference to the term "transubstantiation" which is linked to the traditional Catholic theological explanation of the way in which the elements are transformed so that they become sacrament of Christ's presence.

These omissions manifest the newer sensitivity toward the boundary line between dogmas of faith and theological explanations. In the opinion of this writer the outlook of members of this consultation reflects the more widespread tendency of Orthodox and Roman Catholic scholars to consider the theological explanations of the precise role of the *epiclesis* of the Holy Spirit and the narrative of institution of the Eucharist within the eucharistic prayer as lying outside the scope of that affirmation of eucharistic faith which is a condition for eucharistic sharing.

This consultation is also in agreement with the widespread consensus of Roman Catholic and Orthodox theologians that the Council of Trent affirmed, using the school language of transubstantiation, the same thing that is affirmed by the various canonized formulas of Orthodox theology: that a real transformation of the earthly gifts takes place in the power of the Spirit so that

---

[9]Georges A. Barrois, an Orthodox theologian, affirms this agreement in the following way: "It is important at this point to realize that differences between the teaching of the Eastern Orthodox Church and the teaching of the Roman Church on the Eucharist as such are minimal and do not affect the fundamental Christian tradition" ("Closed Communion, Open Communion, Intercommunion?" *St. Vladimir's Seminary Quarterly* 12 [1968]: 147).

they become sacrament of Christ's presence—a mode of presence which differs from the presence of Christ by faith in the individual believer.

The consultation is likewise in agreement on an important consequence of the fact that the Eucharist is sacrament of the church: the place where the church best expresses its true nature and so can best realize itself. This implies that the condition for regular eucharistic sharing between local churches is a visible, enduring unity which covers the whole range of the essentials of Christian communal life.

III

The Orthodox and Roman Catholic Churches have always agreed on the essentials of eucharistic doctrine and mutually recognized that each church has preserved a pastoral office in historical apostolic succession. Nevertheless, after the separation of the two churches a problem did arise about the recognition of the ecclesial status which each church could concede to the other. Hence the way was open to a denial of the reality of the Eucharist and other sacraments in the other church.

Each church affirms that the integral faith of the *Una Sancta* is expressed only by it. Since the Eucharist is sacrament of the church, the church must be there to celebrate it. What can be said of the Eucharist can also be said of the other sacraments of the church. This reasoning could give rise to the questions: To what extent can both churches mutually recognize the existence of sacraments in each other? What are the theological grounds which can support such a recognition? This topic will be taken up by the consultation during the next year.

Historically this has not been such a serious problem for the Roman Catholic Church as for the Orthodox Church. Since the third century baptismal controversy between Cyprian of Carthage and Stephen of Rome, the West has accepted heretical baptism—provided it was correctly administered. However there was greater sensitivity toward the necessary ecclesial context for the conferment of orders and the celebration of the Eucharist throughout the early middle ages in the West. Augustine's appeal to the use of proper form for the sacraments instituted by Christ and his argument that the efficacy of the sacraments depends on Christ and not on the faith of the minister were not considered sufficient for the recognition of orders conferred without the proper ecclesial context.[10] The concept of "absolute ordination," i.e., conferred without proper ecclesial context, was only accepted in the West in the late middle

---

[10]Cf. H. E. Cowdrey, "The Dissemination of St. Augustine's Doctrine of Holy Orders during the Later Patristic Age," *Journal of Theological Studies* 20 (1969): 448-481. The author gives evidence for the fact that Augustine's position on orders became acceptable in the West only after the middle age discussion beginning with P. Lombard and Master Roland.

ages when the theology of priesthood had been subtly disengaged from its eccle-siological basis.[11] This, in turn, had the effect of isolating the Eucharist from the church and making it a work of the priest who exercises the power of orders independently of the faith of the church.[12]

This development allowed for the recognition of all orders conferred by a bishop in historical apostolic succession even though he had no jurisdiction and received by a candidate without any title of mission. Hence the only problem that could arise about the truth of Orthodox ordinations would concern the liturgical rite used.[13]

On the other hand, the Orthodox have always been concerned with the ecclesial context of sacraments. They never accepted the concept of "absolute ordination." When called on to assess the value of sacraments outside the Ortho-dox Church, instinctively they turn to the context in which the sacraments were celebrated. This explains, in part, the long history of denial by individual Ortho-dox theologians of the existence of true sacraments in the Roman Catholic Church. It is also true that Orthodox Church leaders who have favored the truth of orders of Western churches, Roman Catholic and Anglican, have never con-sistently put their convictions into practice.

At the present time Orthodox bishops and theologians appear to have less difficulty about recognizing sufficient ecclesial basis in the Roman Catholic Church for the celebration of true sacraments. In particular there is more general agreement, based on the Orthodox theology of the local church, that bishops of the Roman Catholic Church have the necessary jurisdiction to ordain bishops and priests. However the Orthodox find it necessary to ask how, in view of Vatican I's teaching about the primacy of jurisdiction of the bishop of Rome over the whole church, and so his role in affirming the jurisdiction of each bishop, the Roman Catholic Church can agree that Orthodox bishops have true jurisdiction and consequently can confer true orders.

This consideration shows how it might be less difficult in theory for the Orthodox to accept the pastoral office of the Roman Catholic Church and so the reality of its Eucharist. On the other hand, there is a question currently being investigated by Roman Catholic theologians which, if officially resolved in a way which goes against the received tradition, could raise insuperable difficulties for the Orthodox recognition of the Roman Catholic pastoral office and so its Eucharist.

---

[11]Cf. E. J. Kilmartin, "Apostolic Office: Sacrament of Christ," *Theological Studies* 36 (1975): 260-261.

[12]Ibid., p. 260.

[13]During the seventeenth century some Roman canonists judged that Orthodox orders were probably not valid because the ordination rite did not include the *traditio instrumentorum* employed in the Latin rite. The Louvain theologian John Morinus was able to prevent a possible official decision against such orders by an appeal to the fact that this rite was introduced into the Latin Church in the tenth century (cf. P. Pourrat, *Theology of the Sacraments* [St. Louis: 1910], pp. 86-87).

The growing consensus of Roman Catholic theologians concerning the possibility of ordination of women to the pastoral office is a source of uneasiness to the Orthodox. It causes the suspicion that Roman Catholics are losing the true understanding of the pastoral office. Given this state of affairs, the theological arguments offered by Roman Catholic theologians for ordination of women will have to be studied seriously in this consultation.

IV

In the ongoing dialogue of this consultation the problem of papal jurisdiction as related to Orthodox pastoral office and Eucharist will have to be discussed. It will necessarily be taken up in connection with the concept of jurisdiction and its christological dimension in relation to the theology of the local church. The problem of the ordination of women is also related to the christological dimension of the church. In both cases it is a question of the function of the structures of the church to manifest that Christ is the one Lord of the church.

Regarding the ordination of women, both the Orthodox and Roman Catholic Churches officially reject the possibility on the basis of the constant contrary tradition which is often interpreted as divine law. Until recently neither church felt the need for a serious discussion of the theological basis of the traditional practice. However the serious questioning of the normative value of this tradition for the modern church has forced theologians to reflect on the grounds for this practice and requires these churches to reconsider the whole question. Are the grounds for exclusion of women from the pastoral office merely cultural or are there solid theological reasons behind the practice which are valid for the modern church?

In seeking to discover the possible christological basis for the rejection of women from the pastoral office, many Orthodox and Roman Catholic theologians have taken as point of departure the traditional doctrine which affirms that the ordained pastor directly represents Christ *and also* the church, as confessing believer, in his official acts. This leads them to conclude that the ordained pastor must be male in order to preserve the symbolic correspondence between the minister of Christ and Christ, who is the one Lord of the church. Only this structure in the pastoral office manifests clearly that Christ remains actually present as the one Lord of the church in the exercise of the official ministry of the church.

At least within the Orthodox-Roman Catholic dialogue this argument has to be dealt with in all its ramifications. It raises a number of serious questions which have been treated in the theological literature of the past few years. One such question is this: Is it correct to say that the pastoral office directly represents Christ *and* the church or should it be said that the pastoral office directly represents the faith of the church and so represents Christ who is the living source of the faith? If one accepts the latter option, the whole argument for symbolic correspondence between Christ and the minister would seem to fall.

But this would entail defining the peculiarity of pastoral office in terms of public guardianship of the common matter of all believers: the mission of Christ. Such a position is unacceptable to traditional Orthodox and Roman Catholic theology.

But even if one accepts the viewpoint that the pastoral office directly represents Christ, how valid is the conclusion regarding the necessity of male candidates in order to preserve the symbolic correspondence between the minister and Christ? A number of difficulties arise at this point. At the very least one can say that the argument for symbolic correspondence is not as persuasive in this case as it is when used to ground the necessity of the presence of pastoral office, an essential element of the structure of church, in the celebration of the Eucharist where the church most perfectly manifests and realizes itself.

Conclusions

1. There is fundamental agreement between Orthodox and Roman Catholics on the meaning of the eucharistic celebration, the necessity of ministry in apostolic succession for the celebration of the Eucharist, and the aptness of the liturgical traditions of the East and West to express the meaning of the Eucharist.

2. There remains the task of investigating the grounds for the recognition of the existence of the Eucharist in both churches. Here the question of jurisdiction of bishop or priest comes into play with special reference to the Roman Catholic explanation of how Orthodox bishops have proper jurisdiction to ordain priests and celebrate the Eucharist.

3. There remains the task of investigating the theological basis for the acceptance or rejection of the ordination of women to the pastoral office. It should be noted that this subject is a major concern of Roman Catholic theologians, not Orthodox theologians, who are not generally open to the view that there may be a theological basis for such ordinations. The growing consensus of Roman Catholic theologians, as well as members of the hierarchy and laity, concerning the acceptability of ordaining women to the pastoral office makes it difficult for the teaching office of the Roman Catholic Church to assure the Orthodox that Roman Catholics are not in the process of acquiring a more "Protestant" concept of pastoral office. This, in turn, can conceivably raise new problems for the Orthodox regarding the recognition of the Eucharist in the Roman Catholic Church, for they regard the priest's intention to act in accord with the traditional Orthodox understanding of his role as an essential element of the eucharistic celebration.[14]

---

[14] An analogous case can be found in the Orthodox understanding of the role of the priest in the marriage celebration. The priest is viewed as minister of the sacrament. Consequently the Roman Catholic understanding of the priest as "official witness" and not minister of the sacrament makes it difficult, in theory, for the Orthodox to accept the sacramental character of the Roman Catholic marriage celebration.

ORTHODOX RESPONSE BY MAXIMOS AGHIORGOUSSIS

In his essay Father Edward Kilmartin presents us with the facts of this dialogue as it takes place in the United States. He is justified in doing this, because only in the U.S. is a continuous dialogue taking place between official representatives of Orthodox and Roman Catholic episcopal committees. Father Kilmartin also gives an interpretation of these facts, reviews the present situation of the dialogue, and interprets its future concerns.

I have nothing significant to add concerning the facts. Their interpretation is to a great extent held in common between him and me. Father Kilmartin is right in his appraisal of the agreement on the Eucharist: a compendium of our common eucharistic doctrine. As for the omissions in it, I concur that they are theological elaborations which do not affect the doctrine as such. For both of our churches the Holy Spirit consecrates the gifts. To state this in the Liturgy and to call upon the Spirit (this is what *epiklesis* is) or to imply the Spirit's operation is a matter of theological expression. As for the term "transubstantiation," it cannot be an issue if it is interpreted to mean the change of the gifts into the real—yet sacramental—body and blood of the Lord, without pretending to explain the mystery of this miraculous change.

As for the theological problems of sacramental sharing, Father Kilmartin is right in establishing the "ecclesial context" of the Eucharist as the Orthodox criterion of acceptance or rejection of eucharistic sharing. The Eucharist is the sacrament of the church. This implies that ecclesial fullness, thus fullness of ecclesial faith, is required so that eucharistic sharing is permitted for the Orthodox. Throughout its tradition, the Eastern Orthodox Church had enough basis for recognizing an ecclesial context in the West, specifically—yet not exclusively—in the Roman Catholic Church. The East has never questioned the validity of the orders of the Roman Catholic priesthood, or even their jurisdiction, as the East has never separated jurisdiction from ordination. The orders, and consequently the Eucharist of the Western church, are "valid." the real problem for the East is to establish if the Roman Catholic Eucharist is licit for the Orthodox, considering the questions the East has about the continuity of genuine apostolic faith in the West in such matters as the procession of the Holy Spirit and the papal primacy.

With regard to the present concerns of the Consultation, I tend to agree with Father Kilmartin that the papal jurisdiction in relation to the Eucharist and the possibility of ordaining women to the priesthood are priority questions. However, I would like to add a third question, which one could even consider first: the procession of the Holy Spirit. For many Orthodox theologians, this question is connected with that of papal jurisdiction. The post-Augustinian theology in the West professes a kind of subordination of the Spirit to Jesus Christ. This subordination is also reflected in the structure of the Western church, where bishops, sharing in the same episcopal "essence," are subordinated to one of them, the Roman pontiff.

For the Orthodox, the papal jurisdiction in relation to Eucharist, and the alleged problem posed to the East because of this jurisdiction, is not a real problem. The real problem is with the theology of the late middle ages, which disengages the priesthood from its ecclesiological basis. If we put the priesthood in its ecclesiological context, it is evident that Eastern Orthodox bishops and priests do not need to have any kind of "jurisdiction" which does not come to them from their ordination.

Finally, regarding the ordination of women, I agree that a change in the traditional understanding of ministry within the Roman Catholic Church would seriously hinder sacramental sharing with the Eastern Orthodox Church. As Father Kilmartin points out, according to this understanding common to the Orthodox and Roman Catholic Churches, the priest represents Christ directly and not because he represents the faith of the church. Thus, "the candidates [for the priesthood] will have to be male to preserve the symbolic correspondence between the minister and Christ." For this and for other theological reasons to be considered in our dialogue, ordination of women to the priesthood seems entirely excluded in the Orthodox Church.

Study and Discussion Questions

1. Discuss why the Eastern Orthodox Church so staunchly opposes intercommunion.
2. What does it mean, in general, to say that the Eucharist presupposes "fulness of ecclesiality"? What conditions are said by the author to be necessary for this fulness to be present? In your opinion, would ecclesiality alone (as opposed to fulness of ecclesiality) be a necessary and sufficient condition for a church's sacraments to be recognized?
3. How would you describe the ancient Eastern church practice with respect to the sacraments of those "outside the church"? How does recent practice compare with ancient practice?
4. Would it be true to say that Rome has officially recognized the ecclesiality of the Eastern Orthodox Church and therefore its Eucharist, while the Eastern Orthodox Church has not officially done the same with respect to Rome? Discuss.
5. Do you share Fr. Maximos' concern that Roman Catholic Trinitarian and papal doctrines constitute a true barrier to full communion between the two churches? Discuss.
6. Does Kilmartin see the differences in Trinitarian theology as being insurmountable? Does he express the same feelings about papal primacy? Discuss.
7. In what areas of eucharistic theology is there fundamental agreement between Orthodox and Roman Catholic churches, according to Kilmartin?
8. Does Kilmartin think that the reasons for prohibiting intercommunion are as serious in 1976 as they were when the 1969 Statement was drawn up? Discuss.
9. In what way did the separation of the Eastern and Western churches open the way to a possible denial of the eucharistic reality of the separated churches? Discuss.
10. If "the Eucharist is sacrament of the church, the church must be there to celebrate it," is it equally true that "wherever there is church, there is Eucharist"? Discuss.
11. Discuss the meaning of "absolute ordination" and its importance in the theology of priestly ordination in the West.
12. Discuss why the question of the possible ordination of women in the West is considered a difficulty in the dialogue between East and West.

ANGLICAN-CATHOLIC DIALOGUE

David A. Scott—Herbert J. Ryan

PRECIS

Scott finds that Anglicans generally: (1) hold the Eucharist to be the central act of worship, (2) understand the Eucharist as a liturgical action to be in some sense a sacrifice, (3) understand the Eucharist to bring about a real communion between Jesus and the members of his Body, and (4) reject transubstantiation and repetitive sacrifice as Anglicans have understood these to have been taught by Roman Catholics. Differences found among Anglicans involve: (1) the frequency of celebrating and attending Holy Communion, (2) the understanding of the sacrificial character of the Eucharist, and (3) the understanding of the real presence.

The contemporary dialogue has led to the 1971 Windsor Statement which, by addressing the eucharistic questions in a way that seems to have been able to transcend the traditional disagreements, has asserted "substantial agreement" in Anglican-Roman Catholic eucharistic understanding.

Ryan provides a general background to the Anglican-Roman Catholic dialogues. Behind all the dialogues is the fundamental assumption that the church is a "eucharistic communion," i.e., that the organic union being sought by the separated churches means finally a visible unity sacramentally celebrated in the Eucharist. Roman Catholic participants in the dialogue have attempted to reflect Vatican II's pastoral understanding of the Eucharist, briefly summarized by Ryan. This understanding is discernible in the Windsor and Canterbury Statements, particularly Vatican II's biblical and patristic thought patterns. Ryan defines this latter approach against the accusation that it abandons the Scholastic and Renaissance theological approach.

David A. Scott (Episcopalian), B.A., Amherst College, B.D., Episcopal Theological School (Cambridge, MA), M.A. and Ph.D., Princeton University, is Associate Professor of Theology at Virginia Theological Seminary in Alexandria. His dissertation (researched at Tübingen University on a Deutsche Akademische Austauschdienst grant) dealt with selfishness in its examination of Martin Luther and Thomas Aquinas.

Herbert J. Ryan, S.J. (Roman Catholic), A.B., Ph.L., M.A., Loyola University (Chicago), S.T.B., S.T.L., Woodstock College, S.T.D., Gregorian University (Rome), is Associate Professor of Historical Theology at Loyola Marymount University, Los Angeles. A member of both the Anglican-Roman Catholic International Commission and the U.S. Anglican-Roman Catholic bilateral, his articles have appeared in a wide variety of periodicals. His books include *The 'De Praedestinatione' of John Scottus Eriugena*, *Episcopalians and Roman Catholics: Can They Ever Get Together?* (with J. Robert Wright), and *Documents on Anglican-Roman Catholic Relations*.

THE EUCHARIST: AN ANGLICAN PERSPECTIVE

David A. Scott

Introduction

To write in a complete way about the Eucharist in Anglicanism, or in any major Christian tradition for that matter, would require including not just doctrinal but also historical and liturgical perspectives. The brevity of this article forbids such a comprehensive presentation. I limit myself to presenting a summary of Anglican belief about the nature and significance of the Eucharist as a liturgical action, as an act of worship by the church.

Even when I aim at a summary of belief rather than trying to trace the historical development of eucharistic thought or review past and present proposals for liturgical change, I must ignore important issues. For instance, I cannot dwell on the relation of Eucharist to priesthood. Nor can I touch on some matters related to the Eucharist itself, such as reservation, benediction, votive masses, and giving the Holy Communion to those in likelihood of immediate death. My purpose is to represent essential Anglican convictions about the Eucharist and their relation to belief in the Roman Catholic tradition.

Eucharistic Doctrine in the Anglican Ethos

Whenever an Anglican writes for non-Anglicans about what Anglicans believe concerning any religious matter, a word must be said about the place of doctrine in the Anglican ethos. The Church of England, and the churches in communion with it composing the Anglican Communion, is not a confessional church. Unlike the Lutheran and Reformed traditions, neither the theology of one leading figure nor an official doctrinal confession functions as a test of correct doctrine. Nor has Anglicanism ever tried to define officially particular doctrines as the Roman Catholic Church did at the Council of Trent.

Every person baptized in the Anglican Church does profess belief in all the articles of the Christian faith, as contained in the Apostles' Creed.[1] But the Articles of Religion, which received their final form in 1571, attempted only to define the Church of England's position in relation to the theological controversies of the sixteenth century. These Articles have been and are used by Anglicans as guides but not as a binding criterion. Similarly, *Doctrine in the Church of England* does not intend to define once and for all matters of belief for Anglicans.[2] That volume attempts to state the boundaries within which

---

[1]*The Book of Common Prayer* (New York: The Church Pension Fund, 1928, 1945), p. 276.

[2]*Doctrine in the Church of England: The Report of the Commission on Christian Doctrine Appointed by the Archbishops of Canterbury and York in 1922* (London: S.P.C.K., 1938), p. 2.

various theological views may still be called Anglican and to elucidate doctrine and doctrinal tendencies present then in the Church of England.

Arthur Balfour, the eminent British statesman and philosopher, once said of the English, "There are a few things on which we agree so deeply that we can afford to disagree even violently on everything else." And Henry R. Luce, the publisher, comments, "It has been part of the charm of the English that just exactly what they may have hitherto agreed on so profoundly has eluded definition." We should keep the comments of both Balfour and Luce in mind as we survey consensus and disagreement among Anglicans about the Eucharist!

Common Anglican Convictions about the Eucharist

1. The Central Act of Worship

The Eucharist (Holy Communion and The Lord's Supper are the terms used in the Prayer Book) is viewed by Anglicans as the single most important act of worship in the church. All Anglicans, therefore, would agree that "the central sacrament of the church and the chief means of spiritual strength in the life of the Christian is the Holy Communion."[3] The Prayer Book Catechism describes the Lord's Supper as one of the two sacraments (baptism being the other) instituted by Christ in his church "generally necessary to salvation."[4] Further evidence of the centrality of the Eucharist in Anglican worship is that Anglicans have made significant contributions to the historical and doctrinal understanding of the Eucharist.[5]

Believing the Eucharist to be the central act of worship of the church is not identical with uniformity about the frequency of celebrating and attendance at the Holy Communion. For example, in the eighteenth century, it was common for English country parishes to celebrate the Eucharist only quarterly, although city churches often had a weekly celebration. The Book of Common Prayer, by providing eucharistic propers for each Sunday, appears to presuppose at least a weekly celebration. And today almost universally every parish celebrates the Eucharist at least once on Sunday, and the Parish Communion (the Eucharist with epistle, gospel, and sermon) has wide popularity.

However often Anglicans celebrate the Eucharist, its essential significance was beautifully expressed in 1550 by Thomas Cranmer, the original architect of the Anglican Book of Common Prayer:

> ... to commend this (Christ's sacrifice on the cross for our redemption) unto all his faithful people, and to confirm their faith and hope

---

[3]W. Pell and P. M. Dawley, *The Religion of the Prayer Book* (New York: Morehouse-Gorham Co., 1943), p. 177.

[4]*The Book of Common Prayer*, p. 581.

[5]For example, Darwell Stone, *A History of the Doctrine of the Eucharist*, two volumes (London: Longmans, Green and Co., 1909); and Dom Gregory Dix, *The Shape of the Liturgy* (Westminster, England: Dacre Press, 1945, 1949).

of eternal salvation in the same, he hath ordained a perpetual memory of his said sacrifice, daily to be used in the church to his perpetual laud and praise, and to our singular comfort and consolation; . . . wherein he doth not cease to give himself with all his benefits, to all those that duly receive the same supper according to his blessed ordinance.[6]

2. Sacrifice and Real Presence

In addition to agreement about the centrality and effectiveness of the Eucharist as a sacrament, Anglicans are agreed, first, that in some sense sacrifice is an element of the Eucharist as a liturgical action and, second, that in the Eucharist real communion occurs between Jesus Christ and the members of the Body of Christ.

Regarding the first of these, the aspect in which the Eucharist is a sacrifice, there is much difference of opinion among Anglicans, and we will attend to those differences below. If, however, sacrifice is defined very generally, as "an act in which man worships God, the form of the act being an expression of the homage due from the creature to the Creator,"[7] then all Anglicans would agree that the Eucharist is in some sense a sacrifice.

With respect to the second element of agreement, Real Presence, there are again important differences among Anglicans about how this Real Presence is to be understood. But all Anglicans agree that the living Christ is really, in a spiritual manner, present at every Eucharist, that Christ is "active and accessible in a special manner as Giver and as Gift, and accordingly that the Eucharist affords a natural and appropriate occasion for the church's thankful adoration of Him as slain Lord for the world."[8]

Thus all main types of Anglican tradition regard the communion aspect of the Eucharist as central and essential. As an action of Christ's self-communication, the Eucharist is, therefore, also in Anglican understanding one in which the union of the Body of Christ with Christ and the unity of all the members of the church is set forth and made real.

3. Rejection of Transubstantiation and Repetitive Sacrifice

A significant element of the Anglican consensus about the Eucharist is the rejection of the doctrines of transubstantiation and repetitive sacrifice as Anglicans understood these to be taught in the sixteenth and seventeenth centuries in the Roman Catholic communion.

---

[6]Thomas Cranmer, *On the True and Catholic Doctrine and Use of the Sacrament of the Lord's Supper* (London: Chas. J. Thynne, 1907), p. xxii.

[7]*Doctrine in the Church of England*, p. 162.

[8]Ibid., p. 171.

There is, as we will see in the next section, much divergence of opinion among Anglicans concerning the sacrificial character of the Eucharist. Quite general agreement obtains among Anglicans, however, that no understanding of Eucharistic sacrifice is admissable which implies that Christ's sacrificial death on the cross can be repeated or added to. F. C. N. Hicks, former Bishop of Lincoln, England, expressed the Anglican view when he wrote, "There can be no sort of repetition of His sacrifice in the Eucharist, no slaying of Him on the altar, no taking away from the uniqueness and all sufficiency of the Cross."[9]

In the sixteenth century the Church of England explicitly rejected the doctrine of transubstantiation as the Church of England understood that doctrine to be understood in the Roman Catholic Church. The doctrine of transubstantiation concerned how the consecrated bread and wine became the Body and Blood of Christ.

Anglicans have never wanted to determine one official doctrine about how Christ's presence is related to the consecrated bread and wine. But most Anglicans have agreed that the theory of transubstantiation as they understood Thomas Aquinas, the Fourth Lateran Council, and the Council of Trent to have meant it, is a misleading doctrine.

The Twenty-eighth Article of Religion includes four traditional objections to the theory: it cannot be proved by Scripture; it is "repugnant to the plain word of Scripture"; it "overthroweth" the nature of a sacrament and has given rise to many superstitions.

Because Anglicans following St. Augustine define a sacrament as having both an outward and visible sign and an inward and spiritual grace, and because the transsubstantiation theory asserts that the substance of the outward and visible sign is annihilated, most Anglicans hold that the theory "overthroweth the nature of a sacrament." In the last section we will see that reconsideration of the function of transubstantiation language helped open the way to rapprochment between Anglicans and Roman Catholics on the Eucharist.

Differences among Anglicans on the Eucharist

Having surveyed convictions about the Eucharist widely shared among Anglicans, we turn now to discuss the areas of eucharistic understanding where differences among Anglicans are most pronounced. These are the sacrificial character of the Eucharist and the relation of the real presence of Christ in the Eucharist to the consecrated bread and wine.

As has been indicated above, Anglicans reject any conception that in the Eucharist Christ is re-immolated, or that a reparational sacrifice additional to Christ's death on the cross is carried out. This conviction has led most Anglicans to reject habitual communions without communion of the people, to reject any

---

[9]F. C. N. Hicks, in *Ways of Worship,* ed. by P. Edwall, E. Hayman, and W. Maxwell (London: SCM Press Ltd., 1951), p. 208.

view of the communion implying that it is a work of the priest and not the whole people of God, and to reject the view that the Eucharist is an effort to propitiate God.

The important differences among Anglicans on the question of the sacrificial character of the Eucharist might be stated this way. All Anglicans agree that the Eucharist is in some sense a memorial of Christ's sacrificial death on the cross. Further, all agree that the benefits of Christ's sacrificial death are received through communion. Third, all Anglicans agree that the faithful worshippers respond to Christ's sacrifice by offering themselves to God to be a "reasonable, holy, and living sacrifice."

A number of Anglicans, however, believe that all this is true but does not say enough. For these Anglicans the eucharistic celebration has a deeper continuity with the once-for-all sacrifice of Christ on the cross and also a real relation with Christ's intercessory work. According to this view the church as the Body of Christ unites, in the Eucharist, its self-offering with Christ's perpetual self-offering as High Priest who eternally makes intercession for us at the right hand of God. What Christ does perpetually in heaven the church in union with Christ does on earth in the Eucharist.[10]

The second area of major disagreement among Anglicans concerns the real presence of Christ, specifically, how Jesus Christ, really present in the eucharistic action, is related to the consecrated bread and wine. While rejecting transubstantiation as a way to describe this relation, Anglicans appear divided roughly into three main groups.

In one group are those who would not identify the presence of Christ in the Eucharist with the consecrated bread and wine. Indeed, one group of Anglicans would want to affirm that, although the Body and Blood of Christ are really received by the faithful, yet Christ's presence is real especially and specifically in the hearts of the receivers, and are not in the elements prior to reception.

A second group of Anglicans would insist that in some sense the bread and wine actually become, through consecration, the Body and Blood of Christ.

Still a third group would place great weight on the Eucharist as an "action." This widely held position among Anglicans affirms that, while Christ's real presence is especially associated with the consecrated bread and wine, he imparts himself to the faithful in and through the whole action of the eucharistic cele-

---

[10]On this issue, see articles by A. H. Couratin, G. W. H. Lampe, and F. C. N. Hicks in Edwall, Hayman, and Maxwell, eds., *Ways of Worship*, pp. 188-209; and C. W. Dugmore, *The Mass and the English Reformers* (London: Macmillan and Co., Ltd., 1958); idem, *Eucharistic Doctrine from Hooker to Waterland* (London: S.P.C.K., 1942); H. B. Green, "Sacrifice in the Eucharist," in W. R. F. Browning, ed., *The Anglican Synthesis: Essays by Catholics and Evangelicals* (Derby: Peter Smith, Ltd., 1964); N. Hicks, *Fullness of Sacrifice* (London: Macmillan and Co., Ltd., 1930); J. L. Houlden, "Sacrifice and Eucharist," in *Thinking about the Eucharist* (London: SCM Press, Ltd., 1972), pp. 81-98; S. Neill, "The Holy Communion in the Anglican Church," in High Martin, ed., *The Holy Communion* (London: SCM Press, Ltd., 1947), pp. 49-66; J. J. Packer, ed., *Eucharistic Sacrifice* (London: Church Book Room Press, 1962); and A. M. Stibbs, *Sacrament, Sacrifice and Eucharist* (London: The Tyndale Press, 1961).

bration. This last view would seem to render less relevant the more familiar difference between an "objective" or "subjective" theory of Christ's real presence.[11]

Anglican and Roman Catholic Understanding
of the Eucharist Today

To indicate in briefest compass the present relationship of Anglican and Roman Catholic understandings of the Eucharist, we do best to focus on the Anglican-Roman Catholic Agreed Statement on Eucharistic Doctrine. This document, often called the Windsor Statement and issued by the Anglican-Roman Catholic International Commission in 1971, affirms "substantial agreement" between present Anglican and Roman Catholic understanding of the eucharistic mystery.[12]

By highlighting a few salient points of the Statement we can indicate the character of this "substantial agreement" and, thereby, illustrate how Anglican and Roman Catholic eucharistic understandings relate today.

The foundation of the agreement represented by the Statement is the view that the Eucharist is a dynamic, personal, liturgical action. The document uses personal, active language to describe what is believed to occur in the celebration of the eucharistic mystery. In this liturgical action Christ is the chief actor. He makes effective his atoning victory among us, he elicits and renews our faith and self-surrender, and he builds up the church's fellowship and empowers its mission. The church's identity as the Body of Christ is both expressed and proclaimed through communion with his Body and Blood. In the Eucharist the church, in an anticipatory way, shares now in the eternal life to come based on what Christ has accomplished once for all. Thus, the Statement's language accents the Eucharist as a liturgical action and so uses a basic category for describing its meaning which is very congenial to Anglican understanding.

On the basis of these shared convictions about what occurs in the Eucharist,

---

[11]On differences among Anglicans on the real presence of Christ, see the previous note and also: P. D. Felton, *Recent Attempts within the Anglican Communion to Understand and Explain the Relation of the Eucharistic Presence to the Elements.* Dissertation (Ph.D.), Marquette University, Milwaukee, Wisconsin, 1968.

[12]Literature relevant to the Statement and the relation between Anglican and Roman Catholic eucharistic theology includes: Julian Charley, *Anglican-Roman Catholic Agreement on the Eucharist* (Bramcote Notts: Grove Books, 1972); Edward P. Echlin, *The Anglican Eucharist in Ecumenical Perspective: Doctrine and Rite from Cranmer to Seabury* (New York: Herder and Herder, 1967); Herbert J. Ryan, "Anglican-Roman Catholic Doctrinal Agreement on the Eucharist," *Worship* 46 (January, 1972): 6-14; idem, "Commentary on the Anglican-Roman Catholic Agreed Statement on Eucharistic Doctrine," in *Documents in Anglican-Roman Catholic Relations* II (Washington, DC: United States Catholic Conference, 1973), pp. 1-48; J. M. R. Tillard, "Catholiques romains et Anglicans: *l'Eucharistie,"* *Nouvelle Revue Theologique* 93 (1971): 606-656; R. E. Turner, "Modern Trends in Anglicanism on Eucharistic Thought and Practise," in Michael Hurley, ed., *Church and Eucharist* (Dublin: Gill and Son, 1966); and John Wand, *Anglican Eucharistic Theology in the Twentieth Century* (London: The Alcuin Club Report, 1972-1973), pp. 5-15.

the Statement addresses the relation between Christ's sacrificial death and the Eucharist and the real presence of Christ in the Eucharist. Both issues, as we say, have been sources of division between Anglicans and Roman Catholics and points of serious disagreement among Anglicans themselves.

In two ways the Statement tries to express the relation of the Eucharist to Christ's atoning death in a way which transcends these divisions and disagreements. First, the Statement asserts emphatically that the eucharistic celebration does not repeat or add to Christ's one, perfect, sufficient sacrifice on the cross. This emphasis expresses a central Anglican conviction about the Eucharist and one many Anglicans have believed Roman Catholics did not share. Second, the Anglican and Roman Catholic authors of the Statement agreed on a word to express positively the relation of Christ's sacrifice on the cross to the eucharistic action. This word is "memorial." The Statement does not say the Eucharist is a sacrifice but that it is a memorial, instituted by Christ, of the totality of God's reconciling action in Christ. The Eucharist as memorial is "no mere calling to mind of a past event or of its significance," but the "making effective in the present of an event in the past." With this notion of memorial the Statement expresses the necessary relation between the Eucharist and Christ's sacrifice without compromising the sufficiency and perfection of Christ's atoning death on the cross.

Two points regarding the Statement's view of the real presence indicate the present relation of Anglican and Roman Catholic understanding of this issue. On the one hand, the objective, real presence of the Lord is stated unambiguously. Thereby, the idea that the communicant's faith makes Christ present is ruled out by implication. As we have seen, the Statement here expresses a traditional Anglican conviction. On the other hand, the Statement does not use the word "transubstantiation" to describe how the bread and wine become Christ's Body and Blood. Indeed, while affirming the association of the consecrated bread and wine with Christ's presence, the Statement avoids localizing or containing Christ in the consecrated elements or specifying a moment when the bread and wine become Christ's Body and Blood. Here, as throughout the Statement, the language of personal action, presence, and encounter is used to express agreement on issues which before have divided the two communions.

CATHOLIC RESPONSE BY HERBERT J. RYAN

Dr. Scott has written an admirable and irenic summary of the wide range of Anglican belief about the nature and significance of the Eucharist as a liturgical action, as an act of worship by the church. He has shown the centrality of the Eucharist in the Anglican tradition. Furthermore, he has specified the two areas, viz., sacrifice and real presence, that have been sources of misunderstanding between the Anglican Communion and the Roman Catholic Church. Dr. Scott emphasizes the Anglican insistence that the eucharist not be understood as a repetitive sacrifice, and stresses that, "In the sixteenth century the Church of England explicitly rejected the doctrine of transubstantiation as the Church of England understood that doctrine to be understood in the Roman Catholic Church." Dr. Scott concludes his article with a brief summary and comment on the Windsor Statement which the Anglican-Roman Catholic International Commission's members believe to have expressed "substantial agreement" on eucharistic doctrine between the Roman Catholic Church and the Anglican Communion.

My difficulties occur in Dr. Scott's generally careful treatment of transubstantiation and his sensitive appreciation of the Windsor Statement. The first difficulty I have is with his statement that "the transubstantiation theory asserts that the substance of the outward and visible sign is annihilated." In the *Summa Theologica* III, 75, 3, Thomas explicitly denies annihilation of the substance of the bread and the wine. Non-annihilation is central to what Thomas means by "conversion of the bread and wine into the Body and Blood of Christ"—and Thomas makes much of this to establish that "conversion" of the elements is a unique case of change.

My second difficulty is in one part of Dr. Scott's treatment of the Windsor Statement. It is true that the Statement does not specify a "moment" when the bread and wine become Christ's Body and Blood. However, the Statement clearly indicates that this occurs during the consecratory prayer (*anaphora*) by the action of the Holy Spirit, so that in communion we eat the flesh and drink the blood of Christ (*WS* 10). This terminology is used out of respect for those Eastern Christian churches which regard the *epiclesis* (the prayer after the words of institution) as the "moment" of consecration.

Two developments in theological scholarship contributed greatly to the Windsor Statement. The authors of the Statement accepted the methods of modern biblical criticism and the viewpoint of contemporary liturgical theology. From modern critical biblical studies they drew their notion of Christ's sacrifice. Christ's sacrifice, in the diverse and descriptive New Testament understanding of that theme, is a notion wider than Christ's death. Christ's sacrifice also includes both his resurrection and his continuing interession for humankind. From liturgical theology the authors of the Windsor Statement accepted the insight that the Resurrected Christ through the Holy Spirit is the principal agent in Christian liturgical action. It is the Holy Spirit who empowers the faithful to fulfill the New Covenant and in Christ Jesus to properly worship the Father.

The sixteenth century founders of the independent Anglican theological tradition did not take this approach to the Eucharist. The same is true of the Council of Trent. Renaissance theology was rather more centered on humanity: humanity's actions, human response, personal salvation. One result of the Renaissance theological approach was the creation of two problems in understanding the Eucharist. Renaissance theology assumed that the Eucharist is primarily human action. Consequently Renaissance theology had a problem of how to relate Christ to the eucharistic action: How could the Risen Christ physically present in heaven be simultaneously present at Eucharist? Based on the same anthropocentric assumption, a second problem arose: How does one relate Christ's past sacrifice to present eucharistic action?

The Council of Trent was aware of the new problems raised by Renaissance theology. It responded to the new problems by affirming old positions that, in truth, did not quite reply to the new concerns. Trent taught the substantial presence of Christ in the Eucharist through the conversion of the bread and wine. Trent did not define a particular doctrine of how the conversion takes place. Transubstantiation is approved as a "most apt" term to designate the conversion of the elements into the Body and Blood of Christ. How the conversion takes place is a mystery of faith that transcends the ability of the human mind. Yet the assertion of "substantial presence" mitigated, from the mediaeval scholastic point of view, the difficulty of Christ's being present physically both in heaven and through the elements. Trent clearly taught that the Eucharist is a sacrifice but never defined what a sacrifice was. In effect, Trent asserted a patristic and mediaeval understanding of the eucharist in the context of the Renaissance problems without really answering them head on.

The mainstream of the Anglican theological tradition until about thirty years ago kept on asking these same two Renaissance questions about the Eucharist. Anglican polemical theology mistook Trent's assertions as answers to the Renaissance problems and prided itself in showing that Trent's assertions did not fit the categories in which the Renaissance questions were framed.

Recent Roman Catholic and Anglican theology, more attuned to biblical and patristic thought patterns, has shown the time-conditioned nature of the Renaissance eucharistic problems. The result has been a lessening of polemics and an increasing theological reflection upon Eucharist as a liturgical action with the hope of discovering a deeper understanding of Eucharist than ever the sixteenth century had.

EUCHARIST IN ANGLICAN-ROMAN CATHOLIC DIALOGUE: A ROMAN CATHOLIC VIEWPOINT

Herbert J. Ryan

Anglican-Roman Catholic Dialogues

Official ecumenical dialogue between the Roman Catholic Church and the autonomous churches of the Anglican Communion is a worldwide phenomenon. Australia, Belgium, Canada, East Africa, France, Japan, Great Britain, Papua-New Guinea, Scotland, South Africa, South America (Argentina), the South Pacific Islands, Uganda, the United States, Wales, and the West European Working Group are but some of the officially appointed regional dialogues that are wrestling with the apparent divergences in doctrine that separate Roman Catholics and Anglicans.[1]

Assisting this regional effort is the Anglican-Roman Catholic International Commission (ARCIC). Drawn from four continents, this group of ten Anglican and ten Roman Catholic scholars, theologians, and pastors—jointly appointed by the Pope and the Archbishop of Canterbury—has been at work since January, 1970.[2] One of the principal tasks of this group is to assist the regional dialogues by providing them with initial study documents or model agreements covering the three doctrinal areas that traditionally have been taken to separate the Roman Catholic Church and the Anglican Communion. These three areas are: (1) Eucharist, (2) Ordained Ministry, (3) Authority (Episcopal office, *magisterium* or teaching authority of the episcopal college in general, and the Bishop of Rome in particular). In its five years of work ARCIC has produced two study documents: at Windsor in 1971, "The Agreed Statement on Eucharistic Doctrine" (Windsor Statement),[3] and in 1973 at Canterbury, "Ministry and Ordina-

---

[1]For a record of this dialogue, cf. Nils Ehrenström and Gunther Gassmann, *Confessions in Dialogue* (Geneva: World Council of Churches, 1972), pp. 1-166; Alan C. Clark and Colin Davey, *Anglican/Roman Catholic Dialogue: The Work of the Preparatory Commission* (London: Oxford University Press, 1974), pp. 1-129; "Anglican/Roman Catholic Working Papers" (The Venice Papers), *Catholic Mind* 69, 1252 (April, 1971): 35-50; Charles H. Helmsing and Edward R. Welles, eds., *Documents on Anglican/Roman Catholic Relations* (Washington, DC: USCC, 1972), pp. 1-50; Herbert J. Ryan, ed., *Documents on Anglican-Roman Catholic Relations*, II (Washington, DC: USCC, 1973), pp. 1-73; Herbert J. Ryan and J. Robert Wright, eds., *Episcopalians and Roman Catholics: Can They Ever Get Together?* (Denville, NJ: Dimension Books, 1972), pp. 1-249; Alan C. Clark and Harry R. McAdoo, eds., *Modern Eucharistic Agreement* (London: SPCK, 1973), pp. vi-89; and Herbert J. Ryan, "La Dichiarazione di Windsor sulla dottrina eucaristica," *La Civiltà Cattolica* 2985 (November 5, 1974): 25-35.

[2]Africa (1 member), Australia (1), Europe (13), North America (5).

[3]Herbert J. Ryan, "Anglican/Roman Catholic Doctrinal Agreement on the Eucharist," *Worship* 46, 1 (January, 1972): 6-14; A. M. Allchin, "Agreed Statement on Eucharistic Doctrine," *One in Christ* 8, 1 (1972): 2-5; Alan C. Clark, *Agreement on the Eucharist* (London: Roman Catholic Ecumenical Commission, 1972), pp. 1-20; Julian W. Charley, *The Anglican-Roman Catholic Agreement on the Eucharist* (Bramcote, Notts.: Grove Books,

tion: A Statement on the Doctrine of the Ministry" (Canterbury Statement).[4] ARCIC is presently at work drafting its third study document dealing with some aspects of authority in the Christian community.

Given the extent and the intensity of official ecumenical dialogue between the Roman Catholic Church and the Anglican Communion, it is impossible in a brief article to give even a summary of the mutual agreements, shared concerns, and continuing tensions that have emerged in the regional and international dialogues. Yet it is possible to investigate the overarching framework of all the dialogues between the Roman Catholic Church and the Anglican Communion. All the dialogues, though each one in its own way, are proceeding on the assumption that the church is a "eucharistic communion." It is the purpose of this article to explain why this occurred and to sketch some of the underlying Roman Catholic concerns that have been brought forward in all the dialogues.

The ultimate purpose of the Anglican-Roman Catholic dialogue is the "organic union" of the Roman Catholic Church and the autonomous churches of the Anglican Communion. In Roman Catholic theology this means the restoration of full, visible, ecclesiastical communion between the Roman See and each of those autonomous churches that maintains historic ties to the See of Canterbury and the Church of England and which makes up with other similar churches that family of churches called the Anglican Communion. Full, visible, ecclesiastical communion is not just an external, paper agreement between or among church authorities. It must be a real type of church unity that shows itself in living community. Genuine, visible church unity is, for Roman Catholics, sacramentally celebrated in Eucharist which is simultaneously cause and symbol of the unity of God's people. This is what is intended by calling the church a "eucharistic communion." Briefly put, full, visible, ecclesiastical communion means full, visible, liturgical participation in celebrating Eucharist together. Thus, given that the ultimate purpose of this dialogue is visible organic

---

1972), pp. 1-24; Avery Dulles, "Consensus on the Eucharist?" *Commonweal* 96, 19 (August 25, 1972): 447-450; and John Coventry, "The Eucharist and the Sacrifice of Christ," *One in Christ* 11, 4 (1975): 330-341.

[4]Herbert J. Ryan, "The Canterbury Statement on Ministry and Ordination," *Worship* 48, 1 (January, 1974): 1-20; J. M. R. Tillard, "A Step Forward: The Canterbury Agreement on Ministry," *Lumen Vitae* 29, 2 (February, 1974): 167-198; Julian W. Charley, *Agreement on the Doctrine of the Ministry* (Bramcote, Notts.: Grove Books, 1974), pp. 1-34; Alan C. Clark, *Ministry and Ordination: An Agreed Statement of the Anglican/Roman Catholic International Commission* (London: Catholic Information Office, 1974), pp. 1-56; Herbert J. Ryan, "Ministry and Its Recognition in Anglican-Roman Catholic Dialogue," in H. Küng and W. Kasper, eds., *The Plurality of Ministries, Concilium*, vol. 74 (New York: Herder and Herder, 1972), pp. 127-133; idem, "Ordained Ministry in Anglican Roman Catholic Dialogue," *Diakonia* 7, 2 (1972): 182-191; and for the pastoral, eucharistic implications, idem, "The Canterbury-Rome Connection," *America* 131, 7 (September 21, 1974): 132-134; A. T. Mollegen and J. H. Rodgers, "Ministry and Ordination," *The Virginia Seminary Journal* 26, 3 (June, 1974): 11-13; J. Robert Wright, "The Canterbury Statement and the Five Priesthoods," *One in Christ* 11, 3 (1975): 282-293; and Herbert J. Ryan, "The Meaning of Ordained Priesthood in Ecumencial Dialogues," in R. Terwilliger and U. Holmes, eds., *To Be a Priest* (New York: Seabury Press, 1975), pp. 91-99.

unity, it was inevitable that the Roman Catholic participants in the dialogue would place Eucharist first on the agenda of items to be mutually discussed.

This theological approach to the question of "organic unity" is somewhat abstract. It corresponds, however, to the actual experience of the members of the first of these official ongoing dialogues to be formed. The Anglican-Roman Catholic Consultation in the USA (ARC) began in 1965, even before Vatican Council II was completed. The influence of ARC on subsequent worldwide Anglican-Roman Catholic dialogue has been profound.[5] ARC chose as its topic for dialogue, "The Church as a Eucharistic Communion." ARC's topic, agenda, and method were adopted by ARCIC and, through ARCIC, have spread to the regional official dialogue groups throughout the world. How did this happen?

On March 24, 1966, Arthur Michael Ramsey, then Archbishop of Canterbury, and Pope Paul VI issued at Rome a *Common Declaration*. The Pope and the Archbishop stated their intention "to inaugurate between the Roman Catholic Church and the Anglican Communion a serious dialogue which, founded on the Gospels and on the ancient common traditions, may lead to that unity in truth for which Christ prayed."[6] To arrange for the dialogue a Preparatory Commission was established. The Roman Catholic co-chairperson of this Commission was Bishop Charles Helmsing of Kansas City-St. Joseph, the Roman Catholic co-chairperson of ARC. The Commission included another ARC member, Fr. George Tavard, A.A., the most influential Roman Catholic theologian of the ARC dialogue. It was Tavard who had persuaded ARC to adopt the topic which it chose.[7] The ARC experience of fruitful official Anglican-Roman Catholic dialogue—a unique experience in 1966—carried great weight in setting the topic for the international dialogue envisioned by the Pope and the Archbishop of Canterbury. When ARCIC was established, three ARC members were named to the International Commission: Dr. Vogel, Fr. Tavard, and Fr. Herbert Ryan, S.J. At the first meeting of ARCIC in January, 1970, ARCIC adopted the agenda and the method of ARC.

Roman Catholic Underlying Eucharistic Concerns

Roman Catholic theologians bring to the Anglican-Roman Catholic dialogues which are exploring the topic, "The Church as a Eucharistic Communion," the pastoral vision of the Eucharist which is found in Vatican Council II. This broad vision may be limned in nine statements of the Council that relate

---

[5] Episcopal Bishop Arthur A. Vogel of West Missouri (Kansas City), who is a member of both ARC and ARCIC, traces the course of ARC in an epilogue to Bernard and Margaret Pawley, *Rome and Canterbury through Four Centuries* (New York: The Seabury Press, 1975), pp. 364-387.

[6] Clark and Davey, *Anglican/Roman Catholic Dialogue*, p. 2.

[7] Two theologians from the Episcopal Church who were familiar with ARC worked with the Preparatory Commission: the Reverend Dr. Massey H. Shepherd and the Reverend Dr. Albert T. Mollegen.

"Eucharist and the Hungers of the Human Family," the theme of the 1976 Eucharistic Congress.

(1) In the Pastoral Constitution on the Church in the Modern World the Council states its belief that all human striving finds its ultimate meaning in the Paschal Mystery (Eucharist). In the Eucharist the fruits of human labor, bread and wine, are changed into Christ's glorified Body and Blood to be both a supper of familial fellowship and a foretaste of the heavenly banquet.[8]

(2) The Dogmatic Constitution on the Church stresses the same theme and joins the human work of baptized Christians to the Eucharist. Christ gives baptized Christians his Spirit. Through the Spirit all their work and their very lives become spiritual sacrifices acceptable to God. In Eucharist Christians offer these spiritual sacrifices to the Father along with the Body of the Lord and thus consecrate the world itself to God.[9]

(3) These spiritual sacrifices, the whole world of human experience, are joined with the perfect sacrifice of Christ, the sole Mediator, through the ministry of ordained priests. In the Eucharist the spiritual sacrifices of the faithful are completed in union with the sacrifice of Christ offered by the priest in the name of the whole church in an unbloody and sacramental way.[10]

(4) Eucharistic celebration establishes and builds up Christian community.[11]

(5) Eucharist ought to motivate the Christian community to active social outreach.[12]

(6) Eucharist is the vital center of the church. In other words, the church is a eucharistic communion.

> But the other sacraments, and indeed all ecclesiastical ministries and works of the apostolate are bound up with the Eucharist and are directed towards it. For in the most blessed Eucharist is contained the whole spiritual good of the Church, namely Christ himself our Pasch and the living bread which gives life to humanity through his flesh—that flesh which is given life and gives life through the Holy Spirit. Thus men and women are invited and led to offer themselves, their works and all creation with Christ. For this reason the Eucharist appears as the source and the summit of all preaching of the

---

[8]"Pastoral Constitution on the Church in the Modern World," in Austin Flannery, ed., *Vatican Council II: The Conciliar and Post-Conciliar Documents* (Northport, NY: Costello Publishing Co., 1975), p. 937, no. 38.

[9]"Dogmatic Constitution on the Church," in Flannery, *Vatican Council II*, p. 391, no. 34.

[10]"Decree on the Ministry and Life of Priests," in Flannery, *Vatican Council II*, pp. 865-866, no. 2.

[11]Ibid., p. 874, no. 6.

[12]"The Constitution on the Sacred Liturgy," in Flannery, *Vatican Council II*, p. 6, no. 10.

Gospel: catechumens are gradually led up to participation in the Eucharist, while the faithful who have already been consecrated in baptism and confirmation are fully incorporated in the Body of Christ by the reception of the Eucharist.

Therefore the eucharistic celebration is the center of the assembly of the faithful over which the priest presides.[13]

(7) Eucharist perpetuates the sacrifice of the Cross and is a memorial of Christ's death and resurrection.[14]

(8) Through the eucharistic celebration the work of redemption continues. Redemption is the reconciling of all human beings and of everything human with God.[15]

(9) Thus Eucharist must be seen as being at the heart of the mission of the church and as helping to promote the unity of the human family.[16]

Anglican-Roman Catholic Mutual Agreement

These nine Roman Catholic theological concerns about Eucharist, expressed in the terminology of Vatican Council II, are discernible in the Windsor and Canterbury Statements of ARCIC. The Second Vatican Council's pastoral understanding of Eucharist is couched in the thought patterns of biblical and patristic theology which uses terms such as "mystery," "sacrament," "communion," and "memorial."[17] The Windsor and Canterbury Statements are written in this same theological style. This type of theological expression was consciously and deliberately chosen by ARCIC. Both of the Statements of ARCIC have, in the words of the 1966 *Common Declaration* of the Pope and the Archbishop of Canterbury, sought to express the fruits of "serious dialogue founded on the Gospels and on the ancient common traditions." This is one reason why the ARCIC Statements also use the thought patterns and terminology of biblical and patristic theology.

One may object that this more ancient and descriptively poetic theology and its categories of thought do not directly deal with the difficulties which Renaissance theology during the sixteenth century raised against the then cur-

---

[13]"Decree on the Ministry and Life of Priests," in Flannery, *Vatican Council II*, p. 871, no. 5, [The Decree's word *"homines"* is here corrected in translation to read "humanity" and "men and women."]

[14]"The Constitution on the Sacred Liturgy," in Flannery, *Vatican Council II*, p. 16, no. 47.

[15]"Dogmatic Constitution on the Church," in Flannery, *Vatican Council II*, p. 351, no. 3.

[16]"Pastoral Constitution on the Church in the Modern World," in Flannery, *Vatican Council II*, p. 942, no. 42.

[17]A good explanation of these terms and the theology that employs them is in J. D. Crichton, *Christian Celebration: The Mass* (London: Geoffrey Chapman, 1975), pp. viii-186.

rently accepted understanding of some Christian doctrines. There is a serious flaw in this objection. The objection is based on the assumption that Renaissance theology had developed a better method and framework to understand the revelation than that developed and employed during the apostolic age and the patristic period. One may well argue the relative merits of medieval scholasticism and Renaissance theology and the value of their methods and ideational frameworks to gain insight into the revelation. However, Christianity is not an abstract, timeless system of ideas. It is an historical religion based on the revelation in Christ. Jesus Christ, the Word of God, was incarnate and lived during a definite time in a specific place. Christ's thought, action, and expression were conditioned by the culture in which he lived. Thus biblical and patristic categories of thought and theology akin to that culture must retain a privileged position in the Christian heritage. Otherwise Christians would not be able to understand Christ's message. This fundamental fonviction, jointly shared by the Roman Catholic and Anglican theological traditions, not only determined the terminology and theological style of the ARCIC Statements but also provided the very basis which made them possible.

ANGLICAN RESPONSE BY DAVID A. SCOTT

My first dialogical comment in response to Fr. Herbert Ryan's article is that it is useful for helping to understand the perspective in which Roman Catholic-Anglican dialogues are carried out. He does this by pointing out that the "overarching framework" for the discussions is the conviction that the church is a eucharistic fellowship. Fr. Ryan clarifies the perspectives in which the dialogue occurs by highlighting nine "concerns" from documents of Vatican Council Two about the Eucharist which Roman Catholics bring to ecumenical dialogue. Furthermore, in the final section of his paper, he suggests that these nine Roman Catholic concerns are "discernible" in the Windsor and Canterbury Statements of ARCIC. He did not substantiate his claims that the Second Vatican Council's concerns are discernible in the Windsor and Canterbury Statements; to do so would be very difficult in the limited scope of these essays. The task of comparing Vatican Two documents and the Canterbury and Windsor Statements appears, however, to be a very necessary thing to do.

But equally important, and this is my second dialogical comment, is the related but different task of determining whether the Windsor and Canterbury Statements of ARCIC contain concerns about the Eucharist which are *not* discernible in the documents of Vatican Two, and especially in the nine concerns highlighted by Fr. Ryan. I wonder whether he would agree with me that, in fact, the Windsor and Canterbury Statements vividly express two concerns not found among the nine concerns he has drawn from the documents of Vatican Council Two.

The first of these is the stress on the ministry of the word *and* sacrament, not just on the ministry of the sacraments. I discern in the Canterbury Statement a concern to highlight the validity of the ministry of the word. The Statement over and over in paragraphs 8-13 speaks of the ministry of word *and* sacrament. Particularly significant in the context of Roman Catholic and Anglican dialogue is the explicit assertion of paragraph 11: "In both word and sacrament Christians meet the living Word of God." In contrast to this, the statement taken by Fr. Ryan from No. 5 of "Decree on the Ministry and the Life of Priests" indicates not a model of balance between ministry of word and sacrament, but one which locates the ministry of the word on the periphery of a circle the center of which is the Eucharist.

A second place where I see tension between the ARCIC Statements and the Council's citations given by Fr. Ryan concerns the relation of the priestly ministry and the lay ministry. The wording of the Canterbury Statement stresses that the ordained ministry *exists to serve* the Christian community and the world. The language and imagery of the Canterbury document recalls the servant imagery of Jesus' teaching in the New Testament, e.g., in Mark 10:45. Thereby, also, the fullness and authenticity of non-ordained ministry is stressed. In rather sharp contrast to this service motif, is the image of the relation between priests and laity in Fr. Ryan's quotations from Vatican Council Two documents. In these citations the priesthood is described as, by implication at least, more "intimately" joined to Jesus' life and mission than the ministry of the laity. (I refer to the citation from the "Dogmatic Constitution on the Church," no. 34.) Further, the language of the quote from "Decree on the Ministry and Life of Priests," no. 2, indicates that without the mediation of ordained priests, the offering of the faithful is incomplete.

In short, the Canterbury Statement and the New Testament present a servant model of the relation between orders of ministry within the Christian community and the lay ministry of the people of God. The citations from Vatican Two given by Fr. Ryan suggest the image of a ladder of intimacy and completeness in sharing in Christ's reality and ministry, a ladder in which the laity are below the ordained ministry.

I believe the pastoral concern of the present Eucharistic Congress is imaged better by the servant model of the New Testament and Canterbury Statement than those Vatican Council texts which reflect a picture of ministry hierarchically conceived, in which the ministry of the laity in the world is pictured as least relevant to the mission and ministry of Christ.

In our age of desperate physical and spiritual hungers, it would be frightening for the Christian community to be liable to Jesus' indictment of the Pharisees reflected in the pericope Matthew 12:1-8 and his prophetic word that God wants mercy and not sacrifice.

Study and Discussion Questions

1. Discuss what Scott means by saying that the Anglican Communion is not a "confessional Communion," and what the relevance of this statement is to the Anglican-Roman Catholic dialogue on the Eucharist.
2. In Scott's view, in what general areas of eucharistic thought is there a consensus and in what areas a difference of viewpoint among Anglicans? Discuss.
3. Discuss on what basis Anglicans have traditionally rejected what they took to be the Roman Catholic teaching on transubstantiation.
4. Specifically, what is meant by saying that transubstantiation "overthroweth the nature of a sacrament"? Have recent Anglican-Roman Catholic discussions dulled the point of this objection? Discuss.
5. In what precise way does Scott think the Windsor Statement has succeeded in transcending the disagreements between Anglicans and Roman Catholics?
6. What omissions of traditional Roman Catholic teaching from the Windsor Statement does Scott find significant? Discuss.
7. According to Ryan, in what way has the Eucharist been a focal point for the Anglican-Roman Catholic dialogues?
8. Ryan refers to the "pastoral vision of the Eucharist" of Vatican II. Discuss to what this expression refers and to what "pastoral" is being contrasted.
9. Ryan finds Vatican II reflected in the Windsor and Canterbury Statements. Scott claims that Ryan's assertion awaits substantiation. Discuss whether you think the assertion can be substantiated.
10. Scott finds tension between the Windsor and Canterbury Statements and those teachings of Vatican II that seem to minimize the ministry of the Word and ministry of the non-ordained. Discuss whether you find the same tension.

LUTHERAN-CATHOLIC DIALOGUE

George A. Lindbeck—Avery Dulles

PRECIS

Despite some exceptions, Lutherans have generally been reticent about intercommunion. The most important consideration in deciding on possible intercommunion has been "agreement in the doctrine of the gospel." This principle, however, is variously understood by Lutherans: from those who seek a virtual unanimity among communicants (Missouri Synod) to those satisfied with a minimal agreement (Swedish-Anglican Agreement, 1920). The Leuenberg Concord (1973) stands midway between. Centuries-old disputes have made it more difficult to achieve "agreement" between Lutherans and Reformed Christians than between Lutherans and Anglicans.

As for intercommunion with Roman Catholics, Lutherans have sometimes followed the Swedish/Anglican model, i.e., basing discussions on the current absence of clear-cut conflict in understanding the center of the gospel, thus suggesting the possibility of limited eucharistic sharing. The U.S. Lutheran/Roman Catholic dialogue, however, resembles the Leuenberg model in that it has confronted several historical areas of disagreement, viz., the Roman Catholic understanding of the Mass, of transubstantiation, and of real presence. Now, as a result, U. S. Lutheran theologians accept the Roman Catholic Eucharist as "in agreement with the gospel." This acceptance does not necessarily lead to intercommunion since various Roman Catholic dogmas may still be considered sufficiently problematic as to discourage even occasional eucharistic sharing.

Lindbeck urges Lutheran and Roman Catholic authorities to draw up cooperative guidelines for occasional sharing so that the fairly widespread pastoral practice of intercommunion may prove to be unitive and not divisive to both churches. For Dulles, occasional acts of intercommunion are an appropriate sign of the partial but growing unity among separated churches and an appropriate remedy for their separation. He discusses the general conditions for intercommunion and finds many of these conditions already verified, in the Lutheran and Roman Catholic situation. The most problematic conditions are: (1) a basic agreement on the nature and meaning of the Eucharist, and (2) agreement that a given service is truly eucharistic.

Official Vatican documents seem to assert that since Protestant churches lack valid ordinations, they do not have a valid Eucharist, and, therefore, that it would be improper for Catholics to receive their Eucharist. The Catholic participants in the U. S. Lutheran/Roman Catholic dialogue have left open the question as to whether Lutheran churches have an authentic Eucharist. These theologians seem more open to the likelihood of a valid Lutheran ministry, and therefore a valid Eucharist, than they are to the argument that there is a valid Lutheran Eucharist even though there are lacking validly-ordained ministers.

Several European initiatives which provide for occasional intercommunion are taken by Dulles to be a positive advance, standing at the center of the previous "all-or-nothing" approach.

George A. Lindbeck (Lutheran), B.A., Gustavus Adolphus College, B.D., Yale University Divinity School, Ph.D., Yale University Graduate School (with additional studies at the Universities of Toronto and Paris), is Professor of Theology in the Yale Divinity School and the Department of Religious Studies at Yale University. An Associate Editor of the *Journal of Ecumenical Studies*, he has published many articles; his books include *The Future of Roman Catholic Theology, Infallibility, Dialogue on the Way* (ed.), and *Divinity and the University*. He was a Lutheran World Federation observer at Vatican II.

Avery Dulles, S.J. (Roman Catholic), A.B., Harvard, Ph.L., S.T.L., Woodstock College, S.T.D., Gregorian University (Rome), is Professor of Theology at the Catholic University of America in Washington, DC, and president of the Catholic Theological Society of America (1975-76). His books include *The Survival of Dogma, A History of Apologetics, Models of the Church*, and *Church Membership as a Catholic and Ecumenical Problem*.

A LUTHERAN VIEW OF INTERCOMMUNION
WITH ROMAN CATHOLICS

George A. Lindbeck

What I shall do in this paper is, first, describe the major Lutheran approaches to the question of intercommunion; second, discuss their implications for intercommunion with Roman Catholics; and, third, comment on the underlying issues.

I

Lutherans as a whole have been more reluctant than other Protestants to engage in intercommunion. Indeed, there are sizable Lutheran bodies who are more restrictive in this respect than any other mainstream Christians. The three-million-member Missouri Synod, for example, comprising one third of American Lutherans, is officially not in communion with most of the seventy million Lutherans in the world.[1] This, to be sure, is not typical. Most Lutheran churches are in communion with each other, and many have moved or are moving toward establishment of some degree of official eucharistic fellowship with various non-Lutheran bodies. The two major current examples of this are, first, the agreement between the Church of Sweden and the Anglicans (which dates from 1920) and, second, the Leuenberg Concord of 1973[2] which is an officially negotiated proposal for the establishment of pulpit-and-altar fellowship between all the major European Reformation churches, whether Lutheran or Reformed. Further, it should be noted that intercommunion between the Reformed and Lutherans has been customary for centuries in some European countries such as Austria where Protestants are a small minority. Nevertheless, despite these exceptions, Lutherans, like the Orthodox, Roman Catholics, and many Anglicans, have in general been reticent about intercommunion.

The reasons for their reticence have, however, been different. Episcopal ordination is not an issue. This is, from their point of view, quite unnecessary for valid eucharistic ministry. Even the Church of Sweden, which has bishops in the apostolic succession, agrees on this point, for it is in full communion with non-episcopal Lutheran churches. All that is required for valid ministers, according to Article XIV of the Augsburg Confession,[3] the most important of Luther-

---

[1] For a full account and documentation of the intercommunion situation among Lutherans as of the early sixties, see Vilmos Vajta, ed., *Church in Fellowship* (Minneapolis: Augsburg, 1963).

[2] The text is in *Lutheran World* 20, 4 (1973): 347-353. For a full discussion, see Marc Lienhard, *Lutherisch-Reformierte Kirchengemeinschaft Heute* (Frankfurt am M.: Lembeck, 1973).

[3] For the text in English of the Augsburg Confession, see Theodore G. Tappart, ed., *The Book of Concord* (Philadelphia: Muhlenburg, 1959), pp. 27-96.

an confessions, is that they be *rite vocatus* ("regularly called"), but this may happen congregationally or presbyterially as well as episcopally. What is required for the unity of the church, and therefore for communion, as Article VII of the same Confession emphasizes, is not common ecclesiastical polity, but rather "agreement in the doctrine of the gospel (*doctrina evangelii*)." This is enough (*satis est*); nothing else is needed. On this point Lutherans have consistently been close to unanimous.

Where they have differed from each other, however, is on the nature of this "agreement in the gospel." Three major positions can be distinguished. The first, exemplified by the Missouri Synod, has, as we have already mentioned, restrictive consequences. Agreement must be comprehensively spelled out in detailed doctrinal formulations, and, furthermore, what is actually taught in the churches must conform to these formulations. One cannot be in communion with churches which, even if officially orthodox, nevertheless tolerate error, or are in communion with other churches which are in error.[4] Such criteria, when rigorously adhered to, lead to a progressive narrowing of the circle of eucharistic fellowship. All non-Lutheran churches, and most Lutheran ones, fail to qualify.

At the other end of the spectrum is a position which assumes "agreement in the gospel" in the absence of evidence to the contrary. One should assume that Christian churches understand the gospel in compatible ways providing they tolerate or do not denounce each others' positions. Such minimal agreement perhaps does not suffice for full church fellowship, but under some circumstances it can be enough to justify reciprocal general admission of the members of two churches to each others' communions and perhaps even some degree of inter-celebration.

Something like this seems to be the position adopted by the Church of Sweden with reference to the Anglicans. The Swedish bishops, in welcoming the approval of intercommunion by the Lambeth Conference, made it clear, first of all, that they did *not* do so for the reasons set forth by the Conference: viz., "succession" and "the conception of the priesthood."[5] While the historic episcopacy is to be regarded "with the reverence due to a venerable legacy from the past," this is not of "decisive importance."[6] The distinction between bishops and other clergy is of human rather than divine law (*de iure humano* rather than *de iure divino*), and so is not essential to the structure of the church or to the validity of ordinations and eucharistic celebrations. For this reason, the Swedish Church can be in full communion with other Lutheran churches which are non-episcopal in polity. What is important for intercommunion is that "the two communities agree . . . as to the content of the message of salvation, founded on the divine revelation, which has been committed to both of them."[7] This in-

---

[4]Fred W. Meuser, "Pulpit and Altar Fellowship among Lutherans in America," in Vajta, *Church in Fellowship*, p. 20.

[5]Vajta, *Church in Fellowship*, p. 180.

[6]Ibid., p. 183

[7]Ibid., p. 184.

volves "reception of Scripture as *norma normans* [a standard-setting norm] both with regard to life and doctrine, and the building of our salvation on God's grace alone received by faith."[8] "Between God and the soul, or which is the same to us, between Christ and faith, nothing, no third principle, no institution, no law, no works of our own, must intervene."[9] The evidence that Anglicans share these convictions is partly found in their doctrinal formulations (the sixth, eleventh, twelfth and thirteenth of the Thirty-Nine Articles are mentioned). The chief consideration, however, appears to be that the Anglicans do not oppose what the Lutherans confess. The English Church does not attempt "to imbue [Lutherans] with other doctrines than those which our Church confesses, or to separate them in any respect from this Church."[10] In short, intercommunion with Anglicans is possible, not because of shared doctrinal formulations, but because Anglican and Lutheran teaching and life are not in conflict.

In addition to the extremes represented by the Missouri Synod and the Swedish Church, however, there is a third intermediate position of which the Leuenberg Concord is the most notable recent example. This does not insist on a comprehensive and detailed consensus in doctrinal formulations, as does the first, nor does it rest content with an unformulated "agreement in the gospel," as does the second. Rather, it deals explicitly with a few issues, viz., those which have historically been disputed between the Reformed and the Lutherans, while for the rest leaving the two sides with their different, even if not contradictory, ways of understanding the faith.

This difference between the Swedish and Leuenberg models, however, is not so much the result of a disagreement regarding the pre-conditions for eucharistic fellowship as the consequence of differences in Lutheran relations to the Anglican and Reformed traditions respectively. Anglicans and Lutherans have been isolated from each other. There have been few if any occasions or opportunities for church conflicts between them. In contrast to this, beginning with Marburg in 1529,[11] the Reformed and the Lutherans have engaged in violent disputes. They have, in effect, anthematized each others' doctrines at important points. The Lutherans have condemned what they considered to be the insufficient realism of Reformed eucharistic teaching, the doctrine of double predestination, and the Reformed tendency toward scriptural literalism and puritanic moralism and legalism (i.e., "the failure to distinguish properly between Law and Gospel"). The Reformed, in turn, have accused the Lutherans, among other things, of remaining semi-Catholic in their sacramental views and liturgical practice, and of moral laxity especially in the sphere of social ethics (where Lutherans have, as a matter of fact, often been more conservative, more establishmentarian, than

---

[8]Ibid.

[9]Ibid., p. 186.

[10]Ibid., p. 182.

[11]For a reexamination of Lutheran-Reformed conflicts, see Paul C. Empie and James I. McCord, eds., *Marburg Revisited* (Minneapolis: Augsburg, 1966).

their Calvinist counterparts). Given this history, the authors of the Leuenberg Concord believed that it was impossible to recommend pulpit-and-altar fellowship between the two traditions without an official explanation of why and how these disputes from the past are no longer church-dividing. Simply a tacit recognition of the Christian character of each others' life and teachings would not be sufficient. Where anathemas have been publicly uttered they need to be publicly withdrawn. Simply to forget about them is ahistorical and individualistic, and in effect amounts to refusing to take seriously membership in the historic traditions and communities.

II

Intercommunion with Roman Catholics combines for Lutherans the difficulties of intercommunion with the Anglicans and with the Reformed. Catholics, like Anglicans, are greatly concerned about questions of apostolic succession and ministerial validity; and in addition, there is with them, even more than with the Reformed, a long history of public polemics and mutual denunciation. In the church-sponsored dialogues with Roman Catholics, Lutherans have sometimes tended to follow the Swedish-Anglican approach to reconciliation. Instead of detailed attention to historic controversies, they have based themselves on the present absence of clear-cut conflict in the understanding of the "center of the gospel," and have moved quickly to the suggestion that this is enough for at least a limited degree of eucharistic fellowship. The international dialogue sponsored by the Lutheran World Federation and the Vatican Secretariat for Christian Unity in some respects took this approach in the so-called "Malta Report" of 1972 ("The Gospel and the Church").[12]

The U. S. dialogue in contrast has, like the Leuenberg discussions, had the time and the resources to enter in greater detail into the historic disagreements. It has, however, dealt with only a few of these, chiefly those centering on the understanding of the Eucharist itself, and has expressed no opinion on whether the convergences it has noted suffice even for minimal intercommunion. These convergences, however, even if not sufficient, are clearly of great importance for the possibilities of future fellowship.

It is affirmed, in the first place, that the contemporary Roman Catholic understanding of the Mass as sacrifice is not in contradiction to the central Reformation insistence on salvation by grace alone through faith. Historically this has been the critical issue. Both Luther and Calvin attacked late medieval theology and practice for, in their view, turning the Mass into a meritorious human work, an unbloody repetition by the church of Christ's sacrifice on Calvary, through which God is placated and grace is acquired. The vast proliferation of private Masses and Mass stipends without any concern for congregational communion was to them decisive proof that the Mass had been turned into an abomination, the greatest of the blasphemies of the "papist" church. What must

---

[12] *Lutheran World* 19, 3 (1972): 259-273.

be done, they contend, is to make clear that the Lord's Supper is entirely God's work and gift to believers, not at all something which we do in order to obtain God's favor. From this point of view, the most important aspect of the U. S. dialogue on the Eucharist is its interpretation of the eucharistic sacrifice. The church or believers offer Christ primarily in the sense that Christ offers them: "members of the body of Christ are united through Christ with God and with one another in such a way that they have become participants in his worship, his self-offering, his sacrifice to the Father."[13] When this interpretation is combined with the liturgical reforms which emphasize the superiority of communal, rather than private, eucharistic celebrations and allow lay communion in both kinds, Lutherans no longer regard the Catholic doctrine of the eucharistic sacrifice as un-Christian, as opposed to the gospel.

A second issue, that of transubstantiation and the real presence, has historically and theologically been less of a problem for Lutherans, although it has become in recent times the major disagreement in the popular mind. Lutherans have traditionally been no less insistent than Catholics on the reality of the presence of Christ's true body and blood "in, with and under" the elements. This often makes them closer in their eucharistic piety to Catholics than to most Protestants. To be sure, they have rejected transubstantiation as an unscriptural and rationalistic (Aristotelian) attempt to explain the mystery of Christ's sacramental presence. But, as the dialogue statement puts it, "What was in dispute . . . was not the *that,* the full reality of Christ's presence, but rather a particular way of defining the manner in which he becomes present. Today, however, when Lutheran theologians read contemporary Catholic expositions, it becomes clear to them that the dogma of transubstantiation intends to affirm the fact of Christ's presence and of the change which takes place, and is not an attempt to explain *how* Christ becomes present. When the dogma is understood in this way, Lutherans find that they also must acknowledge that it is a legitimate way of attempting to express the mystery, even though they continue to believe that the conceptuality associated with 'transubstantiation' is misleading and therefore prefer to avoid the term."[14]

Given these clarifications in understanding and practice, there is no doubt in Lutheran minds that Roman Catholic Eucharists can be celebrated "in agreement with the gospel," that is, validly. Catholic priests are regularly called to their office by Christian communities, and that is all that is needed to empower them to celebrate. For this reason, the Lutheran participants in both the U. S. and the international dialogues found it easy to recommend that their church authorities officially recognize the validity of Roman Catholic Eucharists and ministries. The difficulties on this point are all on the other side. It is Roman Catholics, as Father Dulles makes clear in his article, who are uncertain how far,

---

[13]Lutherans and Catholics in Dialogue, vol. III, *The Eucharist as Sacrifice* (Washington, DC: USCC, 1968), p. 189. Italics added.

[14]Ibid., p. 196.

given agreement in the basic understanding and practice of the Eucharist, Lutheran celebrations may be valid even when the ministers have not been ordained by bishops in the historic succession.

Yet it must be emphasized that even mutual recognition of validity does not, from the traditional Lutheran perspective, automatically lead to intercommunion. There may still be points, such as episcopacy, papacy, infallibility, and the Marian dogmas, in which each side still feels conscience-bound to criticize the other as in error, as opposed to Christian truth. If so, occasional admission to each others' Eucharists in cases of pastoral need, as envisioned in the Strasbourg directives on eucharistic hospitality,[15] might still be possible, but that would be the limit of official intercommunion. Anything more than that would be a "false sign of unity," for it would suggest, in the absence of any responsible communal decisions to that effect, that the two communions no longer considered each other seriously wrong on issues such as those just mentioned. Official approval of general admission to each others' Eucharists is impossible, and inter-celebration even on an occasional basis is highly questionable, until the mutual anathemas of the past have been withdrawn.

III

The difficulty with even this minimal form of the traditional Lutheran insistence on doctrinal agreement, "agreement in the gospel," as a pre-condition for official intercommunion is that it no longer corresponds to the pastoral situation. The practice of intercommunion has become widespread. Simply to condemn or ignore this does not stop the practice. On the contrary, it increases the dangers of irresponsibility. Guidance from the ecclesiastical authorities is needed in order to make the increasing unofficial eucharistic fellowship fruitful for the life and unity of the churches.

For Lutherans, in terms of their tradition, it is important that intercommunion emphasize that the Lord's supper is God's gift, not our work, that Christ is truly present even in his body and blood, and that this sacrament in its unifying function is a central part of Christian worship and witness. As a matter of historical fact, Lutheran resistance to intercommunion has chiefly been in situations where the realism of Christ's presence and the importance of the sacrament have in effect been minimized, rather than enhanced. It is intercommunion with "sacramentarians," that is, with Protestants who are not sacramental realists, which has been seen as the chief danger. Some degree of eucharistic fellowship with the sacramentally realistic churches—with the Anglicans, Catholics and Orthodox—is from this point of view admissible.

The one further condition is that the participants in each other's eucharistic services are not *de facto* seen as abandoning their own understandings of the

---

[15]*Lutheran World* 20, 4 (1973): 353-360. For a fuller treatment of the problems from a Lutheran perspective, see Vilmos Vajta, *Interkommunion mit Rom?* (Göttingen: Vandenhoeck & Ruprecht, 1969).

gospel or embracing the "errors" of the other party. This, however, is not a legal condition, but a psycho-social one which, in the present religious and sociological situation, is almost always present.

Clearly it is impossible to legislate a set of juridical rules which would insure that these conditions are always met. The most that the church authorities can do is to provide pastoral guidelines and urge that they be followed wisely and responsibly.

The greatest question, perhaps, is whether it is charitable for Lutheran churches to take unilateral action in this matter. Would this not be equivalent to allowing or encouraging Lutherans to tempt Catholics, for example, to break the disciplinary regulations of their own church? It would be an immense advantage if the sacramentally realistic churches could, by a process of joint consultations, develop coordinate guidelines in this area. This would greatly increase the possibility that the present surge in unofficial intercommunion would have constructive, rather than disintegrating, consequences for the unity of the church universal.

CATHOLIC RESPONSE BY AVERY DULLES

The major portion of Dr. Lindbeck's paper deals with the conditions under which general eucharistic sharing between Lutherans and Roman Catholics might properly be authorized. Rightly, in my judgment, he favors a middle course between the Missouri Synod, which would insist on virtual theological unanimity, and the Church of Sweden which, by his account, would be satisfied with a minimal "agreement in the gospel." Using the model of the Leuenberg Concord, he holds that altar fellowship would not be appropriate unless accompanied by some agreed explanation of why the major disputes of the past are no longer seen as barriers. He even suggests that the mutual anathemas of the past must be withdrawn.

Lindbeck's line of reasoning points up the importance of the theological consultations between confessional families. Theologians must labor to clarify the distinctions between essential and unessential doctrines and to seek to overcome, by reinterpretation, their disagreements about the former. Generally speaking, the recent efforts to overcome past disagreements have proved beneficial to the participants. The exercise has helped the churches to correct the one-sidedness of their own previous positions and to advance toward a more contemporary understanding of the gospel.

If there were anything to be added to Dr. Lindbeck's lucid analysis, it might be a fuller attention to the non-doctrinal factors. Habitual eucharistic sharing, in my estimation, presupposes a real community of life and charity, so that the congregations no longer view themselves as mutually estranged bodies but as complementary realizations of the one church of Christ.

Dr. Lindbeck and I agree that at the present time it would not be proper to countenance general eucharistic sharing between Lutherans and Catholics, but that occasional admission to each other's Eucharists, along the lines envisioned by the Strasbourg directives on eucharistic hospitality, may be in order. I concur with the statements in Lindbeck's closing paragraphs to the effect that the conditions for mutual eucharistic sharing cannot be strictly legislated, that sound pastoral guidelines are desirable, that these should not be unilateral, and that joint theological consultations should contribute to their formulation. In the United States, I believe, we cannot take over without modification the directives laid down for any European country.

I doubt whether it is possible to compose specific guidelines that do justice to the full complexity of the religious situation in this country. The directives, to be practical, would have to be rather simple, and could not include all the nuances that academic theologians would wish to introduce. It would be impractical, for instance, to make distinctions among the various Protestant denominations, although the differences between them are important. Thus we may have to live with general rules that are inapplicable to particular cases. That is why directives, rather than laws, are to be sought.

As Lindbeck points out, excessive laxity in the practice of the faithful may be at least as harmful as excessive rigidity in the ecclesiastical directives. Efforts must be made to prevent holy communion from degenerating into a mere expression of courtesy, friendship, or solidarity in secular causes. Ideally, eucharistic sharing should be a sign that expresses and enhances the unity of the church as a community constituted by God's enduring gift of himself in the Paschal mystery. If this christological and ecclesial significance is maintained, intercommunion should be encouraged. If this significance is lacking, efforts should be made to restrict the practice of intercommunion. In saying this, I intend to express my agreement with Lindbeck's response to my own article.

INTERCOMMUNION BETWEEN LUTHERANS AND
ROMAN CATHOLICS?

Avery Dulles

Intercommunion—in the sense of eucharistic sharing across confessional lines—is of its very nature problematical. If there are divisions between churches, and if the Eucharist is the sacrament of church unity, intercommunion might seem, at first glance, to be precluded. On the other hand, the Eucharist is not and never can be the sign of a perfectly achieved unity; it is always the sign of an imperfect unity seeking to become more perfect. And the different denominational churches increasingly see themselves as being, notwithstanding their structural and doctrinal divisions, fundamentally one in Christ. Granted, then, that one should normally receive communion in a service of one's own confession, occasional acts of intercommunion may be seen as an appropriate sign of· the partial but growing unity among separated churches and as an appropriate remedy for their present separations.

Because of the ecclesial significance of the Eucharist itself, certain conditions must be respected as preconditions for intercommunion. Without any claim to completeness, the following conditions might be specified: (1) a basic unity in faith, expressed by common creeds understood in a similar way; (2) a sense of somehow belonging, notwithstanding all the divisions, to the one church of Christ; (3) the will to a more perfect union; (4) a basic agreement about the nature and meaning of the Eucharist; (5) and, finally, a shared conviction about what is transpiring at the particular eucharistic service being conducted.

With reference to the Lutheran-Catholic relationship, the first three of these five conditions would not be difficult to verify, at least for certain individuals, parishes, and synods. Theological debate has therefore focused principally on the last two conditions, which are more problematic in character. It is asked, first, whether the two confessions are sufficiently agreed about eucharistic doctrine for sacramental sharing to be appropriate, and, second, whether they can agree that each other's services are true Eucharists.

The Lutheran-Catholic Dialogue in the United States has not formally addressed itself to the question of intercommunion, but two of its published volumes have major implications for this question. Its third volume, dealing with eucharistic doctrine, establishes, to the satisfaction of the authors, that the traditional divergences regarding the sacrifice of the Mass and the real presence are not insuperable. "Despite all remaining differences in the ways we speak and think of the eucharistic sacrifice and our Lord's presence in his supper, we are no longer able to regard ourselves as divided in the one holy catholic and apostolic faith on these two points."[1] The unresolved issues are seen as secondary in

---

[1] Lutherans and Catholics in Dialogue, vol. III, *The Eucharist as Sacrifice* (Washington, DC: USCC, 1968), p.198.

character and as capable of being debated within a united family.

The greatest obstacle to intercommunion, therefore, would seem to be the last one: the difficulty of recognizing each other's eucharistic services as authentic. This question is treated in volume four, in the context of an agreed statement on ministry. The conclusion is generally positive, but there is a certain disparity between the Lutheran and Catholic positions. The Lutherans, for their part, have no difficulty in recommending that the authorities of their churches issue a formal declaration to the effect that Roman Catholic priests are engaged in a valid ministry of the gospel and that Jesus Christ is truly present in their celebrations of the Eucharist.[2] The Catholics, in turn, find "serious defects in the arguments customarily used against the validity of the eucharistic ministry of the Lutheran churches." Without unequivocally recommending recognition, they ask whether "the ecumenical urgency flowing from Christ's will for unity may not dictate that the Roman Catholic Church recognize the validity of the Lutheran ministry and, correspondingly, the presence of the body and blood of Christ in the eucharistic celebrations of the Lutheran churches."[3]

The question form in which this recommendation is put betrays some hesitation. Apparently the Roman Catholic participants, unlike their Lutheran counterparts, felt unable to recommend unreservedly that recognition be extended to Lutheran ministries. They were therefore content to put the question whether such recognition should not be given. While finding defects in the usual arguments against Lutheran orders, they did not affirm that Lutheran orders are in fact valid. Still less did they firmly endorse any particular argument tending to prove this fact. Instead they declared that they had no intention of solving the question of the validity of Lutheran orders in the past and that they were not attempting to decide whether recognition by the Catholic Church today would be constitutive of the validity of Lutheran orders or merely confirmatory of an existing validity.[4] In other words, they left it unclear whether they were asking the Catholic Church to *make* Lutheran ministries valid or to acknowledge that these ministries are *already* valid. In so doing they left open the question whether the Lutheran churches now have an authentic Eucharist.

Without contradicting anything said by the Roman Catholic participants in the Dialogue, one could take any one of the following three positions:

1. The Lutheran churches presently lack both a valid ministry and, consequently, a valid Eucharist.

2. The Lutheran churches already have a validly ordained ministry and, correspondingly, a valid Eucharist.

3. The Lutheran churches, although they do not have a validly ordained ministry, do have an authentic Eucharist.

---

[2] Lutherans and Catholics in Dialogue, vol. IV, *Eucharist and Ministry* (Washington, DC: USCC, 1970), p. 22.

[3] Ibid., p. 32.

[4] Ibid.

The first of these positions would be highly unfavorable to intercommunion. The second and third positions would tend rather to favor intercommunion, although neither of them, by itself, would be sufficient to justify intercommunion.

The first of the three positions seems to be most compatible with the Roman documents issued since the Council. The Ecumenical Directory of 1967 in article 59 says that when a Catholic goes to a Protestant service "reception of the Eucharist is always excluded." The reason is hinted at in article 55, which states that although a Protestant may under certain circumstances receive at a Catholic Mass, "a Catholic in similar circumstances may not ask for the sacraments except from a minister who has been validly ordained." The Roman position seems to be as follows: The Protestant churches do not have valid ordinations; therefore they lack a valid Eucharist and consequently it would be improper for a Catholic to receive at their services.

In contrast to this opinion, the U. S. Lutheran-Catholic Dialogue suggests at least the likelihood that Lutheran ministries, even though they make no claim to a pedigree of bishops standing at the apostolic succession, are nevertheless valid. Some Catholics and Lutherans have contended that ordination can be validly conferred by the community of believers or by presbyters, at least under certain circumstances such as the impossibility of obtaining an ordaining prelate. If this be true, one could take the second of the proposed positions, namely that the Lutheran Eucharist is valid because confected by a minister with valid orders.

The Lutheran-Catholic Dialogue suggests that this view would be neither contrary to the evidence from the New Testament nor demonstrably against the teaching of the Council of Trent. But the Dialogue does not go so far as to assert that this position is true. At the present time, it seems to be contrary to the Roman view, as represented both by the Ecumenical Directory, already quoted, and by the document on Apostolic Succession issued by the International Theological Commission with the approval of the Holy See in April, 1974. This later document states that because the practice of imposing hands was either abandoned in Protestant churches or, if retained, ceased to have the required sacramental significance, "intercommunion [with such churches] remains impossible for the time being, because sacramental continuity in apostolic succession from the beginning is an indispensable element of ecclesial communion. . . ."[5]

There remains the third logical possibility: that the Lutheran churches, even though they lack validly ordained ministers, do have a valid Eucharist. In the Catholic "reflections" included in the U. S. Lutheran-Catholic consensus statement, there are some allusions to arguments tending to prove that unordained ministers can celebrate a true Eucharist—e.g., the argument from the silence of the New Testament regarding the competent minister of the Eucharist and several rather obscure Patristic texts which can be read as acknowledging that in certain cases an unordained person could preside. It is doubtful how much stock

---

[5]See text in *Origins* 4, 13 (September 19, 1974): 200.

the Catholic participants in the Dialogue meant to invest in this position, since their main argument is in support of the recognizability of Lutheran ministries. Possibly this third position is brought in merely as a back-up.

Other dialogue groups, treating specifically of intercommunion, have put greater weight on this third position. For instance, the Joint Lutheran/Roman Catholic Study Commission, in its 1972 report on "The Gospel and the Church," took a position in favor of "occasional acts of intercommunion." As justification the Report declared:

> Unclarity concerning a common doctrine of the ministerial office still makes for difficulties in reciprocal intercommunion agreements. However, the realization of eucharistic fellowship should not depend exclusively on full recognition of the offices of the ministry.[6]

Four of the seven Catholic participants in this dialogue, in putting their signatures to the report, appended explanations in which they dissociated themselves from the paragraph from which I have just quoted, so that this paragraph may not be taken as representing even the majority view among the Catholic signers. Nevertheless, the statement perhaps reflects the views of the Lutheran signers and those of three Catholic signers.

This third position will not easily become the basis for the approved practice of the Catholic Church because it disagrees with the teaching of Vatican II (*Lumen gentium*, no. 10) and with several recent declarations of the Congregation for the Doctrine of the Faith. In a Declaration of February 15, 1975, concerning two books by Hans Küng, the Congregation specifically condemned the view that, even in cases of necessity, the Eucharist could be validly consecrated by baptized persons lacking sacerdotal orders. This view, said the council, cannot be reconciled with the Fourth Lateran Council or with Vatican II.[7]

From what we have said thus far, it might seem that there is no prospect, from the Catholic point of view, of permitting officially any kind of reciprocal eucharistic hospitality with Lutherans. Since the Lutheran-Catholic volumes on Eucharist and Ministry, however, there have been significant developments opening up new possibilities apparently not envisaged in the publications of the American Dialogue.

In a set of pastoral directives on eucharistic hospitality issued in November, 1972, Bishop Léon Arthur Elchinger of Strasbourg set forth a nuanced position that seems to do full justice to the teaching of Vatican II and at the same time to make room for occasional intercommunion. A Catholic accepting eucharistic hospitality from a Protestant church, says the bishop,

---

[6]*Lutheran World* 19, 3 (1972): 259-273; quotation from no. 73, p. 271.

[7]Text in *Origins* 4, 37 (March 6, 1975): 577, 579. The same point was made in section 6 of the Declaration, *Mysterium Ecclesiae*, issued by the Congregation for the Doctrine of the Faith on June 24, 1973.

would recall that certain deficiencies exist—greater or lesser according to the particular church—on the plane of the sacramental orga-
nism by which the Church visibly constitutes itself as the Body of
Christ.

He would know, however, that in spite of these deficiencies, those
who celebrate the Eucharist in faith and fidelity to the Lord's testament may really share in the life of Christ who gives himself as food
to his own for the building up of his one Body.[8]

Such a Catholic, then, would receive communion at a Protestant service
with the consciousness "that this celebration—in a mysterious and real manner,
difficult to specify precisely—gives him a share in the unique eucharistic reality
which he is certain, according to his faith, of approaching in all its sacramental
plenitude in his own church."

Since Bishop Elchinger's courageous initiatives, some other individual
bishops and groups of bishops have begun to take similar positions. Bishop
Schmitt of Metz, on July 10, 1973, authorized certain Catholics of his diocese to
receive communion at Protestant services "under the conditions anticipated in
the Guidelines of the Bishop of Strasbourg, Msgr. Elchinger."[9] The French
Bishops' Committee for Christian Unity, in a recent commentary on a document
by the Groupe des Dombes,[10] accepts the possibility of limited intercommunion
with Protestants. We have not yet reached the day, they declare, when eucharistic hospitality and especially reciprocity present no problems. In the present
ambiguous situation it is important to avoid an "all or nothing" mentality. It is
the responsibility of the local bishop to exercise discretion in particular cases.

Even more significant for its detail is the Pastoral Instruction adopted on
March 1, 1975, by the Swiss Interdiocesan Synodal Assembly and subsequently
approved by the Swiss Episcopal Conference.[11] This instruction holds, in conformity with the Decree on Ecumenism (no. 22), that any church which has not
retained the episcopate and the sacrament of orders lacks the "full reality of the
eucharistic mystery." In such cases the general rule is that of the Ecumenical
Directory (no. 55), that a Catholic may not ask to receive the Eucharist from a
minister who has not validly received the sacrament of orders. But if a Catholic

---

[8]Text in *Documentation Catholique* 1626 (February 18, 1973): 161-170; for English
translation, see *One in Christ* 9, 4 (1973): 371-387. I have given some reflections on this
statement in my article, "Ministry and Intercommunion: Recent Ecumenical Statements
and Debates," *Theological Studies* 34, 4 (1973): 643-678. See also G. A. Ansons, "Intercommunion in Anticipation of Greater Unity," *Journal of Ecumenical Studies* 11, 2 (Spring,
1974): 315-321; and Joseph Hoffman, "Eucharistic Hospitality," *One in Christ* 11, 3
(1975): 266-281.

[9]The statement of Bishop Schmitt is quoted in "Reports and Documentation,"
Lutheran World 22 (1975): 151.

[10]Text of the statement of the French hierarchy may be found in *Documentation
Catholique* 72, 3 (1975), no. 1669: 126-129.

[11]Text in *Documentation Catholique* 72, 11 (1975), no. 1677: 529-531.

in an exceptional situation arrives at the conviction that his or her conscience authorizes him to her to receive the Eucharist, "this step should not be interpreted as necessarily implying a rupture with his own church, even though common sharing of the Eucharist remains problematical as long as the separation of the churches continues."

These recent statements seem to me to represent a positive advance. In the past most discussions of ministry and Eucharist have been hampered by an all-or-nothing understanding both of church office and of "real presence." Current theological probings into the nature of the apostolic ministry and the real presence increasingly stress the many dimensions of both. The apostolic ministry is constituted not simply by a bishop laying on hands, but by a personal vocation of the ordained to the ministry, by charisms recognized by the community, and by solidarity with the presbyterate.[12] Christ's presence in the Eucharist involves not only the action of the ordained priest repeating the words of institution over the elements, but the faith and worship of the entire assembly, including their openness to the action of Christ through the Holy Spirit.[13]

In this multidimensional view there is room for many distinctions regarding the various modes and degrees in which the "real presence" can occur. In the absence of a minister who has been ordained by a bishop in the apostolic succession, something pertaining to the full sacramentality of the eucharistic action is no doubt lacking. But there are solid grounds for believing that something—even very much—of the eucharistic mystery may be present. Hence the reception of holy communion by a Catholic in a Protestant church need not be regarded as a meaningless gesture or a false sign.

The differences between Lutherans and Catholics regarding the ministry and the Eucharist are far from being wholly solved. But on the basis of the agreements thus far reached it is possible to go beyond the present provisions of the Ecumenical Directory, which seem to prohibit Catholics from ever receiving communion at a Protestant service. If the discipline of both churches were to permit this, occasional acts of reciprocal eucharistic hospitality between Lutherans and Roman Catholics would seem to correspond to the possibilities and exigencies of the present ecumenical situation.

LUTHERAN RESPONSE BY GEORGE A. LINDBECK

Fr. Dulles' objectives are much the same as mine, although our approaches are different. Both of us wish to enlarge the area of intercommunion, but he

---

[12] See E. J. Kilmartin, "Apostolic Office: Sacrament of Christ," *Theological Studies* 36, 2 (June, 1975): 243-264.

[13] See J. H. McKenna, "Eucharistic Epiclesis," *Theological Studies* 36, 2 (June, 1975): 265-284.

speaks from a Catholic perspective, and I from a Lutheran one. His chief problem is apostolic succession, while mine is "agreement in the gospel"; but neither of us has, as far as I can see, any reason to quarrel with the other. The Reformation concern with the *doctrina evangelii* is clearly also important to Catholics such as Dulles; and the apostolic succession, when presented as he does, is compatible with a stress on salvation "by grace alone through faith."

Instead, therefore, of pursuing our minor differences, it seems better in this comment to deal with a difficulty which we both confront, a difficulty which is common to all those who are interested in increasing intercommunion.

Intercommunion sometimes harms rather than helps eucharistic worship and the unity of the church. It functions on occasion as what in the past would have been called "a false sign of unity" rather than as a cause or impetus toward greater ecclesial fellowship. We need to ask much more fully and systematically than is usually done how this danger arises and how it can be combated. What is needed, in addition to the usual discussions, is an improved pastoral theology or social psychology of eucharistic practice. All that can be done here, to be sure, is to try to define the problem.

What makes the Lord's Supper a false sign in our day is rarely or never the same as in the past. Then the danger was a discrepancy between the sign and the reality signified (the *sacramentum tantum* and the *res sacramenti*). Falsity arose when those who shared communion were thereby understood to be united in faith and/or governance when in fact they knew themselves not to be. Now, however, the problem is that although the reality and unity which those who intercommunicate intend to celebrate may quite genuinely be there, this reality and unity may not be eucharistic. It may rather, for example, be a unity in shared sentiments of friendship and respect, or in common commitments to such cases as justice or peace and struggles against poverty or oppression. When this is the case, it is not surprising that occasionally the invitation to commune may be extended even to those who are adherents of other religions or of no religion at all. Not to do this is felt under these circumstances as somehow unfriendly or discourteous. Even when this does not happen, however, even when all the communicants are baptized, they may not in fact be celebrating or intending to celebrate that reality of which the Eucharist is properly the sign.

This reality is not subjective attitudes of love or common actions to improve the world. It is rather God's initiative in giving us Christ in his very flesh and blood through which believers are united to God and to each other in a single body, a body which is an enduring community whose members have lasting responsibilities and obligations to each other. Shared sentiments and commitment to movements and causes may flow from this eucharistic gift; but even when they are absent, the gift is there; the body and blood are there; the ecclesial community is there. Those who communicate together are united by ecclesial and communal bonds which are, in a sense, quite objective, quite independent of feelings and actions, just as the members of a family or of a people may remain bound to each other even when affections fail and wills conflict.

This, at least, is the view of those who hold, as Catholics and Lutherans traditionally have, to a realistic interpretation of the sacrament.

It follows from this that intercommunion is to be encouraged only when and where this objectivity and realism are not undermined. What is important in ensuring that this does not happen, however, is not so much explicitly formulated doctrines of the real presence (although these have their uses—and abuses), as the communal and ecclesial experience of being united to fellow communicants by the gift of God which far transcends the vagaries of our feelings and of the particular causes and movements to which we may from time to time adhere. This might be called the experience of the real presence, and its occurrence and non-occurrence do not by any means entirely coincide with the line between correct and incorrect doctrines.

In conclusion, intercommunion is to be recommended when it promotes enduring habits, patterns, and structures of mutual concern and responsibility among divided Christians and churches. When this does not happen or is not intended, it may well be more destructive than constructive. It then threatens to become an expression of subjective attitudes of togetherness, rather than an efficacious sign of God's gift, and can lead to views of the church as evanescent fellowships of the like-minded, rather than as a universal and perduring community sustained by transcendent loyalties.

Study and Discussion Questions

1. What importance does "agreement in the doctrine of the gospel" have for Lutheran views on the unity of the church and for the question of intercommunion?
2. In your personal judgment, is there a minimum consensus in doctrinal matters that is a necessary prerequisite for intercommunion? If so, discuss how you would specify this minimum consensus.
3. Discuss what historical factors, according to Lindbeck, have led to the different approaches found in the Swedish and Leuenberg models.
4. Has the Lutheran/Roman Catholic historical experience most resembled the Lutheran/ Anglican or the Lutheran/Reformed experience, according to Lindbeck? Would the U. S. Lutheran/Roman Catholic experience dictate any special approach to dialogue? Discuss.
5. In discussions on eucharistic sharing, what is meant by a "false sign of unity"? According to Lindbeck, what makes the Lord's Supper such a false sign in our day as compared to other eras? Discuss.
6. Discuss Dulles's statement: "The Eucharist is not and never can be the sign of a perfectly achieved unity; it is always the sign of an imperfect unity seeking to become more perfect."
7. What general conditions does Dulles suggest for intercommunion? Discuss and evaluate.
8. Dulles considers two conditions for intercommunion to be the most problematic in the Lutheran/Roman Catholic context. What are these two conditions and, in light of Lindbeck's article, do you think he would agree with Dulles? Discuss.
9. Does it seem to you that the Roman Catholic Church would officially accept a position maintaining that there can be a valid Eucharist even where there are not validly ordained ministers? Discuss.
10. In the multidimensional approach to intercommunion discussed by Dulles, reference is made to "various modes and degrees in which the 'real presence' can occur." How is this statement to be understood?

REFORMED-CATHOLIC DIALOGUE

Ross Mackenzie—Christopher Kiesling

PRECIS

Calvin, while holding that we should achieve as far as possible a clarity of thought and expression about the Eucharist, acknowledged a mystery beyond human understanding. According to Mackenzie, Calvin rejected any doctrine of local presence, considered the doctrine of transubstantiation inconsistent with the rest of Christian teaching, and stressed the necessity of maintaining a true eschatological tension in all eucharistic teaching.

Reformed teaching has emphasized Jesus' role as the one true worshipper, through whom one enters God's presence. Following Calvin, the tradition holds the sacraments to be signs of a present reality; thus, the eucharistic presence of Christ is a true presence. Because the Lord's Supper is related to the Holy Spirit, it is spoken of as "spiritual"; "spiritual" is not to be taken as opposed to a "real" presence. For the Reformed tradition, the "conversion" of the Supper lies in the transformation of one's humanity in the life, death, and resurrection of Jesus, in which one participates in the Spirit. Finally, the corporate, ecclesial nature of the Supper plays an important role in Reformed belief.

Kiesling sees the nuances in the eucharistic teaching of each tradition deriving from a different theological matrix. Protestant, and specifically Reformed, theology developed in the service of preaching which, in turn, aimed at generating or confirming faith. Thus, there is an emphasis in Reformed teaching on Christ's eucharistic presence in the community, the act of worship, and communion. In contrast, Roman Catholic theology has been more objective than existential; its emphasis has been on the eucharistic presence even while it has acknowledged other presences and its eucharistic theology has been particularly concerned with the question of the "conversion" of the elements. Transubstantiation was a Roman Catholic effort at a particular time to achieve the most adequate expression of the eucharistic faith inherited from the tradition.

For Kiesling, the Roman Catholic and Reformed doctrines regarding the nature of the eucharistic "conversion" are more complementary than antithetical. Mutual benefit will come from a deeper understanding of the emphases of each tradition, not least by Reformed Christians attempting to understand the Roman Catholic practice of reserving the Eucharist.

J. A. Ross Mackenzie (Presbyterian), M.A., B.D., Ph.D., University of Edinburgh, is Professor of Church History at Union Theological Seminary in Virginia. He has been a participant in the Roman Catholic/Reformed and Presbyterian Consultation for several years, and was a Presbyterian Church, U.S., delegate to the Consultation on Church Union, 1966-73. His books include *The Word in Action* and *Trying New Sandals*.

Christopher Kiesling, O.P. (Roman Catholic), S.T.D., Dominican House of Studies (Washington, DC), is Professor of Liturgy and Sacraments at Aquinas Institute of Theology, Dubuque, IA, and is student formation director of the Dominican Province of St. Albert the Great. A member of the Roman Catholic/Presbyterian and Reformed Bilateral Consultation in the U.S. from 1965-1975, he has written numerous articles and books, most recently *Confirmation and Full Life in the Spirit*.

REFORMED AND ROMAN CATHOLIC UNDERSTANDINGS OF THE EUCHARIST

Ross Mackenzie

It will be helpful in any ecumenical discussion of the Eucharist to be clear about the purpose and method to be followed in the procedure. In his study of Calvin's doctrine of the Lord's Supper, Ronald S. Wallace indicated some of the main considerations that were in Calvin's mind in formulating his own doctrine.[1] Adapting his language, we may summarize these as follows.

First, we should achieve as far as we can a clarity of thought and expression in our understanding of the Eucharist. "The knowledge of this high mystery is very necessary," Calvin wrote in the *Institutes*, "and in view of its greatness it demands a careful explanation." Since the nature of Christ's presence in the Supper has been in dispute among Roman Catholic and Reformed theologians, this essay will deal later with the clarity which Calvin sought in explaining that presence.

Second, even in seeking clarity, we must recognize that at the heart of the Supper there remains a mystery which is quite beyond human thought to understand.

Third, though he was willing to accept that the action of God in the sacrament goes far beyond our comprehension, Calvin refused to admit any doctrine or interpretation that was inconsistent with other parts of the Christian faith. "We reverently embrace what human reason repudiates. We only shun absurdities abhorrent to piety and faith." One of these "absurdities" for Calvin was the idea that the body of Christ was locally present in the elements, and on both theological and moral grounds he rejected the doctrine of transubstantiation. It may appropriately be asked in the ecumenical dialogue whether what Calvin rejected has not also been rejected by Roman Catholic theologians themselves, for instance, Edward Schillebeeckx or Karl Rahner. The objection of Reformed Christians to transubstantiation has not been so much the elevation of philosophical or metaphysical speculation to the status of a dogma of faith as its inconsistency with the rest of the Christian teaching.

Fourth, therefore, any discussion of eucharistic doctrine must be in conformity with the rule of faith. By this Calvin meant that no doctrine should assert anything contradictory to any other part of the faith, and that our interpretation of the Lord's Supper should be determined by what scripture teaches as a whole. A clear implication of this is the indissoluble relationship in Reformed worship between Word and sacrament. Christ's presence in the Eucharist is not to be separated from his presence in the proclamation of his gospel. In

---

[1] Ronald S. Wallace, *Calvin's Doctrine of the Word and Sacrament* (Edinburgh: Oliver and Boyd, 1953), pp. 217-226.

Calvin's words, the Supper is "adioustée avec" the Word.

Lastly, it is necessary in our thinking about the Eucharist to maintain a true eschatological tension. The Christ with whom we have communion is risen, has ascended, and has poured out upon the church the gift of the Holy Spirit. Through the Holy Spirit the members of the church are already being introduced into the glory of God's reign and given a pledge of their future inheritance. Whenever we eat this bread, we do so both in memory and in hope. As Calvin wrote in his Commentary on I Corinthians 11, the Supper is "a kind of memorial which must always be maintained in the church until the final coming of Christ."

Now we may turn to see the lines which emerge as Calvin sought to explicate the Lord's Supper. By way of preface we may say that in general the Reformed churches today remain in agreement with the Reformer's eucharistic teachings. It must also be said that Calvin was a eucharistic theologian, as it were, when the opportunity was offered. Very often his thought was expressed in dialectical terms, as part of his continuing efforts to reconcile the eucharistic views of the Reformed communities in Germany and Switzerland.

In the first place, the Reformed churches have characteristically understood worship by looking at Jesus Christ as the one true worshipper. Jesus Christ is the new being, in whom is our salvation. This means that in our salvation Christ acted for us not only as God, but also as human. In our humanity he has already offered our sacrifice to God. He is, as Calvin wrote in his Commentary on Hebrews 8:2, the minister, *leitourgos*, of the sanctuary and of the true tent of meeting. Our risen and ascended Lord is the one true *leitourgos*, who leads us in our worship. As J. B. Torrance has pointed out, this was the heart of Calvin's interpretation of baptism and the Eucharist, as of all worship: "that Christ's baptism is our baptism, set forth in our water baptism; that Christ's sacrifice is our sacrifice, set forth at the table; that Christ's worship is our worship, set forth in our worship and prayers."[2]

In its liturgical meaning the Reformed doctrine of justification by grace implies that in worship God provides for us what we cannot provide for ourselves, the worship that is in spirit and in truth. As John Knox put it, even when we pray or offer ourselves as a living sacrifice, we do so only "by the hand of Christ." All our prayers are "through Jesus Christ," or "in the name of Christ," because Jesus has already offered up prayers of thanksgiving at his Supper for us, has already died and risen for us. When Reformers such as Calvin and Knox spoke of the uniqueness of Christ's priesthood, they meant that in Christ access to God is open to us. In Christ, we have already entered into God's presence.[3]

Secondly, in the Reformed understanding the Eucharist is the *anamnesis* of

---

[2] J. B. Torrance, "The Place of Jesus Christ in Worship," in the Church Service Society *Annual*, May, 1970, pp. 41-62. Citation on p. 43.

[3] See John Calvin, Commentary on Ephesians 2:18 and 3:12, and also the Commentary on Hebrews 8.

Christ's death and resurrection. Calvin is therefore one with the constant tradition of the church in teaching the presence of Christ in the Eucharist. No doubt many Presbyterians today understand that presence in a subjective or "spiritualizing" sense, or conceive of the Eucharist as a memorial, the confession of faith by the community of the past sacrifice of Christ. No support for such views can be found in Calvin. The one who is present with us when we "do this" in remembrance of him is the one in whose self-consecration we are consecrated, in whose death we have died, and in whose resurrection and ascension we have passed from death to life.

In contrast to the somewhat simple realism of Luther, Calvin and the other Reformed theologians indicate that the *esti* of the narratives of the institution—*touto mou estin to soma*, "this is my body"—cannot be properly explained in metaphorical, symbolical, or parabolic terms. The sacraments are signs, but they are not bare signs. They are signs of a present reality. In his answer to Tilemann Hesshusen on the thorny doctrine of Christ's presence in the Eucharist, Calvin wrote: "We too reject the sentiments of all who deny the presence of Christ in the Supper." And the controversy between Calvin and the Lutheran, Joachim Westphal, dealt with not the question of presence but the mode of communion in Christ's body. Over and over again in his *Short Treatise on the Supper of our Lord* (1541) Calvin laid stress on the true communication of Christ's body and blood. These sentences are typical: "The communion which we have in the body and blood of the Lord Jesus . . . is therefore figured to us by visible signs, according as our weakness requires, in such manner, nevertheless, that it is not a bare figure but is combined with the reality and substance. . . . The internal substance of the sacrament is conjoined with the visible signs; and as the bread is distributed to us by the hand, so the body of Christ is communicated to us in order that we may be made partakers of it."[4]

As early as the first edition of the *Institutes* (1536), Calvin had rejected the idea that Christ is "really and substantially" (*realiter ac substantialiter*) present. Twenty years later he repeated the objection to Westphal: "Though I have classed among opinions to be rejected the idea that the body of Christ is really and substantially present in the Supper, this is not at all repugnant to a true and real (*vera et reali*) communion, which consists in our ascent to heaven, and requires no other descent in Christ than that of spiritual grace."[5] But if the word "real" is used—and Calvin would have preferred a term such as "true"—this can only mean "not fallacious or imaginary." Christ is to be sought by faith, and though we do not bring down the substance of Christ's body from heaven to give us life, yet we are far from excluding it from the Supper.

This teaching of Calvin, and of the churches which have followed him, is of

---

[4]John Calvin, *Short Treatise on the Supper*, 15, 17, in *Tracts and Treatises on the Doctrine and Worship of the Church* (= *TT*), vol. II (Grand Rapids: Wm. B. Eerdmans Publishing Company, repr. 1958), pp. 171-172.

[5]John Calvin, *Second Defence of the Faith Concerning the Sacraments*, in *TT*, vol. II, p. 281.

such central importance that the discussion must be prolonged a little more. It might even be said that for Calvin the Eucharist is the sacrament of ascension. Christ is in heaven, bearing our human nature. "He is not here, he is risen." He is in the place of power, holding and exercising universal empire. If we ask how he can be present, Calvin says, we must answer: "through his grace and virtue." In his *Last Admonition to Joachim Westphal* Calvin summarized his views: "Our view is, that though Christ in respect of our human nature is in heaven, yet distance of place does not prevent him from communicating himself to us—that he not only sustains and governs us by his Spirit, but renders that flesh in which he fulfilled our righteousness vivifying to us. Without any change of place, his virtue penetrates to us by the secret operation of his Spirit, so that our souls obtain spiritual life from his substance."[6] Thus Calvin understands Christ's presence in dynamic terms. But if it is objected that his language implies the presence of the Holy Spirit rather than of the body of Christ, Calvin always had his answer: "I do not simply teach that Christ dwells in us by his Spirit, but that he so raises us to himself as to transfuse the vivifying vigour of his flesh into us. Does not this assert a species of presence, viz., that our souls draw life from the flesh of Christ, although, in regard to space, it is far distant from us?"[7]

In the third place, the theologians of the Reformed churches have characteristically understood the Lord's Supper in relation to the Holy Spirit. If the Spirit is lacking, the sacraments can accomplish nothing. We can speak about a double representation of the Spirit in the Eucharist. Through the Holy Spirit God comes to us in the ministry of Word and sacrament. But it is through the Holy Spirit also that we come to God.

As we have seen, the Reformed churches have taught from the first that in the Lord's Supper we receive Christ's body and blood. But the language which has been used to express this truth has often been misunderstood on the Roman Catholic side. For instance, the Geneva Catechism (1536) speaks of the Supper of our Lord as "a sign by which under bread and wine he represents the true spiritual communion which we have in his body and blood." Amongst some Reformed writers and frequently in the more popular expressions of Presbyterian faith the word "spiritual" has meant "metaphorical," "imaginary," or "fanciful," and it has been set in contrast with "real," But it is clear in the primary Reformed documents that the term "spiritual" refers to the activity of the Holy Spirit. This has been carefully noted by a Roman Catholic writer, Kilian McDonnell, who shows that in Calvin's thinking the communion is spiritual in the sense that it is by the agency of the Holy Spirit. A typical explanation of this "true spiritual communion" is to be found in the "First Sermon Upon the Sacraments" by Robert Bruce, Knox's successor at St Giles' in Edinburgh. The flesh of Christ, he said, "is called spiritual, in respect to the spiritual end whereunto it serves to my body and soul; because the flesh and blood of Christ serves to

---

[6] John Calvin, *Last Admonition to Joachim Westphal*, in *TT*, vol. II, p. 384.

[7] John Calvin, *Second Defence*, in *TT*, vol. II, p. 286.

nourish me, not to a temporal life, but to a spiritual and heavenly life."[8]

It was on this ground that the Roman Catholic doctrine of transubstantiation was set aside by the Reformed churches as "overthrowing the nature of the sacrament." The objection of the Reformers was grounded on what they took to be a true Christology, and for them the doctrine of transubstantiation represented a Nestorian fusion of the divine and human elements, that is, it was not properly based on the New Testament doctrine of the incarnation.

This being said, it is nonetheless true that for Calvin and his successors there is a "wonderful conversion" in the Lord's Supper. As God comes to us through the Holy Spirit, so even in our brokenness the Holy Spirit lifts us up to Christ, the "minister of the sanctuary," *ton hagion leitourgos.* Jesus took our broken and sinful human nature, and perfected it through his obedience, death, and resurrection. Now in the Eucharist he comes again to us in the power of the Holy Spirit, and gives us *his* broken body: "This is my body, which is for you." As Calvin expressed it in the *Institutes:* "For the Lord so communicates his body to us there that he is made completely one with us and we with him." Or again, "By declaring that his body is given for us and his blood shed for us, he teaches that both are not so much his as ours. For he took up and laid down both, not for his own advantage for for our salvation."[9]

So for Calvin—and for the Reformed churches this has been at the center of their attack on transubstantiation—the wonderful conversion, *mirifica commutatio*, of the Lord's Supper is not what takes place in the elements of bread and wine, but the transformation of our humanity in the life, death, and resurrection of Jesus Christ. In the Spirit on the Lord's day we participate in that conversion.

Lastly, the Reformed churches have followed Calvin also in stressing the corporate nature of the Supper. There is an integral bond between the church and the Eucharist; for the Eucharist is *communion*, holy communion with Jesus Christ and with all that he was and is, and communion also with all who are in Christ. Fr. McDonnell has understood Calvin well at this point, and has shown that Calvin's doctrine of the Eucharist is not to be separated from his concept of the church. By this he means not only that the Lord's Supper is the activity of the church, but also that it is to be understood within the concept of the God who elects: "Election in Christ is the basis of the church, and it is this basis which establishes the lordship of Christ in the church, and is the guarantee that in the church neither ecclesiological divinization nor sacramental divinization, with its inevitable sacramental Pelagianism and structural churchmanship, has

---

[8]"The First Sermon Upon the Sacraments in Generall," in *Sermons by The Rev. Robert Bruce,* ed. by William Cunningham (Edinburgh: Wodrow Society Edition, 1843), p. 13.

[9]John Calvin, *Institutes,* Book IV, ch. 17, sects. 38 and 3, in *Calvin: Institutes of the Christian Religion,* tr. by Ford Lewis Battles, vol. II, Library of Christian Classics, vol. XXI (Philadelphia: Westminster Press, 1960), pp. 1414-1415, 1362.

any validity."[10] The Supper is the spiritual banquet of those whom God has received into his family. For this reason the Supper has always had the character of a meal in the Reformed churches. Even if it has been celebrated with comparative infrequency in most Presbyterian churches, the white cloth on the Holy Table is a *table* cloth, and the crowds who approach with hearts prepared, to quote an older hymn for the Lord's Supper, are "joyful guests."

Not inappropriately for Presbyterians, the last word on theology can be drawn from John Knox, of whom it may be said that he helped to make the Reformed church a church not only of the Word but also of the sacrament. In a little document presented to a council when he was summoned to stand trial in 1550 he wrote: "Herewith [in the Supper], also, the Lord Jesus gathers us unto one visible body, so that we be members one of another, and make altogether one body, whereof Jesus Christ is the only Head." Jesus Christ not only gathers and creates the church, but gathers it by the Supper. By this sacrament we are gathered into one visible body, and by it we are constituted the one body of which Jesus Christ is the only Head.

Some conclusions may be drawn from this study of the Reformed understanding of the Eucharist for the contemporary ecumenical dialogue.

First, in his thinking about the sacraments Calvin sought to be faithful to the doctrine and custom of the primitive church. Since theology reflects critically on the interpretations of the faith which have been handed down from one age to another, any criticism of Calvin's eucharistic thought must deal with the question of whether or not he has been true to the New Testament and the teaching of the early church.

Second, in their thinking about the Eucharist most Presbyterian churches remain officially loyal to Calvin. That is, in their "espoused" theory they still reflect in their confessional documents the eucharistic theology of the Reformer. But their "pragmatic" theory indicates that many Reformed churches today have moved away from Calvin in several directions. Studies such as Arthur C. Cochrane, *Eating and Drinking with Jesus* (Philadelphia: Westminster Press, 1974); Franz J. Leenhardt, *Parole Visible* (Neuchatel: Delachaux & Niestle, 1971); and Jean Jacques von Allmen, *The Lord's Supper* (Richmond: John Knox Press, 1969), are written by Reformed theologians, but represent quite divergent understandings of the Eucharist. In the minds of many laypeople the presence of Christ in the Eucharist is often understood, when it is articulated, in a kind of Zwinglian "spiritual" sense. The Reformed churches will be enriched by returning to the sources of their espoused theology, and that should be one of the starting points in the movement toward a genuinely ecumenical theology.

Third, recent theological conversations with Roman Catholics about the Eucharist have presented the Reformed churches with possibilities for advance as well as with difficulties. One good possibility is that a common re-examination

---

[10]Kilian McDonnell, *John Calvin, the Church, and the Eucharist* (Princeton: Princeton University Press, 1967), p. 170.

of the faith and practice of the early church may lead to agreement concerning the meaning of the Eucharist. One danger is that Reformed church people and their theologians will give decreasing place to the Eucharist in their congregational life and theological formulations. Presbyterian churches, at least in the United States, are not "eucharistic" in the sense in which the term can be used of the Roman Catholic Church. And with notable exceptions Reformed theologians and pastors have tended to assume that the Roman Catholic mass, in Calvin's troublesome phrase, is "poles apart" from the Holy Supper of the Lord. The heat of polemic has often inhibited serious theological reflection on the Eucharist within the Reformed churches. The resumption of conversation with theologians of the Roman Catholic Church may help to lead eventually to the *communicatio in sacris.*

CATHOLIC RESPONSE BY CHRISTOPHER KIESLING

A growing conviction of mine has been that, if Roman Catholics did not have their particular conceptual tools for expounding Christian faith, they would speak very much like John Calvin when they attempt to convey to others their belief in the real presence of Christ in the Eucharist. Dr. Mackenzie's exposition of Reformed understanding of the Eucharist strengthens that conviction.

If I wished to avoid a crass notion of Christ's presence in the Eucharist, if I could not use concepts of substance and accidents or appearances to describe reality as I experience it, and if the word "transubstantiation" connoted crude images of Christ's eucharistic presence, then I would have to affirm repeatedly with Calvin's vigor that Christ is indeed bodily present and truly feeds us with his body and blood in the Lord's Supper. His eucharistic presence is not merely our subjective awareness of him, our memory of him; nor is it merely the divine omnipresence of Christ as God, but the presence of Christ as human. I would have to say, on the other hand, that the bread and wine remain as they seem to be, for that is the obvious fact to human perception; yet I would repeatedly insist that in partaking of them we really and truly spiritually feed upon, and are nourished by, the humanity of Jesus in his heavenly glory. Like Calvin, I would have to affirm in all kinds of ways the value of the elements as sure vehicles of our spiritual nourishment by the body and blood of Christ. When asked how this could be, what the conditions of the possibility of such an event are, I would have recourse to the action of the Holy Spirit, as I do ultimately even when using my Roman Catholic conceptual tools, for I confront an ineffable divine mystery here.

I am more convinced than ever that Roman Catholic and Reformed doctrines on the real presence of Christ in the Eucharist are trying to affirm the same faith. In regard to Calvin's considerations in expounding eucharistic doctrine and the characteristics of the Eucharist in the understanding of Reformed theology—all of which Dr. Mackenzie sets forth—Roman Catholics have to say "Amen" to their general thrust, though we may have differences of expression or even deeper disagreements as we move into the various areas delineated by these considerations and characteristics.

For Calvin, according to Dr. Mackenzie, the Eucharist is the sacrament of ascension. I believe that Roman Catholic understanding is ultimately the same. Roman Catholic liturgical texts put worshippers in the presence of a risen, glorious, triumphant Christ who reigns at the right hand of the Father. A view of Christ as "the Prisoner of the tabernacle" has been at times widespread in popular piety, but it has no place in liturgical texts, official teaching, or theology generally. Significantly, Roman Catholic doctrine speaks of the conversion of the substance of the elements into the substance of the body and blood of Christ, not the other way around. Christ does not change. Christ is present, not because he comes down, but because the bread and wine are raised up to him, so that *we* may be raised up to him in his glorious humanity to be nourished by it—all, of course, by the power and action of the Holy Spirit.

In speaking of the Lord's Supper being understood in relation to the Holy Spirit, Dr. Mackenzie says that Reformed churches set aside the doctrine of transubstantiation as "overthrowing the nature of the sacrament." He goes on to say that this doctrine "represents a Nestorian fusion of the divine and human elements, that is, it was not properly based on the New Testament doctrine of the incarnation." I need more exposition here. I do not understand these objections. Roman Catholics obviously do not see a conflict between the nature of this sacrament and transubstantiation, and I do not see how Dr. Mackenzie's statements in the previous paragraph lead to his affirmations here.

Transubstantiation, further, presupposes the New Testament doctrine of the incarnation, but does not imply either a Nestorian or a monophysitic interpretation of the incarnation. (Nestorianism was an early heresy stating that the human and divine natures in Christ were linked by only a moral bond; the monophysite heresy taught that there was only one—divine—nature in Christ.) On the other hand, according to my understanding of Nestorianism, I would qualify some Reformed explanations of the Lord's Supper as tending in that direction. I suspect that lurking in the background here is the question of the metaphysical nature of signs.

I would like to explore further with Dr. Mackenzie his understanding of J. B. Torrance's words which he quotes, namely, "that Christ's sacrifice is our sacrifice, set forth at the table." In what sense and how is Christ's sacrifice ours? I would hope that also in this controversial matter of the sacrificial nature of the Lord's Supper we would discover much more mutually shared faith than our theological expressions and practices of piety lead us to think we have.

ROMAN CATHOLIC AND REFORMED UNDERSTANDINGS OF THE EUCHARIST

Christopher Kiesling

This essay is devoted to responding to difficulties which I, a Roman Catholic, perceived Reformed Christians to have with Roman Catholic doctrine and practice in regard to Christ's real presence in the Eucharist. The limitations of an essay prevent dealing with other aspects of Eucharist. The essay invites two questions about the general topic and each of its parts. First, are we Roman Catholics correctly understanding the difficulties which our Reformed brothers and sisters have? Second, do the answers offered overcome the difficulties to any extent?

Some Reformed Christians—it is my impression—think that Roman Catholic teaching affirms Christ's presence under the appearances of bread and wine apart from communion to the neglect of Christ's presence in the gathered community of believers, in the act of worship, and especially in the partaking of the elements.

One reason for the Roman Catholic emphasis is a general orientation of Roman Catholic theology and doctrinal pronouncements. This orientation contrasts with the general thrust of Protestant theology and confessional statements. The latter are directed to preaching and finally to the response of faith more than Roman Catholic theology and doctrinal statements.

The church in the centuries preceding the Reformation was in sorry condition because of a lack of preaching and impoverished faith. The Reformers set out to fill that void. Protestant theology developed in the service of preaching which would generate and confirm people's faith. Consideration of the mysteries revealed by God for the sake of rendering them intelligible to the inquisitive human mind was not part of the theological endeavor. The Schoolmen were castigated for idle speculation. Theologizing was directed to edifying faith through preaching. The believer was, and is, always a prominent factor in Protestant theology, even when not the explicit topic. In other words, Protestant theology tends to be practical, or existential. In this light, we can easily understand Reformed emphasis on Christ's eucharistic presence in the gathered community, the act of worship, and the partaking of the elements. In these "places," especially the last, any presence of Christ in the Eucharist makes its impact upon the individual believer.

Roman Catholic theology, on the other hand, flowered with the rise of the universities in the thirteenth century and in the light of St. Anselm's understanding of theology as faith seeking understanding.[1] As a result, Roman Catholic theology and doctrinal statements tend to be descriptions of an objective

---

[1] *Proslogion* (Migne, *Patrologia Latina*, vol. 158, col. 225).

world revealed by God, seen by faith, and articulated in the language of the time. Roman Catholic theology and doctrine leave it to the preacher, much more extensively than Protestant theology and confessions, to make this world a stimulus to, and a support of, the act of faith. The gathered community, the act of worship, and the partaking of the elements are, to be sure, parts of the objective world revealed by God. But they are regarded objectively rather than existentially; moreover, they are ordered to, and dependent upon, another more important factor in that world, namely, Christ present by means of the elements in virtue of his words pronounced over them: "This is my body given for you. . . . This is my blood shed for you." I suggest that Roman Catholic theology has a natural propensity to emphasize this presence of Christ in the Eucharist over other presences, without thereby denying the other presences, even as Protestant theology has an inclination to stress other presences more immediately related to the believer.

As a result of the renewal sanctioned by Vatican Council II, appreciation of the richness and extent of Christ's presence in the Eucharist has entered into official church teaching. The *Instruction on Eucharistic Worship,* for example, says: "In the celebration of the Mass the principal modes by which Christ is present to his church are gradually revealed. First of all, Christ is seen to be present among the faithful gathered in his name; then in his Word, as the Scriptures are read and explained; in the person of the minister; finally and in a unique way under the species [appearances] of the Eucharist."[2] The same document states: "When the faithful adore Christ present in the sacrament, they should remember that this presence derives from the sacrifice and is directed toward both sacramental and spiritual communion."[3]

A second reason for the Roman Catholic emphasis, especially in the past four hundred years, has been the tendency among some Protestants to reduce the real presence of Christ in the Eucharist to the mere recollection of him, a presence in the minds of the worshippers, evoked by the bread and wine regarded as mere signs or symbols of Christ's body and blood. The Roman Catholic conviction—and that of the vast majority of Christians in the world and most churches—is that such a presence does not do justice to Christ's words declared in his name over the elements. The reduction of Christ's presence to mere remembrance in the common modern understanding of the word is a rationalistic demythologizing of biblical faith. John Calvin reacted against it.[4] Roman Catholicism can be credited with striving to maintain a truth which Calvin sought to uphold, though Roman Catholicism does so in a different way.

Christ's real presence in the gathered community has always been part of

---

[2]Congregation of Rites, May 25, 1967, no. 55 (Washington, DC: USCC, 1967), p. 32.

[3]Ibid., no. 50, p. 30.

[4]*Institutes of the Christian Religion* IV, xvii, 5, 11, 19, John T. McNeill, ed., Ford Lewis Butler, trans., Library of Christian Classics, vol. 21 (Philadelphia: Westminster Press, 1960), pp. 1364-1365, 1372-1382.

the Roman Catholic Church's belief, though it has not always been emphasized in pastoral preaching and teaching for the reasons mentioned. It is implied in the doctrine of the church as the body of Christ, the Head—a doctrine which has endured in Roman Catholicism, though it was lost to view somewhat after the Medieval period until the nineteenth century, when it reassumed significance leading to great prominence in the twentieth century.

Christ's real presence in the act of worship is included in the belief in Christ as Head of the church, as well as in the Roman Catholic doctrine that by baptism the faithful are incorporated into the body of Christ, the priest, becoming ministers of the worship which Christ, through his Spirit, effects in the church. Vatican II's *Constitution on the Liturgy* affirms: "He is present . . . when the church prays and sings, for he promised: 'Where two or three are gathered together for my sake, there am I in the midst of them' (Matt. 18:20)."[5]

Christ's presence in the partaking of the elements follows upon his real presence under the appearances of bread and wine, for he gives himself under those appearances precisely to be present to us in communion. This Roman Catholic position does not mean that Christ, present under the appearances of bread and wine, is present in communion effectively, i.e., unto salvation, regardless of the disposition of the recipient. The recipient's living faith is necessary to appropriate the presence of Christ offered under the appearances of the elements.

It can be said that the presence of Christ in the Eucharist is only initiated by his presence under the appearances of bread and wine and is consummated in partaking of the elements in faith. Certainly Christ's eucharistic presence is fully realized in its finality only in the faith-filled communion of believers.[6] In this sense Roman Catholics can accept the Reformed affirmation that Christ is present in the Eucharist in the partaking of the elements. Any other presence of Christ, however special it may be, falls short of being the ultimate presence intended by Christ, namely, his union with us in faith and love. This union has traditionally been regarded in Roman Catholic theology as the reality ultimately signified and effected by the Eucharist.

The Roman Catholic and Reformed emphases as to "where" in the Eucharist Christ is really present are, therefore, not opposed to one another but complementary.

Still Reformed Christians have difficulty with speaking of Christ as present or giving himself "under the appearances of bread and wine." They prefer to

---

[5]No. 7, Walter M. Abbott, ed., *The Documents of Vatican II* (New York: Guild Press, 1966), p. 141.

[6]Edward Schillebeeckx writes: "Only a eucharistic presence that is personally *offered and accepted* becomes an altogether complete presence. The presence of Christ in the tabernacle is therefore real, but as such it is only offered, and in this sense is secondary in relation to the complete, reciprocal presence to which it is directed as to its end and perfection" ["Transubstantiation, Transfinalization, Transignification," *Worship* 40 (1966): 336, emphasis in original].

speak of Christ's being present or giving himself through the power of the Spirit "with" the elements. The Roman Catholic expression implies a non-empirical change of the substance of the elements into the substance of the body and blood of Christ, the so-called doctrine of transubstantiation. Reformed Christians, I gather, regard this doctrine to be nonbiblical, the elevation of philosophical, or metaphysical, speculation to the status of a dogma of faith. I suspect that some of them, if perfectly frank, would say that the doctrine implies that communion is cannibalism of some sort.

Recent debates in Roman Catholic theology over transubstantiation vs. transignification have brought out that the doctrine of transubstantiation is not the result of philosophical speculation but a corollary or explicitation of the doctrine of the real presence of Christ in the Eucharist and therefore, like that doctrine, a matter of faith based on the Scriptures.[7] They maintain that we must distinguish between, though we cannot separate, faith's insight and the language which expresses it. Greek philosophical literature was the cultural matrix in which theology arose in the early Middle Ages. A new flood of it inundated Europe in the twelfth and thirteenth centuries as that theology flowered. Seeking to deepen the cognitive aspect of faith, Medieval theologians naturally used terms such as "substance," "species" or "appearances," and "transubstantiation" to express, not their speculations, but their biblical faith's insight.

In this short essay we cannot develop in detail this argumentation. But Roman Catholics can ask their Reformed brothers and sisters to be open to the possibility that the Roman Catholic doctrine of transubstantiation is not a departure from biblical faith or a human addition to it, any more than is the Chalcedonian doctrine about the one person and two natures in Jesus Christ. The Roman doctrine may be a valid insight of Christian faith which has been obscured for some or even many Christians because of the difficulties of the language in which it has been expressed and because of the generally rationalist milieu of the modern era.

Reformed Christians—and many Roman Catholics too—can be asked not to conceive of Christ's real presence under the appearances of bread and wine in a materialistic manner which implies a kind of cannibalism in communion. As the Reformed Scottish theologian Donald Baille has noted, the Roman doctrine does not mean that the body of Christ is contained locally or spatially in the bread, inside it, so to speak, so that if the surface were peeled off, the flesh of Christ would be found.[8]

The language of the Schoolmen and Roman Catholic documents is very precise: they do not speak of the change of the bread and wine into the body

---

[7]See Edward Schillebeeckx, *art. cit.* and also *The Eucharist* (New York: Sheed and Ward, 1968). Pertinent matter, though in another context, is also found in Karl Rahner, "The Presence of Christ in the Sacrament of the Lord's Supper," *Theological Investigations*, vol. 4 (Baltimore: Helicon, 1966), pp. 287-311 *passim*.

[8]*The Theology of the Sacraments* (New York: Charles Scribner's Sons, 1957), p. 100.

and blood of Christ but the change of the *substance* of the former into the *substance* of the latter. In the language available to the Schoolmen and church leaders for expressing their inherited insight of faith, spatial and all sensible properties belong to the accidents or appearances, not to substance. Substance is not, strictly speaking, in space at all or visible or tangible. In choosing to speak about a conversion of the substance of bread or wine into the substance of the body or blood of Christ, the Schoolmen and ecclesiastics were obviously attempting to express a non-empirical, unimaginable, inconceivable mysterious effect upon the elements by a transcendent divine action in which they believed because of Jesus' words recorded in Scripture, not to which they concluded on the basis of rational speculation.

There was, of course, rational argumentation in the eucharistic controversies which resulted in the doctrine of transubstantiation. But the argumentation was over the manner in which the whole of eucharistic faith inherited through tradition from the primitive church would be most adequately expressed; the argumentation was not directly over that faith's perception.

John Calvin insisted that we are truly fed on the body and blood of Christ when we partake of the eucharistic elements.[9] He reverted to the mysterious, incomprehensible action of the Holy Spirit as effecting this feeding, without any change in the bread and wine.[10] Roman Catholic doctrine also invokes the action of the Holy Spirit to explain our being nourished on the body and blood of Christ, but it sees—in faith in Christ's words over the bread and wine—this action converting the elements so that they are, beyond their appearances, truly the body and blood of Christ in a mode of being beyond our intellectual comprehension.

One reason for Calvin's not having this latter vision of faith is his theory or speculation about the nature of signs and implicitly about the ontological structure of things such as bread and wine.[11] The bread and wine, precisely as bread and wine, are signs of Christ's body and blood. If they are changed so that they no longer are bread and wine, then they cease to be signs of Christ's body and blood; transubstantiation removes the possibility of the Eucharist's being the sign of Christ's body and blood rather than provides that possibility.

But are things such as bread and wine signs in virtue of their appearances or their radical identity, their "substance," or is such a distinction invalid? To answer either question, as Calvin did explicitly or implicitly, is metaphysical speculation. If Roman Catholic doctrine about the real presence of Christ under the appearances of bread and wine and about the change of the substance of the elements into the substance of Christ's body and blood is conditioned by philo-

---

[9]*Inst.* IV, xvii, 10, in McNeill, p. 1370-1371; "Short Treatise on the Lord's Supper," II, in *Calvin: Theological Treatises*, J. K. S. Reid, trans., Library of Christian Classics, vol. 22 (Philadelphia: Westminster Press, 1954), pp. 145-148.

[10]*Inst.* IV, xvii, 10, 12, 33, in McNeill, pp. 1370, 1373, 1405.

[11]*Inst.* IV, xvii, 14, in McNeill, p. 1376.

sophical theory, the same must be said about Reformed doctrine. Neither Roman Catholics nor Reformed Christians can boast of being in possession of pure faith undiluted by metaphysical presuppositions.

In regard to the conversion of the elements of the Eucharist, perhaps Roman Catholic and Reformed doctrines should be regarded as complementary rather than antithetical. Certainly Roman Catholics can find in the Reformed doctrine a corrective to tendencies to conceive of the doctrine of transubstantiation in a too materialistic or too mechanical manner, or to think that it explains away the mystery of Christ's presence by means of the bread and wine in the eucharistic celebration. Roman Catholics can profit from the Reformed emphasis on the Holy Spirit's operation in making the Eucharist truly nourishment by the body and blood of Christ. Reformed Christians can find in Roman Catholic doctrine an emphasis to prevent the mystery of the Eucharist from becoming overly spiritualized, out of line with the principle of incarnation employed by God in dealing with humanity, and even reduced to mere thinking piously about Christ.

Reformed Christians also have difficulty with the Roman Catholic practice of reserving the eucharistic elements. I suspect this difficulty arises because reservation implies belief in a change in the elements, a belief which Reformed doctrine rejects. Reservation also implies that the Eucharist is being viewed as not directed to communion, a view also opposed to Reformed doctrine. I wonder if reservation does not also suggest to some Reformed Christians that Roman Catholics indulge in idolatry, worshipping material objects.

The Roman *Instruction on Eucharistic Worship* states: "It would be well to recall that the primary and original purpose of reserving the sacred species in church outside Mass is the administration of the Viaticum [communion for the dying]. Secondary ends are the distribution of communion outside Mass and the adoration of our Lord Jesus Christ concealed beneath these same species."[12] "When the faithful adore Christ present in the sacrament, they should remember that this presence ... is directed toward both sacramental and spiritual communion."[13]

In Roman Catholic thought and practice, the Eucharist is always ordered ultimately to communion. If it is reserved, it is for future communion. Christ present in the reserved Eucharist—note: Christ, not the elements or their appearances—may be adored, his love contemplated, his friendship cherished, and our prayers and our lives offered to him in thanksgiving; in other words, we may feed in faith upon him who is the Bread of Life in spiritual communion, extending or preparing for sacramental communion.

No idolatry is involved in reservation. The purpose of the Eucharist, communion, is not subverted by reservation. If the Roman Catholic doctrine that Christ's presence, or one mode of his presence, is "located" in the eucharistic

---

[12]No. 49, op. cit., p. 30.

[13]No. 50, ibid.

elements resulting in their change—if this doctrine is possibly a valid insight of authentic biblical faith—then Roman Catholics can ask Reformed Christians to respect the Roman Catholic practice of reservation and even to adopt it, or at least to adopt the practice of disposing of the elements used in eucharistic celebration in a way that corresponds to the possibility that they are no longer ordinary bread and wine.

To ask Reformed Christians so to treat the elements used in the Eucharist is, I know, asking very much of them. But I suspect that refusal will speak louder against future shared Eucharists than many doctrinal positions. If Reformed Christians were to treat the elements used in the Eucharist with special respect, they would be saying in action that they acknowledge at least the possibility that Roman Catholic doctrine about the real presence of Christ in the Eucharist is authentically Christian belief. Until Roman Catholics and Reformed Christians can recognize in deed as well as word the possibility of the authenticity of each other's faith and doctrine, the achievement of unity will remain an extremely distant goal.

At this limit of space allotted to me for this essay, I feel great frustration. So much more remains to be talked through by Roman Catholics and Reformed Christians in regard to even the above topics, to say nothing of other aspects of the Eucharist. What has been said suggests—to me at least—that much, though not all, of our disagreement is based on confusion between faith and the expression of faith. We have condemned each other's words and concepts without endeavoring to appreciate the faith which they are feeble attempts to articulate. There is reason to hope, therefore, that through continuing dialogue Roman Catholics and Reformed Christians can eventually be reconciled fully to one another in Christ, their one Lord and Savior.

REFORMED RESPONSE BY ROSS MACKENZIE

Solvitur acris hiemps—"Melts Winter now," wrote Horace; and Fr. Kiesling's work in the Roman Catholic/Reformed and Presbyterian Consultation has helped to disclose how changed are the bitter frosts of the older "Catholic-Protestant" disagreement. Thanks are therefore due to Fr. Kiesling for his irenical spirit and for what he has achieved.

Are Roman Catholics correctly understanding the difficulties which their Reformed brothers and sisters have? At this level in the dialogue, yes. Catholic historians such as Joseph Lortz have spoken of the "historical necessity" of the Reformation; and Fr. Kiesling sees, too, that whatever other factors may have been involved, the "revolt" of Martin Luther and those who came after him was a *religious* revolution, as it were a *metanoia* within the heart of the church. The tragedy was that, whereas at an earlier time protest and renewal movements could be contained and fructify the church, the rupture of the sixteenth century remained unhealed.

Do the answers offered overcome the difficulties to any extent? Undoubtedly, they do. With much, perhaps even most, of what Fr. Kiesling says about the Eucharist I would cordially agree, and do so in reference to Calvin himself, especially in the *Institutes*, Book IV, chs. 14 and 17.

Some undeveloped comments may now be made about particular ideas in this essay.

The writer contrasts Roman Catholic and Protestant theology by saying that, where the former flowered with the rise of the universities, the latter developed in the service of preaching. Karl Barth certainly saw theology as a servant of the church in its witness to the Word of God. In this sense Protestant theology is akin to patristic theology in its quest to discern the appropriate language by which the church may proclaim and witness to the Word of God in both liturgy and life. To this extent, therefore, Reformed theology has often and even characteristically tried to explicate the Calvinistic axiom that the life of faith and the political sphere alike are to be ordered "under the Word of God."

Much more discussion needs to go on about presence. In speaking of the "modes by which Christ is present"—an odd-sounding Latinism, one suspects, for many Presbyterians—Fr. Kiesling suggests that there is a kind of hierarchy of presence, Christ being present "finally and in a unique way" in the Eucharist. One must ask: Could *any* presence of Christ be other than "unique"? That said, in what particular sense can we say that Christ is known to us in the breaking of the bread? Granting their failures, Reformed theologians have at least tried to avoid at this point drawing the extreme inferences which, it appears to them, Roman Catholics draw from the words, "This is my body."

The Reformed rejection of the doctrine of transubstantiation was a consequence of its understanding of the mystery of the sacramental union. As in Christ, so in the Eucharist, there is a union without confusion or separation. In the Eucharist the sign and the reality, while they are to be distinguished, are not to be separated; and while they are to be united, they are not to be converted or transubstantiated into one another. Fr. Kiesling asks that Reformed Christians "be open to the possibility that the Roman Catholic doctrine of transubstantiation is not a separation from biblical faith," but may be a valid insight of Christian faith which has been obscured because of the difficulties of language." Good; and Reformed theologians will gladly continue the discussion. They will do so, first, in the light of what they take to be a biblical understanding, and in reference to what they find in Calvin's eucharistic theology that appears good to them. They will also discuss the question by asking our contemporary questions about the meaning of time, space, and incarnation. As Reformed interpreters see the matter, transubstantiation has sometimes been taught and popularly understood in terms of *what is contained* in what, and *how* Christ is present. Does Fr. Kiesling mean that the question of *who* is present is a prior one, and that therefore the idea of relation, of *koinonia*, and not spatial categories will give us a fuller understanding?

Presbyterians have much to learn in the conversation. They have not listened to Calvin on the Eucharist as much as they should. They have too often narrowed down their spirituality of the Word to a spirituality of the sermon. And they have frequently been insensitive to nuances of Catholic theology and to deeply felt Catholic attitudes. Nothing but good can come for both sides by continuing the conversation.

Study and Discussion Questions

1. In what way has Roman Catholic teaching on transubstantiation been thought by Reformed Christians to be inconsistent with the rest of Christian teaching? What teaching in particular? In the light of Kiesling's article, do you feel there is such an inconsistency?
2. Discuss how the Reformed church's views on Jesus as the one true *leitourgos* might connect with the Roman Catholic teaching on the Mass.
3. In Mackenzie's explanation, Calvin does not hold a symbolic, metaphorical, or spiritual (as opposed to real) view of the Eucharist. In what way is the term "spiritual" used by Reformed theology and in popular Reformed usage?
4. In what way is the Eucharist the "sacrament of ascension" in Reformed tradition? Is there any comparable usage in Roman Catholic tradition? Discuss.
5. How is the "wonderful conversion" of the Lord's Supper understood in Reformed teaching? How is the *corporate* nature of the Supper understood? Discuss whether these views are in any way similar to Roman Catholic teachings.
6. Is it generally accurate to say that Roman Catholic theology has emphasized the eucharistic presence of Jesus to the detriment of other presences? Would it be equally true to say that Protestantism generally, and Reformed theology in particular, has stressed presences other than the eucharistic? If so, what have the consequences been?
7. How does Kiesling answer Reformed questions about reserving the eucharistic elements? Do you find the explanation satisfactory; if not, why?
8. Kiesling states that recent Roman Catholic debates have brought out that the doctrine of transubstantiation, like the doctrine of the real presence, is a matter of faith. Discuss whether you agree with this statement.
9. How do you react to Kiesling's suggestion that Reformed Christians might consider a different way of disposing of the elements remaining from a eucharistic celebration? Discuss.
10. Discuss Kiesling's contention that much, though not all, of the disagreement between Roman Catholics and Reformed Christians is based on "confusion between faith and the expression of faith."

METHODIST-CATHOLIC DIALOGUE

J. Robert Nelson—Gerard S. Sloyan

PRECIS

According to Nelson there has been a certain inconsistency between the Reformation and early Wesleyian sacramental life and the later neglect of the Eucharist within Methodism. The liturgical and ecumenical movements are forcing a reassessment of this situation within Methodism. The Wesley brothers saw the Eucharist as so important that their revival can be called not only evangelical but also eucharistic, based as it was on word and sacrament. The strong eucharistic thrust of early Methodism can be found in the Wesleys' sermons and particularly in their hymns. While the authority of the Wesleys may not be sufficient to bring about a contemporary Methodist eucharistic revival, ecumenical influences may well bring Methodists to a deeper appreciation of their own eucharistic tradition.

Sloyan traces the early post-biblical history of the Eucharist with its double emphasis on offering and eating. Sloyan suggests that Protestants have much to learn from Roman Catholic eucharistic tradition and contemporary experiences in eucharistic reform. Among these contemporary challenges are: (1) the relative place of the ordained and unordained in the celebration of the Lord's Supper, (2) the tension between joy and solemnity in the liturgy, and (3) the balancing of the rational and the emotional in worship.

Sloyan is heartened by early Methodist eucharistic theology, the fidelity of the Wesleys to church "order," and the emotive element in Methodist worship. Nelson agrees with Sloyan's call for a balance between offering and meal, and with his suggestions for greater eucharistic participation by the laity and greater emotional expression in the liturgy. Nelson, however, takes issue with Sloyan's attributing to Protestantism a disregard of post-biblical eucharistic tradition and with his discussion of the relationship between Christology and the reservation of the Blessed Sacrament.

J. Robert Nelson (United Methodist), A.B., DePauw University, B.D., Yale University, D. Theol., University of Zurich, is Professor of Systematic Theology at the Boston University School of Theology. Long a participant in Faith and Order concerns for the National and World Councils of Churches and in the Consultation on Church Union, his writings on ecumenicity have appeared in many journals and books, including *Overcoming Christian Divisions, Fifty Years of Faith and Order*, and *Church Union in Focus*. He is an associate editor of the *Journal of Ecumenical Studies* and a participant in the United Methodist-Roman Catholic bilateral discussion.

Gerard S. Sloyan (Roman Catholic), A.B., Seton Hall University, Ph.D., Catholic University of America, a priest of the Diocese of Trenton, NJ, is Professor of Religion at Temple University and an associate editor of the *Journal of Ecumenical Studies*. A member of the United Methodist-Roman Catholic bilateral discussion, he is the author of many books, most recently *Jesus on Trial: The Development of the Passion Narratives and Their Historical and Ecumenical Implications*, and *A Commentary on the New Lectionary*.

METHODIST EUCHARISTIC USAGE: FROM CONSTANT COMMUNION TO BENIGN NEGLECT TO SACRAMENTAL RECOVERY

J. Robert Nelson

Uncertainty and Inconsistency

American Methodism[1] follows the Reformation tradition of defining the church as the congregation where the Word is rightly preached and the sacraments duly administered. But it is a matter of honesty to question how "duly" the sacraments are now either practiced or understood. The pure flowing eucharistic waters of John Wesley's eighteenth century revival have become during two centuries a murky trickle. This negative judgment, as will be shown, is made on the basis of two criteria: Wesley's own theological convictions, and the eucharistic doctrines and habits of most other churches.

Some regretable signs of Methodism's condition—apart from many healthy exceptions—are the following:

- Celebrations every three months.
- Deliberate absenteeism by members who feel alienated from Holy Communion.
- Individualistic piety apart from communal experience.
- Vigorous preaching displaced by soothing Communion meditations.
- Liturgies truncated by the arbitrary choice of ministers.
- Carelessness with the handling of the elements, and innovations of dubious merit.

Obviously, such abuses are not found in Methodism only. But, taken together, they seem to be more the rule than the exception; and they must be subjected to theological and historical criticism.

Stimulus to Recovery of Integrity

There is a new seriousness about liturgy and sacraments, thanks to the indirect effects of the liturgical movement and the direct effects of the ecumenical movement. It is important that ecumenical involvements have acquainted many Methodists with the practices of other Protestant churches, and increasingly with those of Catholic and Orthodox churches. Equally important is the way by which ecumenical encounter has perforce driven Methodist theologians and

---

[1] Although there are several Methodist denominations, this discussion refers mainly to The Methodist Church and its successor since 1968, The United Methodist Church.

historians to rediscover those purer springs of eighteenth century Wesleyanism. This is not a venture into archaism, but recognition of perennial authenticity of meaning. It is now possible that the same degree of sacramental seriousness which characterized Wesley in his time may find an appropriate expression in changing Methodist practice in this time.

Anglican Earnestness of John and Charles Wesley

Neither too little nor too much should be made of the Anglican origins of Methodism. Two centuries of divergent development have shown that Methodism is not just a variant form of Anglicanism. But the vital sap still flows from its rootage in two extraordinary priests of the Church of England, the brothers Wesley. And none could be more devoted than they were to communion with the living, present Christ through liturgical action.

All writing about John Wesley's view of the Eucharist refers to his sermon on "constant Communion" as well as to his own exemplary demonstration of its values. "I advise," he wrote, "all the Methodists in England and Ireland, who have been brought up in the Church, constantly to attend the services of the churches, at least every Lord's Day."[2] This frequency he commended, not in a legalistic way, but in strong belief that so great a gift of God as the Eucharist should not be despised carelessly. In the nine decades of his own extraordinarily busy life, he either celebrated or received Holy Communion on an average of once every four days.[3] And he thought it no imposition to admonish the newly-formed Methodist Episcopal Church in America to make weekly celebration its rule.[4]

The Methodists of Britain seem to have been more appreciative of his example than those in the independent American nation. Historical data in Wesley's copious journals and conference records show the truth of the claim that Methodism was not only an *evangelical* but a *eucharistic* revival. The saving Gospel was conveyed as much by Holy Communion as by preaching the Word. The adverbs "rightly" and "duly" were honored. The records tell of many persons who testified to inner conversion to Christ during the Holy Communion. Wesley called it a "converting ordinance," a veritable means of the grace of God. This is why he was open and flexible about admitting sincere people to the service, sometimes extending the invitation also to little children, if he was satisfied as to their faith.

In the face of indifferent or faithless attitudes, he could be strict and exclusive, confining Communion to members or those specially admitted; but these conditions were no obstacle to any who had a sincere desire to be saved, for the

---

[2]*Minutes of the Methodist Conferences from the First*, vol. I (London, 1812), p. 58.

[3]John C. Bowmer, *The Lord's Supper in Early Methodism* (London: Dacre, 1951), Ch. V.

[4]Wesley's letter of September 10, 1784.

conditions of membership included them. Wesley bade them all to come. And the Methodists came! By the hundreds and, at times, by thousands they came to receive the bread and wine, causing services to last several hours. As John Bishop shows, this devotion to Communion prevented early Methodism from falling into extreme revivalism and losing its connection with the historic church.[5] True revival meant the whole Gospel—Word *and* sacrament—for wholeness of life of the community.[6]

The Oxford students who had ridiculed the young Wesleys and their "Holy Club" with the name "Methodists" were, in fact, recognizing an aspect of the Wesleys' Anglicanism: *order*. The rules and canons of the Established Church were to be honored, obeyed, and put in service of revival. Thus it was strict policy among Methodists that preaching and prayer meetings must not be scheduled to compete with Holy Communion or Morning Prayer in the parish churches. Only those Methodist preachers who had been ordained as Anglicans could celebrate at other times. Brother Charles was even more adamant than John on this critical point. Had the Established hierarchy appreciated what was happening for the health of Christianity in the realm, the ultimate schism might have been avoided. When, at last, the bishops refused to permit Wesley to preach and celebrate in parish churches and, more categorically, refused to ordain Methodist candidates for orders, the aging Wesley reluctantly took what he regarded to be the necessary action. He ordained men as presbyters, not because he despised the Church of England's canons concerning ordination by bishops only, but because he was fully convinced of two things: (a) that Methodists should not remain sacramental orphans in America and in some parts of Britain, and (b) that in the New Testament church there was a parity of presbyter and bishop, giving the bishop no exclusive prerogative to ordain.

If other Anglicans dismissed Methodism as a crude display of that "horrid thing" called "enthusiasm," they should have seen John and Charles themselves as eucharistic enthusiasts. Their zeal for Communion was matched, however, by the strength and clarity of their doctrinal interpretation. This they taught, not in learned monographs or catechisms, but in sermons and in devotional hymns. Charles was the gifted poet of the movement, and John was not lacking talent. In 1745 they published the first of nine editions of *Hymns on the Lord's Supper*, a collection of 166 hymns for use by Methodists. The fact that very few of these are remembered, much less sung, by modern Methodists is an indication of the defection from their sources.

The hymns were composed and systematically planned to be an exposition of a short writing by the erstwhile Anglican Dean of Lincoln, Daniel Brevint. This was just an instructional tract, entitled *The Christian Sacrament and Sacrifice*. It so impressed the Wesley brothers that J. Ernest Rattenbury, who has

---

[5]*Methodist Worship* (London: Epworth, 1958), p. 18.

[6]Paul S. Sanders, "Wesley's Eucharistic Faith and Practice," *Anglican Theological Review* (April, 1966): 4.

done the most extensive study on it, asserts that it "must be accepted as the sacramental doctrine of the Wesleys."[7] Indeed, they reproduced the text of Brevint's tract in the volume of hymns, so that all Methodists might study and accept it. Then the hymns were arranged according to Brevint's outline as follows:

— As a memorial (*anamnesis*) of the suffering and death of Christ.
— As a sign and means of grace.
— As a pledge of heaven.
— As a sacrifice of ourselves joined to that of Christ.
— After the Sacrament, our appropriation of the benefits.

Only a few comments are here permitted, to emphasize these historic ingredients in Methodist eucharistic theology.

First, Wesley laid great emphasis upon the passion and death by crucifixion of Jesus Christ. The hymns keep reminding worshippers of the dreadful cost of atonement in terms of Jesus' agony and suffering. Here he followed the tradition of Western Catholic mysticism and Lutheran pietism. The symbol of the bread, for example, was not only "gathered from the mountainsides," as in *The Didache*, but was "made of corn which was cut down, beaten, ground and bruised by men."[8] The language of sorrow and contrition used in the hymns was unrestrained.

Second, his doctrine was saved from maudlin recollection—as though every day were Good Friday—by his Easter faith in Christ's risen presence. With all seriousness he believed and taught the real presence of Christ against any so-called Zwinglian interpretation of memorial. However, the true presence of the risen, living Christ could not be localized in the elements, as in either the Roman Catholic or Lutheran teaching.

> No local Deity
> We worship, Lord, in Thee.

Third, Wesley spoke of "presenting" Christ's saving work to the Father, and thus virtually employed the concept of "re-presentation" long before it became popular in the present ecumenical discussions. The presentation of Christ's life, death, and resurrection is more than a sacramental representation of a past event. The sacrament, in Wesley's view, "does more than re-present what Christ did and does. It effects what it re-presents."[9] Christ is made known to the community because of the present work of the Holy Spirit; he is revealed and effectual for changing lives through these given means. A characteristic hymn expresses this:

---

[7] *The Eucharistic Hymns of John and Charles Wesley* (London: Epworth, 1948), p. 15.

[8] Ibid., p. 25.

[9] Ibid., p. 33.

> Now, Saviour, make Thyself reveal,
> And make Thy nature known,
> Affix the Sacramental Seal
> And stamp us for thine own.
> The tokens of thy Dying Love,
> O, Let us All receive,
> And feel the Quick'ning Spirit move,
> And *sensibly* believe.

Fourth, the hymns give more importance to the power of the Holy Spirit in the Eucharist than does the Anglican liturgy in *The Book of Common Prayer*. This involves the prayer for the Spirit, the *epiklesis*, which is so prominent in the Orthodox Churches. Only by the Spirit's work can the memorial of Christ's sacrifice become the present appropriation of divine self-giving; only so can the sacramental sign convey the reality of Christ's presence.

> The Sign transmits the Signified,
> The Grace is by the Means applied.

How? By the Spirit, as in this hymn-prayer:

> Angel and Son of God come down,
> The Sacramental Banquet crown,
> The Power into the means infuse,
> And give them now their Sacred use.
> "Come, Holy Ghost, thine Influence shed,
> And realize[10] the Sign,
> Thy Life infuse into the Bread,
> Thy Power into the Wine.

These strong words express unconditional faith in the Spirit's power and purpose to conjoin the worshipping community to Christ: the self-offering of the people with Jesus Christ's unique, once-for-all sacrifice on Calvary. Time is bridged, history unified, in the Eucharist, so that faithful worshippers receive the benefits of Christ and also offer themselves as a living sacrifice. As Sanders observed, "Nowhere is Wesley's sacramental theology more obviously evangelical; nowhere do there come more acutely to focus the distinctive emphases of his preaching: the universal love of God, justification by grace through faith, and the pursuit of holiness."[11]

American Methodism's Defection from Wesley

Two centuries after Wesley's commendation of Brevint's theology and the

---

[10]Rattenbury is sure that "realize" for Wesley meant "real make." Ibid., p. 49.

[11]Sanders, "Wesley's Eucharistic Faith," p. 16.

publication of the eucharistic hymns, it is evident that American Methodists, by and large, have not seen an integral connection between Holy Communion and those evangelical emphases of God's love, justification, and holiness. Methodists' movement on the American frontier, with its rough and tumble life and the dominance of revivalism, surely contributed to this sacramental distortion. Were it not for the fortunate fact that doctrine is best preserved in liturgy, the present situation might have been even less acceptable. The familiar Anglican ritual in *The Book of Common Prayer* with some amendments has served the Methodists as well. But it has suffered significant verbal changes according to shifting theologies. In the nineteen-thirties, for example, when Protestant liberalism was at its height, the words conveying sacrificial and eschatological meanings were excised. Thirty years later they were restored.

Most Methodists would probably consider such questions of liturgy to be far less important than the preservation of the nineteenth century rubric which specifies "unfermented" grape juice to be used. This rule resisted amendment in 1968, when the United Methodist Church was inaugurated.

Those who would like to see a resurgence of the eucharistic theology of the Wesleys, refined by recent ecumenical studies, can feel no confidence that it can be effected by a formal appeal to the authority of Wesley: There remains an unamended rule that the Methodist standards of faith and doctrine are the writings of Wesley and his abridgement of the Thirty-nine Articles of the Church of England. And a 1972 report on doctrinal standards, adopted by the United Methodist Church, gave the Wesleyan tradition a new enhancement. But, in actuality, there can be no imposition of that past authority.

More helpful and hopeful are the newer ecumenical influences, which have shown to Methodists themselves what an authentically catholic tradition they have available to them. During the 'sixties, those charged with preparing a new text of ritual apparently considered the familiar rite of *The Book of Common Prayer* to be narrow and archaic, in language as well as in structure. An Alternate Text was issued in 1972 by the denomination's commission on worship. Though commissioned by the General Conference of 1968, this text is not intended to replace the official ritual of the *Book of Worship*. It would not be fair to describe it as a typically Methodist order. Rather, its composers deliberately included elements found in the Western Catholic liturgies of the patristic period as well as those generally recognized today as being of ecumenical validity.[12] If that is the direction in which ecumenism is pressing United Methodists, so much the better. They will probably find their own heritage becoming more viable in this direction rather than in a private denominational effort to reappropriate it.

---

[12] See *One Baptism, One Eucharist and a Mutually Recognized Ministry* (Geneva: World Council of Churches, 1975), p. 26.

CATHOLIC RESPONSE BY GERARD S. SLOYAN

Professor Nelson's review of the eucharistic doctrine and piety of early Methodism cannot but be congenial to the Roman Catholic reader.

Dean Brevint's tract, as it is reflected in the ordering of the Wesleys' hymns, inevitably brings to mind a gospel antiphon from the office of Corpus Christi found in the York breviary of 1493 (and in a *Processional* of a century earlier):

> O sacrum convivium in quo Christus sumitur,
> Recolitur memoria passionis eius,
> Mens impletur gratia,
> Et futurae gloriae nobis pignus datur.

("O holy, convivial meal in which Christ is received, the memorial of his suffering cherished, the spirit filled with grace, and the pledge of future glory given us.") Of the four elements that characterize the Wesleyan hymns, only our sacrifice joined to that of Christ is missing from this Latin verse, until recently so familiar to Catholic choirs and worshipers. (Paradoxically, it was the most often sung part from the *sacrum convivium*.) Yet Tridentine teaching has kept the conviction vigorous that the Mass is Christ's sacrifice. That it is one in which we associate ourselves with him sacramentally, the text of the "prayer over the gifts" (*secreta*) frequently makes clear. Further, it is common doctrine that the "Sign transmits the Signified."

It was Aquinas's teaching that the sacrament does more than re-present what Christ did and does but "effects what it re-presents," as Rattenbury puts it. This cannot be called the heritage of every schoolchild, however. Anscar Vonier, a popularizer of Aquinas, was saying things like that in the 1940's, but the teaching was not widely available to Catholics in the 1740's. Pope Pius XII moved things along notably by incorporating into his *Mediator Dei* (1947) a better eucharistic theology than had prevailed. While giving satisfaction to many with that encyclical letter, he also disappointed many by retaining the Carolingian symbolism of the separate consecration of bread and wine ("blood from body") as conveying the reality of the sacrifice. The "corn ... beaten, ground, and bruised" and the crushed grape are not featured strongly in the Catholic liturgical renewal, despite the lead provided by Ignatius of Antioch with his body "crushed by the teeth of wild beasts" to make him Christ's pure bread. The secondary symbolism of Amalarius of Metz takes the believer needlessly away from what is primary, namely the nourishment given by food, in the direction of its appearance, or the preparation process.

The fidelity of the Wesleys to church "order" is important to Roman Catholics, who have the same principle and consider it apostolic. Leadership at the meal is confined to those who have been constituted leaders by the imposition of hands. There are lively theological inquiries current about broadening the ranks of candidates for ordination to those of both sexes, married and single, but one does not hear in theological circles the question sometimes put by Catholic enthusiasts, "Why can't anyone say the words at a fitting time in the gathering and the people have the Eucharist?" It is a serious question whether those who require fidelity to the tradition of ordination are consistant in entertaining departure from the tradition of ordaining men (even as the West once departed from the tradition of ordaining the married). It is not a serious question whether ordination can be omitted altogether. No matter how many thousands may be chosen for the role, the practice of ordination is sufficiently traditional that Catholic theology cannot conceive of departure from it.

John Wesley's decision to ordain, although not on bishop's orders, was a disciplinary and a theological question for him and for the Church of England. It hinged on whether the latter was derelict in its duty by refusing to ordain Methodist candidates. Catholics need not have any opinion on the facts in dispute but they have long held the pastoral principle, "*Salus animarum, suprema lex.*" The ordination of priests by other priests is a fact of the Catholic past and not simply an aberration. The theological uncertainty of the distinction between a New Testament *episkopos* and *presbyteros* lies at the heart of the problem. There are numerous sober theologians who hold that the priesthood is an absolute in the realm of order, and that what is called "fullness" in the episcopate is jurisdictional. This view is supported by the fact that a bishop is never ordained without service to a particular church, however fictive the device of sees *in partibus infidelium.* His bishopric is thereby defined in jurisdictional terms.

The great concern of the Wesleys for the tepid, the ignorant, and the unchurched is a lesson to the onlooking Roman Catholic. The elongated Eucharists of early Methodists, marked by an emotional display that caused unease to some, are extremely instructive. The last decade in the Roman communion has witnessed distressing sanctions against certain celebrations that have encouraged emotive expression. There has even been the suspicion that any outsized and enthusiastic eucharistic assembly must be doing something wrong in the realm of liturgical law, since religion is basically not thought to be an interesting business.

All in all, the Methodist vision with which Professor Nelson supplies us is entirely heartening. It is medieval Catholic, largely, in its eighteenth century phase, but marked by a readiness to gain help from any Christian quarter, lest eucharistic life languish in the twentieth century.

ROMAN CATHOLIC EUCHARISTIC REFORMS: A BASIS FOR DIALOGUE?

Gerard S. Sloyan

The *New York Times* of November 30, 1975, carried a story reporting the removal of Father Oswald Baker from his pastorate of the Roman church at Downham Market in the diocese of Northampton. The bishop, Charles A. Grant, had evidently been in long communication with him over his persistent celebration not only in Latin (which can be permitted) but in accord with the Tridentine formula (which is not permitted, from the time of its succession by the *Ordo Missae* of 1969). Father Baker's reasons for his conduct will stand as typical of the main theological division in the Roman Church—weddedness to the familiar quite apart—ever since attention to a renewed eucharistic liturgy was required by the *Constitution on the Sacred Liturgy* of the Second Council of the Vatican promulgated December 4, 1963. He is quoted as objecting chiefly to "softening the Mass," which is his description of the emphasis of the new form on "a man-centered and convivial gathering—the meal aspect of the eucharist" in place of the emphasis of the old Mass on the "sacrifice aspect—an act of worship directed to the honor of God."

Readers will recognize immediately the centuries of ritual and theological history compacted in those statements. The researches of Hans Lietzmann in *Messe und Herrenmahl*, whatever may be questionable about his conclusions, have at least established the joyously eschatological and anticipatory character of the primitive Eucharist. To this, commemoration of Jesus' death had already been added by the time St. Paul received the tradition he reports on in 1 Corinthians 11:23-26. To speak of "the meal aspect" of this piece of religious behavior would seem to be like speaking of the moist aspect of water or the caloric dimension of fire, were it not for the adventures the Lord's supper underwent in its early transition from table to altar. At all points it was cultic or worshipful activity, *eucharistia* and *eulogia* being the vocabulary of thanks and praise. The Jewish temple liturgy which the Jerusalem Christians continued to take part in along with their table fellowship was a rite of *korban*, "approaching" so as to offer. It provided eucharistic practice with the language of offering (*prospherein, prosphora, anaphora*).

In the mid-second century Justin (100-165 A.D.) could describe the one who stood before the assembly as taking bread and cup and "sending up praise and glory to the Father of the universe through the name of the Son and of the Holy Spirit, and offering thanksgiving at some length that we have been deemed worthy to receive these things from him" (1 *Apology* 65). An initial kiss of peace to open the assembly is spoken of both here and in the earliest complete eucharistic liturgy we possess, that of Hippolytus in his *Apostolic Tradition* of ca. A.D. 215 (I, 4). If the formula of the *Didachē* (first or second century), ch. 9, spoken over cup and fragment, is a true liturgy, we then have an earlier instance than Justin of behavior that is demonstrably a meal. Ritual stylization has set in, however, as was already the case with the formularies found in the three synoptic gospels and Paul.

The employment of the Jewish vocabulary of priesthood and cult in a context of the episcopal/presbyteral order is familiar from 1 Clement (96 A.D., ch. 40-44) and Ignatius (d. 107 A.D.–*Ephesians* 5; *Magnesians* 7; *Philadelphians* 4). Justin, in his *Dialogue with Trypho* (ch. 117), spoke of "sacrifices pleasing to God" which are offered at the "thanksgiving for bread and cup celebrated by Christians everywhere." By A.D. 348, St. Cyril of Jerusalem could speak freely in *Mystagogical Catecheses* V, 2 of the priest (*hiereus*) and presbyters standing around God's altar (*thysiastērion*, V, 2) in a church (V, 4). Again, the holy kiss of peace is the warmest interpersonal gesture described (V, 3). Careful instructions are given for accepting the "sign" (*antitypon*, V, 20) of the body and blood of Christ respectfully:

> Make your left hand as if a throne for your right, which is about to receive the King, and having hollowed your palm, receive the body of Christ, saying after it, Amen. Then, after you have carefully hallowed your eyes by the touch of the holy body, partake of it; for what you lose is a loss to you as if of one of your own members. Tell me, if anyone gave you gold dust, would you not hold fast to it with every safeguard, being careful not to mislay it and thereby suffer loss? How much more cautiously, therefore, will you observe that not a crumb falls from you of what is more precious than gold or precious stones?

This awesome behavior reached its zenith in injunctions such as those of St. John Chrysostom (d. 407 A.D.) to approach the eucharistic altar in fear and trembling. This same church father summarized the sacrificial language about the Eucharist that had become accepted practice by his time when he wrote of "the Lord being sacrificed and laid upon the altar and the priest standing and praying over the victim" (*On the Priesthood* 3, 4, 177). Already in A.D. 200, St. Irenaeus of Lyons was speaking of the whole church making an "offering" of the eucharistic sacrifice (*Against Heresies* 4, 17, 5-6). The word offering or sacrifice (*thysia*), in turn, goes back to the *Didachē* (14, 1).

The complaint of Father Baker and Catholics like him is against two basic changes they perceive, one in form and the other in content. As to *form*, they favor speech in a hieratic tongue or silence, the celebrant's face expressionless or solemn, his stance directed away from the congregation in symbol of his leadership of them toward God (an effect achieved in the East by the iconostasis), the prayers addressed to the All-Holy in accents of the honor or "external glory" due him. Regarding the *content* of the rite—both prayers and actions—a stress on the eating and drinking of the elements is seen by them to have replaced the representation of a body broken and blood poured out in atoning sacrifice for the world's sins. This representation is visual as much as it is in the order of nourishment. There is an important sense in which the texts of the "new Mass" are not basically in question here. The Roman Canon with its added Frankish and Gallican elements remains in use (Canon I). The three new canons can be shown to be anything but "soft" on the worshipful and sacrificial character of the rite, once the language of the early centuries has been exposed to contemporaries more familiar with the diction of the medieval than the patristic age.

A basic difference remains, however, and so long as it does the two camps in Roman Catholicity are not likely to come close over this central sign of unity and charity. The difference is whether the Lord is to be commemorated through food and drink consumed (the "meal aspect") or a gift offered to God and upheld to view (the "sacrifice aspect"). Hope of reconciliation lies only in a persistent catechesis in the spirit of the first three centuries. Presumably all parties to the Catholic debate accept the witness of tradition. In that tradition, the twofold action of offering and eating were somehow reconciled.

The initial Protestant response to this internal problem of the Roman Church may be impatience. Largely feeling no need of recourse to post-biblical tradition, some Protestants are able to say that their radical response to the problem four centuries ago was to return to the practice recorded by Matthew, Mark, Luke, and Paul, without theological subtlety or attention to the changing emphases of ritual history. Yet they cannot escape quite so easily, and this not simply for reasons of participation in contemporary ecumenical dialogue. The "mere commemoration" of Zwingli has been deeply influential on all the churches, regardless of their official doctrine of the Lord's supper. Moreover, they have inherited from the New Testament not simply a meal but a meal that had already become ritualized. Any remembrance of the Lord in bread and cup they engage in, however starkly confined to New Testament wording, is bound to both recall and look forward, in the doubly ambivalent symbol of a meal that is also a cultic rite. There is, finally, pressure from within and without Protestant congregations to celebrate the Lord's supper more often than heretofore, and to do it in some ritual form that includes biblical proclamation, speech, song, movement, and the reverent consuming of the elements. In a word, the present experience of the Roman Church can be instructive for all the churches, quite apart from the ninth century debates on realism and symbolism, and without regard to the sixteenth century struggle over one "real presence" of Christ rather than his total real presence.[1]

Churches in the tradition of the Reformers are normally free of the compli-

---

[1] Ernst Käsemann writes in "The Pauline Doctrine of the Lord's Supper," commenting on Jesus' words over the cup in 1 Cor. 11:25ff. in context of 10:16ff., that it is not possible to distinguish between the two dimensions, food and sharing (*koinōnia*), as modern thought distinguishes between a thing and its image: "According to the understanding of antiquity, the representing dimension does actually bring about the presence of what is represented and therefore mediates participation in it. Thus, whatever objections may be raised against the term 'Real Presence,' it expresses exactly what Paul wants to say." *Essays on New Testament Themes* (1964), p. 128.

cation of a visual approach to the Holy Bread (cf. E. Dumoutet's historical study, *Le Désir de Voir l'Hostie*; and recall Queen Elizabeth's "Higher, sir priest, higher!"). In eliminating the veneration of the reserved sacrament, they removed an internal tension between Christ as mediator of grace and as recipient of divine honors. Or at least they seemed to, though common commitment to Chalcedonian (451 A.D.) Christology means that the tension remains. But certain persistent problems in current Roman eucharistic reform cannot but be instructive to churches such as the United Methodist Church, which are attempting similar reforms in their eucharistic practice.

The first of these is the relative place of ordained ministers, unordained ministers, and the laity in the celebration of the Lord's supper. The sociological threat of clerical dominance is but a reflection of unsolved theological problems regarding the relationships among all the baptized. The imposition of hands on some makes them ministers of Word and sacrament, either as bishops, presbyters, or deacons. What skill in leadership in ritual behavior was assumed in the candidates for that ordination? And what is to be done in practice when they are demonstrably less gifted in that area than others in the congregation not ordained to such a leadership function?

The problem is not simply that some in the community are gifted as readers, singers, dramatists, and even potential expositors of the Word, but that nothing has been stipulated in the sacramental structure (i.e., by virtue of baptism and confirmation) that gives them a clear title to participate as that which has been given to the ordained. Yet the faithful, in receiving those two sacraments, were not constituted bystanders in worship but active participants. It seems important, therefore, that the Roman Church place the welcome development of a laity serving on diocesan liturgical commissions and parish liturgy committees and as directors of local worship programs on some sacramental basis. This is needed not merely as a device to protect them against the arbitrariness of the clergy but for the deeper theological reason that a relation already exists between their rite(s) of initiation and the active eucharistic life they were initiated into. In former times the minor orders of doorkeeper, lector, exorcist, and acolyte served the function of further commissioning the baptized. With the recent suppression of these minor orders as steps on the way to the priesthood, they should be revived on a realistic basis for other ministers of both sexes.

A second area of needed exploration is that of the tension between joyous celebration in an eschatological mood and solemn reflection on two tragedies in a quite different order: the sinfulness of humanity and the reconciling death of Jesus on the cross that can overcome it. The temperamental differences among worshipers—the joyous and the solemn—are not primary here, even though they are what bring the tension most to public notice. The general unfamiliarity of Christians with their own eucharistic history lies at the root of the confusion. In an important sense, the recent text of the Mass of the Resurrection for the dead highlights the problem by replacing one imbalance with another.

Nowhere in the revised rites of the Roman Church is it proposed that

seriousness be replaced by frivolity or worship of the divine by human conviviali-
ty. Yet the fact that such a caricature is widespread in circles of the "scandal-
ized" must mean that careful instruction on the point has been lacking. That
instruction cannot be given thoughtlessly. Perhaps the reason for its widespread
omission is the paucity of theological inquiry into the transition from the *agapē*
tradition of 1 Corinthians (2 Peter 2:13 also, if the correct reading is *agapais*)
and the *Didachē* to the more structured liturgies that followed, in which ordinary meal behavior is less discernible. The Christian *seder* (the term for the
Jewish Passover meal), a recent Holy Thursday development outside of liturgical
boundaries, while a helpful bridge, is no substitute for liturgical scholarship that
has not yet been done.

In former times, the feasts and seasons of the Christian East and West, with
their alternating moods of joy and sorrow, dealt with this problem in part. Now
that people of the West are little touched by any lively study of the history and
meaning of festivals (heortology), the problem is heightened. The human events
of birth, marriage, and death lend a tone to the liturgical observances that mark
them. The weekly celebration of the Lord's supper may profit by a major season
or some designated theme. Overall, however, the character of the celebration of
the ordinary Sunday Eucharist is in a kind of limbo because the profound
differences between communal rejoicing (*socia exultatione*) and formal praise
(*offerimus praeclarae maiestati tuae*) have not been sufficiently explored. A
simple return to what is supposed to have been the meal behavior of Jesus and
his disciples or the Corinthian church in a disciplined state do not comprise
"sufficient exploration."

Lastly, there is the problem of the rational and the emotional in Christian
worship, with which the Roman Church is today struggling mightily. As is well
known, the Reformers worked for a vernacular liturgy on a comprehensibility
principle, with Paul's clear preference of prophecy over speech in a tongue to
support them (see 1 Corinthians 14). Despite their efforts to rescue medieval
Europe from religious behavior that was uncomprehended in terms of the biblical word, the laws of religious behavior inevitably reasserted themselves. Great
chorales and organ music replaced Latin motets and the chant, with the rationality of the texts of interest to only the few. The cadences of Luther's Bible and
the Authorized Version became fitting music to the ear. It was a conceit of the
learned to suppose that the actual text of the Scriptures was what gave satisfaction. In fact, the religious needs of the congregants were being met in another
order, that of their feelings and emotions. Bible reading and preaching beyond
doubt had some of the salutary effects hoped for, but these effects were rational
only in part. Witness the success of the drama of revivalism or its American
counterpart, the camp meeting; the preaching of Black Christians which is more
often song than speech; and the structured interplay of hymnody and verbal
utterance at divine service.

All of this authentic religious behavior—for it is that—had its matching
phenomena in the Roman Church, whether in the incomprehensible Latin or five

or six hymns universally known or familiar experiences in aroma, sight, and sound. Much of this is temporarily in decline in the Roman Church on the initial principle of the Reformers, the rationality of religion. Unfortunately, those who have official oversight of the revised liturgical books (verbal *texts*, notice) tend to have no matching interest in the arts. They are men of ideas and words and laws, not of great song and language and movement. The result of this official disinterest in art forms as vehicles of religious feeling has been the filling of the vacuum everywhere by debased arts: spoken and sung language of poor quality, bouncy or whiny music, casual or embarrassed postures where the discipline of a ballet captain or lead tenor is called for.

The Roman Church can do no better in its search for renewed authentic religious behavior at the Lord's supper than to invite attention to what it has left undone, as well as the important matters it has lately, and at some cost, done.

METHODIST RESPONSE BY J. ROBERT NELSON

Why is it that until very recently most American Protestants were loathe to employ the words "Eucharist" and "celebration"? To be honest, because their anti-Catholic prejudice prevented them from applying words which connoted "the popish Mass" to their Holy Communion. Instead, and quite deliberately, most Protestants of the Reformed and Evangelical persuasion spoke of the "ordinance" of "the Lord's Supper," which was never "celebrated" but rather "administered." As often happens in religious discourse, it was connotation rather than meaning alone which determined the choice.

One positive gain of ecumenism has been the general acceptance of "Eucharist" and "celebration" into the Protestant lexicon. But many who use them freely have yet to learn that they mean literally the joy of thanksgiving to God for the gift of Christ Jesus. In fact, the sacrament is still administered as a mournful commemoration of the crucifixion, with psychological emphasis upon the worshipper's sense of personal unworthiness and contrition. More often than not, it seems to be more elegiac than eucharistic.

Sloyan discusses the tension within the Catholic community between those who emphasize almost exclusively the cultic sacrifice and those for whom the reenactment of Jesus' last meal with the disciples is preeminent. His answer is correct: both dimensions are legitimate, indispensable, and highly valued. He cites Lietzmann's noted research, but could have made his point by indicating that the title of that book was not *Mass "or" Lord's Supper (Messe "oder" Herrenmahl)*. Such a dichotomy is manifestly false. This is what the contemporary ecumenical rapprochement makes clear to us. As it was in the beginning—first three centuries—it ought to be now and evermore. If Protestants are again learning to appreciate the Eucharist as sacrificial thanksgiving, Catholics are appropriating again the great value of a Holy Communion of the people gathered for the meal of the Bread of Life.

Sloyan does an injustice, however, to two dimensions of prevalent Protestant thought and doctrine: namely, Tradition and Christology. It is just not the case with many Protestants that they ignored Tradition and went "back to the Bible" for a simple, pre-traditional form and doctrine of the Lord's Supper. Lutherans, Reformed, Anglicans, and Methodists have all consciously maintained continuity with early cultic traditions. It is true that many, probably too many, have been indifferent toward the official rubrics and doctrines of their own denominations. They have allowed and encouraged the introduction of practices which at best are unfortunate and at worst deplorable. Is this not due to a double lack on their part: the lack of theological seriousness and the lack of respect for church discipline (because it is seldom enforced in this area)? Thus, what is supposedly normative in theory becomes abnormal in practice. We are fully aware of these aberrations and of the need for cleansing the temple of both recklessness and frivolity. Sloyan may be right in crediting the Roman Catholics with influencing Protestants (other than Episcopalians and Disciples of Christ) toward more frequent celebrations; but he is wrong in claiming the same cause for Protestants' use of "biblical proclamation, speech, song, movement, and the reverent consuming of the elements," since these have always been the ingredients of their rituals.

A second question must be raised about the relation of Christology to the veneration of the reserved eucharistic bread. Certainly Protestants who are committed to Chalcedonian Christology believe that Jesus Christ is the "mediator of grace" and the "recipient of divine honors." But Sloyan's assertion that the tension between these two dimensions of Christology is removed by the rejection of reservation (and benediction) of the Blessed Sacrament is, to this reader, an opaque statement. It implies the reopening of debates about transubstantiation, which for a good number of years have been considered unrewarding. The theological insights of Eastern Orthodoxy have helped both Catholics and Protestants in this regard. Suffice it to say that a "high" Christology conjoined with a realistic belief in the eucharistic presence of Christ does not require the practice of veneration of the Host.

More agreeable is Sloyan's strong proposal for all churches that an unequivocal recognition be given to the participation of the laity in eucharistic worship, not merely as passive recipients, but as readers, expositors, and servers, and justifying this on the basis of the theology of baptism and confirmation. Protestant churches are not consistent in this regard, despite their common affirmation of the "priesthood of all the faithful." Indeed, some Protestant churches allow less formal participation to laity than do Catholic and Orthodox churches, but this is seldom due to considered theological reasoning.

Sloyan's appeal for more amplitude for emotional expression as the counterpart to reason expressed in liturgical diction is likewise to the point. Celebration and cerebration should be in balance. This has been the *intent* of much liturgical reform in recent years, even though not easily realized. The diversities of aesthetic taste and cultural conditioning make it impossible anymore to prescribe one rite only for all people of the same denomination, and much less one rite for all Christians. Africa has become an interesting and instructive testing ground for ritual expression in which authentic celebration can combine with acceptable rationality. What appear to be innovations in the eucharistic worship—dance, movement, song, and color—are not really new, but the sanctifying of familiar elements of distinctive cultures. Since European and American Christianity has already appropriated traditional culture for worship (and, indeed, Christian worship has formed much of that tradition), it is difficult to know whether innovations employing currently accepted and popular modes of music, language, and motion can aid authentic celebration or not.

Such experimenting and testing, in any case, for many Protestants will be just a liturgical diversion, a curious dilettantism, unless and until the Eucharist is restored to the place of primacy and centrality in the life of the congregation. This is something which some Protestants have learned, and are learning, from Catholics and Orthodox and certain Anglicans. It is to be hoped that Catholics who are disposed or eager to appropriate some of the manifest values of Protestant sacramental practice will not weaken their own power to exemplify the primacy of the Holy Communion in their lives.

Study and Discussion Questions

1. Do you agree with Nelson's questioning the faithfulness of Methodist eucharistic practice to the basic Reformation emphasis on the church as the congregation where the word is rightly preached and *the sacraments duly administered*? Discuss.
2. Among the "regretable signs of Methodism's condition," Nelson mentions "carelessness with the handling of the elements." What is meant by this statement? What assumptions of a eucharistic theology does it contain, and would you agree that its merits listing as an abuse?
3. In what specific ways does Nelson document the eucharistic concern of the Wesley brothers? Discuss.
4. Discuss how Wesley understood the "presenting" of Christ's saving work to the Father in the Eucharist.
5. If "doctrine is best preserved in liturgy" does Nelson consider Methodist liturgy to have been a good guardian of eucharistic doctrine? Discuss.
6. How optimistic is Nelson that Methodism can reappropriate its own eucharistic tradition? Do you agree with him?
7. Sloyan points out that some Catholics today are complaining about what they perceive to be changes in the form and content of the eucharistic liturgy. To what is Sloyan referring? Discuss.
8. What does Sloyan conclude from his survey of the tradition of eucharistic practice in the early centuries? Discuss.
9. What does Sloyan mean by a "visual approach to the Holy Bread"? What influence did this approach have on eucharistic practice?
10. In what way are Christologies related to questions of the eucharistic presence of Christ? Discuss.
11. Do you agree with Sloyan that blending joyousness and solemnity in the liturgy is an important contemporary challenge? Discuss how ecumenical dialogue might help meet this challenge.

BAPTIST-CATHOLIC DIALOGUE

Arthur B. Crabtree—John A. Hardon

PRECIS

After discussing the Baptist terminology for Eucharist, Crabtree outlines Baptist eucharistic tradition. Presbyterian influence led to a monthly celebration, while Zwinglian and Calvinistic influence led to an emphasis on the commemoration and communion aspects of the rite. In the U. S. until recently, the Lord's Supper was thought of chiefly or exclusively as the commemoration of the death of Jesus. In the last thirty years, U. S. Baptists have reexamined their understanding of the Eucharist and, as a result, the concepts of "presence of Christ" and "sacrifice" have reentered the theological discussion. Crabtree believes all current Baptist terminology inadequate. In his view, any adequate eucharistic theology must include considerations of mystery, acted gospel, liberation, celebration of covenant, participation in Christ, sacrifice, sacrament, and grace.

Hardon summarizes traditional Roman Catholic eucharistic teaching on real presence, the sacrifice of the Mass, and communion. Regarding real presence, the Catholic Church has taught that the whole Christ is truly, really, and substantially present, that the term transubstantiation is an appropriate term to describe the change that takes place, that the whole Christ is present under each species and under each and every portion of each species, and, since this presence continues beyond the time of communion, that true adoration is to be given to the sacrament. As for the sacrificial aspect of the Eucharist, official church teaching has frequently asserted that in the Mass there takes place the application to humanity of the blessings of salvation won on the cross. After a primitive church custom of frequent reception of communion, there was a decline in the custom, leading eventually to annual communion prescribed in 1215. Pius X was instrumental in restoring the custom of frequent communion, a practice reinforced by Vatican II teaching.

Arthur B. Crabtree (American Baptist), B.A., B.D., University of Manchester, Dr. Theol., University of Zurich, is a Professor in the Department of Religious Studies at Villanova (PA) University. He is the North American Academy of Ecumenists' editorial liaison with the *Journal of Ecumenical Studies*, and a member of the Baptist Committee on Christian Unity. Author of *The Restored Relationship,* his most recent article is "Baptist Spirituality" in *The Month* (1976).

John A. Hardon, S.J. (Roman Catholic), A.B., John Carroll University, M.A., Loyola University (Chicago), S.T.L., W. Baden College (Indiana), S.T.D., Gregorian University (Rome), is a Professor of the Jesuit School of Theology in Chicago, on a visiting professorship at St. John's University in New York in the Institute for Advanced Studies in Catholic Doctrine (1974-76). A member of the Bishops Commission for Ecumenism and Inter-religious Affairs, he has written hundreds of journal and encyclopedia articles and several books, most recently *The Catholic Catechism* (Doubleday).

THE EUCHARIST IN BAPTIST LIFE AND THOUGHT

Arthur B. Crabtree

The purpose of this essay is mutual understanding and dialogue, which will probably be served best if I proceed by the following steps: first, a comment on Baptist terminology; second, a short survey of Baptist eucharistic traditions; third, a revue of contemporary trends in Baptist eucharistic theology; fourth, an outline of my own eucharistic theology.

Baptist Terminology

Consonant with the Calvinistic tradition, Baptists customarily term the Eucharist the "Lord's Supper." The English Baptists, influenced apparently by the Anglican tradition, sometimes call it "Communion." The General Baptists called baptism and Eucharist "sacraments." The Particular Baptists termed them "ordinances."[1] Today there is a tendency, led by English Baptists, to return to the word "sacrament."

Baptist Eucharistic Tradition

There is some evidence, according to Horton Davies,[2] that the earliest Baptists celebrated the Eucharist every Sunday in conjunction with the liturgy of the Word. Soon, however, they began to follow the Presbyterians in celebrating it only occasionally, usually once a month. This is still the custom.

The manner of celebrating the Lord's Supper is relatively uniform. It is usually conducted by an ordained Baptist minister with the assistance of deacons (who are laypeople), sitting behind a table, facing the congregation. The words of institution are read from 1 Corinthians 11 or one of the Gospels, thanksgiving (that is, eucharistic) prayers offered for the bread and wine, and bread and wine distributed by the minister and deacons, and eaten and drunk. A "fellowship offering" is contributed for the needy, and the Supper closes with a hymn and benediction.

The interpretation of the Lord's Supper has been influenced not by the Lutheran but by the Zwinglian and Calvinistic traditions. According to the Zwinglian tradition, which stresses the words "do this in remembrance (*anamnesis*) of me," the Supper commemorates the Lord's death, the bread and wine signifying, but not being, the body and blood of Christ, since Christ is now

---

[1]Cf. Norman H. Maring and Winthrop S. Hudson, *A Baptist Manual of Polity and Practice* (Valley Forge: Judson Press, 1963), p. 125.

[2]Quoted by John W. Brush, "Baptists and the Lord's Supper," *Foundations* (October, 1958).

in heaven and not with us on earth. According to the Calvinistic tradition, the Supper is both commemoration and communion—a "witness of the union which we have with Christ, inasmuch as he not only died and rose for us once, but also feeds and nourishes us truly with his flesh and blood, so that we may be one in him, and that our life may be in common."[3]

The earliest Baptists, such as Smyth and Helwys, followed the Calvinist tradition of the English Separatists and Dutch Mennonites. This Calvinistic tradition was presented in the General Baptist Orthodox Creed of 1679 which affirms that the Supper means remembrance of Christ's sacrificial death, spiritual nourishment and growth in Christ, communion with Christ and one another, obedience to Christ, and thanksgiving to God for God's benefits.[4]

It similarly found expression in the Particular Baptist Second London Confession of 1677, which in 1742-1743 was adopted by Baptists in the United States as the Philadelphia Confession of Faith. This Confession declares that "the Supper of the Lord Jesus, was instituted by him ... for the perpetual remembrance, and shewing forth the sacrifice of his death, confirmation of the faith of believers in all the benefits thereof, their spiritual nourishment, and growth in him ... and to be a bond and pledge of their communion with him, and with each other."[5]

In England, however, according to Payne, "during the eighteenth century Zwinglian views seem to have become somewhat more general."[6] In the United States there was a similar Zwinglian trend. The New Hampshire Confession of 1833 says tersely that baptism is prerequisite to "the Lord's Supper, in which the members of the Church, by the (sacred) use of bread and wine, are to commemorate together the dying love of Christ; preceded always by solemn self examination."[7] During the late nineteenth and the early twentieth centuries, the New Hampshire Confession became immensely influential both among Northern (now American) and Southern Baptists. In 1925 the huge Southern Baptist Convention "worked over the Confession, adding ten new sections, and published it as the expression of the faith generally held by Southern Baptists."[8] We thus discern during the eighteenth and nineteenth centuries both in England and in the United States a general shift from the Calvinistic to the Zwinglian tradition. For most Baptists, particularly in the United States, the Lord's Supper became until recently merely a commemoration of the death of Jesus.

---

[3]*French Confession of Faith*, 1559, composed by Calvin and his pupil Chandieu. Phillip Schaff, *The Creeds of Christendom*, III (New York: Harper and Brothers, 1877), p. 380.

[4]William L. Lumpkin, *Baptist Confessions of Faith* (Philadelphia: Judson Press, 1959), p. 321.

[5]Ibid., p. 291.

[6]Ernest Payne, *The Fellowship of Believers* (London: Carey Kingsgate Press, 1948), p. 64.

[7]Lumpkin, *Baptist Confessions*, p. 366.

Recent Thinking

By "recent" I mean the past thirty years. During this period the trend toward Zwinglianism has been reversed. The trend is now toward Calvinism—and even beyond it in the direction of Anglicanism and Catholicism. This recent trend began in England and is being followed in the United States.

In 1948, the Council of the Baptist Union of Great Britain and Ireland approved the following statement:

> The Communion Service is more than a commemoration of the Last Supper and a showing forth "of the Lord's death until He comes." Here the grace of God is offered and is received in faith; here the real presence of Christ is manifest in the joy and peace both of the believing soul and of the community; here we are in communion, not only with our fellow-members in the Church, not only with the Church militant on earth and triumphant in heaven, but also with our risen and glorified Lord.[9]

In 1951, the Baptist Principals' Conference, at the request of the Council, published a fuller declaration entitled: *The Lord's Supper, a Baptist Statement*, which interprets the Communion or Supper in a sevenfold manner:

First, "The Lord's Supper is a service of Remembrance."

Second, "such remembrance embodies also a Proclamation" in which "we proclaim anew the eternal reality of His suffering and redeeming love."

Third, it is "a service of self examination and repentance, of confession and judgment."

Fourth, "when approached in this spirit, the service is truly a 'sacrament,' for then its actions and words become to us 'the outward and visible sign of an inward and spiritual grace.'"

Fifth, "there is much help to be gained from the idea of Sacrifice, when used with due care. Baptists repudiate any notion of repeating, or adding to, the one perfect and all sufficient offering for the sins of mankind made by our Saviour upon the Cross." Nevertheless, we remember at the Table "the eternal self offering of Christ to God on our behalf" and offer ourselves to God in such a manner that we so "identify ourselves by faith with Him in what He does on our behalf that even our imperfect offering is transformed, and being taken up into the perfection of His, is made acceptable and well pleasing to God."

Sixth, the Lord's Supper is a "Covenant-rite" in which there is "a perpetual renewing of the Lord's covenant with His people, and so of our covenant with Him and with one another."

Seventh, the Lord's Supper has universal and ecumenical significance, since

---

[8]Ibid., p. 361.

[9]Quoted in *The Lord's Supper, A Baptist Statement* (London: Carey Kingsgate Press, 1951), p. 9.

it reminds us of "the bond that unites us in Christ with all the people of God, and not least with those who are sundered from us by distance or by ecclesiastical divisions."

In light of this bond, the Statement, while permitting "close communion" (that is, the restriction of holy communion to Baptists), recommends "open communion" (that is, the sharing of holy communion with non-Baptists). In other words, it recommends shared communion or intercommunion on the grounds that, though severed by ecclesial boundaries, we are united in Christ and recognize one another and collaborate with one another as brothers and sisters in Christ. "What right therefore have we to deny them access to the Table of the Lord?"[10]

In the British periodical, *Baptist Quarterly*, H. W. Trent, in 1957, emphasized three aspects of the Supper: retrospectively, it is a commemoration of the crucified Christ; presently it is participation (*koinonia*) in the risen Christ; proleptically, it is an anticipation of the consummation of the kingdom of God.[11]

In the United States the need for Baptist rethinking on the Eucharist was pointed out by Samuel H. Miller in 1958, when he wrote that in light of our modern understanding of symbol and sacrament, Baptists "may need a new doctrine in regard to the Lord's Supper."[12] A step in this direction was made by Thorwald W. Bender in an address delivered to the American Baptist Convention at Detroit in May, 1963. "The Communion Service," he said, "stands for far more than 'bare memorialism.'. . . We must recognize its sacramental dimension. . . . This remembrance looks backward to Calvary; it looks forward to the glorious, victorious return of Christ; and it takes place in the joyous awareness of the Risen Lord's present ministry."[13]

A further step was taken by Eric C. Rust, a former British Baptist now teaching in Southern Baptist Seminary, Louisville, Kentucky, in an article entitled "The Theology of the Lord's Supper" in a special issue of *The Review and Expositor*, Winter, 1969, devoted to the question of the Lord's Supper and edited by David Mueller. Rust begins by remarking that until recently Baptists have relegated the Supper to a minor place and interpreted it in the Zwinglian manner as merely a memorial meal. He now wishes to accord it to larger place and broader meaning. In particular, he stresses six aspects of the Supper:

First, it is acted gospel, *dabar* in action, a proclamation of the death of the Lord.

Second, it is living presence—the presence of Christ with his people—"the living presence of the Risen Lord."

---

[10]Ibid., p. 34.

[11]H. W. Trent, "Ourselves and the Ordinances," *Baptist Quarterly* (January, 1957).

[12]Samuel H. Miller, "Reducing the Reality of the Lord's Supper," *Foundations* (October, 1958).

[13]Thorwald W. Bender, "A Theological and Functional Understanding of the Ordinances," a paper presented to the American Baptist Convention meeting in Detroit, 1963.

Third, it is Eucharist, that is, thanksgiving.

Fourth, as Eucharist it is sacrifice, since "our thanksgiving is an offering, a sacrifice. Hence in the great church tradition, the Lord's Supper can be described as both Eucharist and Eucharistic Sacrifice." It is a sacrifice since "the once-for-all atonement on Calvary's hill is also an eternal reality. . . . Christ ever stands in the divine life offering eternally his sacrifice for us and for all men," and we join our sacrifice to his "not alone the sacrifice of our praise but also "the sacrifice of ourselves to his service."

Fifth, it is a fellowship meal in which "we commune with one another and with God though his sacrifice."

Sixth, it is an eschatological feast which we celebrate "until he shall come, when the whole universe will display the glory of the Lord."[14]

Summarizing these trends, we may say that Baptist theologians are gradually recognizing that the Eucharist is not merely a memorial meal but also communion with Christ and Christians, a sacrifice of thanksgiving and of consecration to his service, a visible and acted word proclaiming the gospel of redeeming love, a sacrament which signifies and communicates God's grace to all who participate in faith, and an eschatological sign of the culmination of God's reign.

From this historical survey it becomes manifest that Baptist views of the Eucharist have varied and still vary. Today they are very much in flux. My own view is but one element in that manifold flux and should not be regarded as representative of all Baptists. It is written from the standpoint of an ecumenical Baptist who tries to take account of "the living tradition of the whole Church."[15]

A Personal Interpretation

1. Terminology.

All three names in common use are good: Eucharist, Holy Communion, Lord's Supper. Each expresses an important aspect of the rite: Eucharist, the aspect of thanksgiving; Holy Communion, the aspect of communion with God and one another; Lord's Supper, the aspect of a common meal in Christ. But neither singly nor in combination do they exhaust the meaning of this rite, which is essentially a mystery transcending comprehension and formulation.

2. Eucharist Is Mystery.

Actually everything is mystery. Reality transcends our grasp. Everything is marvelous. *Mir ist alles Wunder* (Schleiermacher). The marvel and mystery of reality leaves us "lost in wonder, love and praise" (Charles Wesley). The Eucha-

---

[14]All quotations are from Eric C. Rust, "The Theology of the Lord's Supper," *Review and Expositor* (Winter, 1969): 36ff.

[15]Vatican II, *Document on Revelation,* 12.

rist is no exception. It is one of the "mysteries of Christianity" (Scheeben), unfathomable, ineffable, indefinable. Every attempt to formulate it, including the present one, is inadequate.

3. Eucharist Is Sacrament.

As the language of Western Christianity became Latin rather than Greek, the word *mysterion* was translated *sacramentum* rather than *mysterium*. What Eastern Christians called (and still call) "mysteries," Western Christians term "sacraments." "Sacrament" was understood by Augustine as a sign of the sacred and by Peter Lombard and the Scholastics as a sign of divine grace—a sign which both signifies and conveys grace when received in faith.

To me the Eucharist is both mystery and sacrament—an ineffable divine-human mystery which, through the sacramental signs of bread and wine, signifies and conveys grace when received in faith.

4. Eucharist Is a Means of Grace.

Such a sacrament is manifestly a means of grace—not automatically—but when received in faith, hope, love, penitence, and humility. Now grace is *charis*, the gracefulness and graciousness of God which graces us (*charitein*, Eph. 1:16) and evokes our gratitude (*eucharistia*).

5. Eucharist Is Visible Word or Acted Gospel.

Grace manifests itself in Christ and Christ meets us in the gospel. This gospel is communicated to us by the written word of Scripture, the spoken word of proclamation, and the acted word of Scripture, the spoken word of proclamation, and the acted word of the Eucharist (the *verbum visibile* of Augustine). "For as often as you eat this bread and drink this cup, you proclaim the Lord's death until he comes" (1 Cor. 11:26). Participation in the Eucharist is proclamation of the gospel. Actions speak no less than words. (The Hebrew word *dabar* means both word and action.) The proclamation of the gospel begins in the liturgy of the Word and continues in the liturgy of the Eucharist. This continuity underlies the unity of Word and Eucharist in the Orthodox and Catholic liturgies—a unity which many Protestants have lost and need to recover.

6. Eucharist Is Liberation, Salvation, Rectification, Reconciliation.

Eucharist is essentially the Jewish Passover christologically interpreted. Passover means liberation from the bondage of Egypt; Eucharist, from the bondage of sin—both from its guilt and from its power. And liberation from sin is liberation for righteousness. It is redemption, salvation, rectification of our relationship with God and one another, reconciliation with God and one another, health, wholeness, fullness of life, *shalom*.

7. Eucharist Is Covenant Celebration.

This rectification of relationships with God and one another is called in the Scriptures a covenant, and covenant is associated with Eucharist (Mt. 26:28; Mk. 14:24; 1 Cor. 11:25). Eucharist is accordingly a covenant celebration, a covenant of love and peace with God and all of God's creatures.

8. Eucharist Is Commemoration.

In this covenant celebration we commemorate the one who makes the covenant—Jesus Christ. "Do this in my remembrance (*anamnesis*)" was Christ's precept to his church (1 Cor. 11:25). *Anamnesis* is unforgetfulness, consciousness of Christ, commemoration of Christ, both of the dying Christ of Calvary and the living Christ who is present in our covenant celebration.

9. Eucharist Is Communion.

Our commemoration of Christ is at the same time communion with Christ. "The cup of blessing which we bless, is it not a communion (*koinonia*) of the blood of Christ? The bread which we break, is it not a communion (*koinonia*) of the body of Christ? Because there is one loaf, we who are many are one body, for we are all partakers of the same loaf" (1 Cor. 10:16f.).
Eucharist is a sacrament of unity in community—unity in Christ in the community of Christ's people. Eucharist is Holy Communion: communion with God, the Father, Son, and Holy Spirit, in the mystical unity of the body of Christ—of that body of Christ which is both the bread and the church.

10. Eucharist Is Anticipation.

This eucharistic unity is glorious, yet fleeting and inperfect, like all things in this mortal life. It is but a foretaste, an anticipation of that richer, fuller, more abiding communion still to come when the *telos* is reached and God is all in all (1 Cor. 15:24-28).

11. Eucharist Is the Continuation of Christ's Priestly Work
    of Reconciliation.

Christ's work has many facets: prophetic, priestly, kingly, ministerial, etc. Presently we are concerned alone with his priestly work, which began with the incarnation, which enabled Christ as the God-human to mediate between God and humanity and to reconcile us with God and one another (Eph. 2:11-22). This incarnational ministry of reconciliation climaxed in the passion in which "he died once for all (*hapax*), the righteous for the unrighteous, that he might bring us to God" (1 Pet. 3:18). This sacrificial offering in the blood of the cross was unique and unrepeatable. This unicity of Calvary was stressed by the Protestant Reformers, affirmed by the Council of Trent,[16] and reaffirmed in the recent bilateral conversations.[17]

That does not mean, however, as the Protestant Reformers tended too readily to assume, that the sacrificial priestly work of Christ ended with the cross. It continues, as the Council of Trent rightly affirms,[18] in the Eucharist. It continues actually in the whole work of the church which, together with Christ, its living head (Eph. 1:22f.; Col. 1:18), is a "royal priesthood" (1 Pet. 2:9). It continues *par excellence* in the liturgy of the church, in the liturgy of the Eucharist no less than in the liturgy of the Word. How does it continue? By way of intercession, oblation, and reconciliation.

(a) *Intercession*: On the ground of this reconciling sacrifice offered once for all on the cross, Christ continually intercedes for us (Heb. 7:25), and in union with Christ we intercede for one another.

(b) *Oblation*: This intercession is a continuing oblation of Christ, a constant sacrificial consecration to his priestly work of reconciliation, an oblation offered no longer in the blood of the dying Christ but in the priestly ministry of the living Christ. And as Christ continually offers himself in sacrificial service, we who participate in his body and blood (1 Cor. 10:16) offer ourselves as a living sacrifice to God (Rom. 12:1).

(c) *Reconciliation*: The effect of this sacrificial priestly work of Christ, begun in the incarnation, climaxed in the cross, and continuing in the Eucharist, is reconciliation: reconciliation with God and one another in the mystical unity of the body of Christ (Eph. 2:11-22). In the sacrifice of the cross Christ was effecting reconciliation *for us*. In the Eucharist he is effecting reconciliation *for us and with us,* since we share with him in the ministry of reconciliation (2 Cor. 5:18).

12. Eucharist Is Thanksgiving.

For all the blessings of God's grace, for the common bread of our daily life and the eucharistic bread of our liturgical life, we raise our sacrifice of praise and thanks. Our response to *charis* is *eucharistia*. Eucharist is Eucharist, thanksgiving.

CATHOLIC RESPONSE BY JOHN A. HARDON

I am happy to respond to the invitation of commenting on Dr. Crabtree's very lucid presentation of "The Eucharist in Baptist Life and Thought." It is

---

[16]Is igitur Deus et Dominus noster, etsi semel se ipsum in ara crucis, morte inter-dedente, Deo Patri oblaturus est. . . . (Denziger, *Enchiridion Symbolorum,* 1740).

[17]Ehrenström and Gassmann, *Confessions in Dialogue* (Geneva: World Council of Churches, 1972), p. 123.

[18]Denzinger, *Enchiridion Symbolorum,* 1743.

surely a tribute to the grace of the Holy Spirit that we can calmly reflect on the Holy Eucharist, as Catholics and Protestants, and trust that with the help of the same Spirit we can speed the day when dialogue will give place to unity of faith in the Mystery of Faith. In my comments I wish to concentrate on the last part of Dr. Crabtree's essay, on what he calls "A Personal Interpretation."

For a Catholic the eucharistic sacrifice certainly is liberation, celebration of covenant, and participation in Christ. But it is all of these with a reality and literalness that Dr. Crabtree's interpretation does not declare. Since Christ is really, truly, and substantially present in the Eucharist, Catholics believe the Mass is correspondingly a true sacrifice. It is not merely a commemoration of the sacrifice accomplished on the cross. It is a true propitiatory sacrifice which truly benefits not only those who physically assist at Mass but all the faithful and, in fact, the whole human race.

It was heartening to read how Dr. Crabtree explains his understanding of how the Eucharist means sacrifice. He says that the Eucharist does not repeat the sacrifice made once for all. The Catholic Church likewise teaches that the Mass is not a new or separate sacrifice which is independent of the cross. On the contrary, all the efficacy of the Mass derives from the cross since in the Mass we have the same priest and victim now on the altar as shed his blood on Calvary. We now receive a share in the graces he merited for us on the cross. It is at this crucial juncture of his explanation that Dr. Crabtree states what I consider to be so encouraging. After stating that in the Eucharist we recall or remember Christ's sacrifice on the cross, he adds these other meanings to the Eucharist as sacrifice:
— Christ who continues the priestly work of interceding for us is present with us to heal and bless.
— We so identify with Christ's sacrifice that we present ourselves a living sacrifice, being transformed by the renewing of our mind that we might discern and do the will of God.

We, too, believe that in the Mass Christ continues the priestly work of healing and blessing humanity. This enables us to identify with Christ's sacrifice by presenting ourselves as a living sacrifice in union with Christ's. But all of this, as the Catholic Church believes, is no mere symbolism, nor mere commemoration, nor mere recollection or remembrance. Christ does here and now truly continue the priestly work of interceding for us through the Mass. There is a real causal efficacy, instrumental no doubt but real, by which the blessings of Calvary are channeled to us through the eucharistic sacrifice.

The reason for being encouraged by what Dr. Crabtree declares is his recognition that Christ instituted the Eucharist as an "outward and visible sign of an inward and spiritual grace," in fact that "it signifies and effects grace when received in faith, hope, and love."

Needless to say, I consider this statement a reflection of the faith of the ancient, undivided church, notably the declaration that the Eucharist *effects* grace. So it does, and so the Catholic Church has always believed to be the meaning of the sacrament of the altar.

There is one important proviso, however, that must be added, and it pertains to the essence of the mystery of the Eucharist. True enough, the Eucharist confers grace on those who receive it in faith, hope, and love. But their faith, hope, and love do not make Christ present in the Eucharist. He is there, once the words of consecration have been pronounced by a duly ordained priest. He is duly ordained if he derives his priestly powers ultimately from the Last Supper through the historical episcopate that comes down to us from Christ when he first ordained the priests of the New Covenant.

Consequently, while I respect Dr. Crabtree's closing observations about intercommunion, I must dissociate myself from what he concludes, that "there are good theological and practical reasons for shared Eucharist." Like him, I hope that one day all Christians will share in the one communion of Christ's body and blood. But it should be evident that not all Christians believe the same about what this communion means. For Catholics it is Christ himself, present under the sacramental species, no less truly than when he walked the streets of Palestine. For many others it is bread and wine signifying, but not being, the body and blood of Christ. How can we speak of a "shared Eucharist" when that which is proposed to be shared is not the same Eucharist?

THE HOLY EUCHARIST IN THE CATHOLIC CHURCH

John A. Hardon

The Holy Eucharist is the center of life and worship in the Catholic Church. Lavish titles have been given to this mystery, of which the best known is the Eucharist, or thanksgiving, either because at its institution Christ "gave thanks," or by the fact that this is the supreme act of Christian gratitude to God. Other familiar names are the Lord's Supper, the Table of the Lord, the Holy Sacrifice, the Holy of Holies, the Blessed Sacrament, or simply the Liturgy. Each of these and similar names concentrate on one or another of the three main aspects of the eucharistic mystery, as real presence, as the sacrifice of the altar, or as the sacrament of Holy Communion.

Building on the biblical foundation, the Catholic Church has ever kept the faithful mindful of their great privilege in possessing the Holy Eucharist and their duty to avail themselves of the graces which Christ intends to confer through this treasury of his mercy.

Real Presence

When Catholic Christianity affirms, without qualification, that "in the nourishing sacrament of the Holy Eucharist, after the consecration of the bread and wine, our Lord Jesus Christ, true God and true man," is present "under the appearances of those sensible things," it rests its faith on the words of Scripture and the evidence of sacred Tradition.[1]

The beginning of this faith comes from the discourse recorded by St. John. Christ had already worked the miracle of multiplying the loaves and fishes. He had also spoken at length about the need for faith in him and his words as a condition for salvation. Then Jesus continued:

> I am the bread of life. Your fathers ate the manna in the desert and they are dead; but this is the bread that comes down from heaven, so that a man may eat and not die. I am the living bread which has come down from heaven. Anyone who eats this bread will live for ever; and the bread that I shall give is my flesh, for the life of the world (Jn. 6:48-51).

The evangelist explains that Christ taught this doctrine in the synagogue, but that after hearing it "many of his followers said, 'This is intolerable language. How could anyone accept it?'" Jesus was fully aware that his followers were complaining and, in fact, asked them, "Does this upset you?" But he took nothing back. Rather he insisted that "The words I have spoken to you are spirit

---

[1] Council of Trent, *Decree on the Most Holy Sacrament of the Eucharist*, I, H. Denzinger, *Enchiridion Symbolorum* (Freiburg, 1953), no. 1636.

and they are life. But there are some of you who do not believe." At the same time he explained that such faith is not of human making, since "no one could come to me unless the Father allows him."

Following this animated dialogue, we are prepared for the statement that, "After this, many of his disciples left him and stopped going with him." Then, to make absolutely certain there was no mistaking what he was saying, Jesus said to the Twelve, "What about you, do you want to go away too?" To which Simon Peter replied, "Lord, who shall we go to? You have the message of eternal life, and we believe" (Jn. 6:59-68).

The church's decisive revelation on the real presence is in the words of institution, "This is my body—This is my blood," whose literal meaning has been defended through the ages. They were thus understood by St. Paul when he told the first Christians that those who approached the Eucharist unworthily would be guilty of the body and blood of the Lord.

The first serious ripples of controversy came in the ninth century A.D., when a monk from the French Abbey of Corbie wrote against his abbot, St. Paschasius (785-860). Ratramnus (died 868) held that Christ's body in the Eucharist cannot be the same as Christ's historical body once on earth and now in heaven, because the eucharistic body is invisible, impalpable, and spiritual.

Within two centuries the issue had reached such a point of gravity that a formal declaration was evoked from the Holy See. In 1079, the archdeacon Berengar of Tours, who favored Ratramnus' position, was required by Gregory VII to accept the following declaration of faith in the eucharistic presence:

> I believe in my heart and openly profess that the bread and wine placed upon the altar are, by the mystery of the sacred prayer and the words of the Redeemer, substantially changed into the true and life-giving flesh and blood of Jesus Christ our Lord.[2]

In the sixteenth century, the controversy over the church's traditional teaching was revived. Theories ranged from complete symbolism to some kind of spiritual presence. It was to meet this new and more serious challenge to the historic faith that the Council of Trent defined the real presence in a series of four canons that covered the major aspects of the faith that were being called into question.

1. Responding to the claims of merely symbolic or spiritual presence, the church condemned "anyone who denies that the body and blood, together with the soul and divinity, of our Lord Jesus Christ and, therefore, the whole Christ is truly, really and substantially contained in the sacrament of the Holy Eucharist, but says that Christ is present in the sacrament only as a sign, or figure, or by his power."[3]

---

[2] Fourth Roman Council, *The Most Holy Eucharist*, Denzinger, no. 700.

[3] Council of Trent, *Canons on the Most Holy Sacrament of the Eucharist*, Canon 1, Denzinger, no. 1651.

The expression *whole Christ* proved to be decisive. Since the whole Christ is present in the fulness of his divine and human natures, this implies that he is present under the sacramental appearances with the totality of his divine attributes as well as his human properties.

2. By the thirteenth century the term *transubstantiation* had come to be used to identify the change that occurs at the time of consecration of the eucharistic elements. At the Fourth Lateran Council, this term was part of the conciliar creed professing belief in the Eucharist. But Trent went a step further. It not only used the term but declared the fitness of the expression. The reason was that some were ready to admit a real presence, even a corporeal one, but claimed that Christ was present along with the elements of bread and wine. Not so, the council held, as though "the substance of bread and wine remains in the holy sacrament of the Eucharist together with the body and blood of our Lord Jesus Christ." This would be to deny "that wonderful and extraordinary change of the whole substance of the bread into Christ's body and the whole substance of the wine into His blood, while only the species of bread and wine remain, a change which the Catholic Church has most fittingly called transubstantiation."[4]

3. Again what may seem to have been a refinement actually touched on the essence of the sacrament, namely, the double question of whether Christ was entirely present under the form of bread or wine, and to what extent. Hence the church's affirmation that "in the venerable sacrament of the Eucharist the whole Christ is contained under each species and under each and every portion of either species when it is divided up."[5] Communion under both species had been customary everywhere, and was then the practice in the Eastern rites. But in the sixteenth century, the strong insistence that the chalice be given to everyone occasioned this definition, which was also the doctrinal foundation for receiving only under the form of bread.

4. Still another theory was the notion that the real presence is to be identified with the liturgical action. This was explained with different nuances, but at their center was the denial of an objective reality that is independent of the faith or piety or devotion of the participants. The church countered from every angle. Thus one cannot say that the body and blood of our Lord Jesus Christ are "present only in the use of the sacrament while it is being received, and not before or after, and that the true body of the Lord does not remain in the consecrated hosts or particles that are left over after Communion."

Given this perdurance of Christ's presence as long as the species remain, it was only logical for the church to worship the Blessed Sacrament as it would the person of Jesus himself. As a result, he is to be adored "in the holy sacrament of the Eucharist with the worship of *latria*, including the external worship." Concretely this means that the sacrament is to be "honored with extraordinary festive celebrations" and "solemnly carried from place to place" and "is to be

[4]Ibid., Canon 2, Denzinger, no. 1652.
[5]Ibid., Canon 3, Denzinger, no. 1653.

publicly exposed for the people's adoration."[6]

The teachings of Trent ushered in a renascence of faith in the real presence that affected many facets of the Catholic liturgy. Notable among these was the renewed impetus it gave to the worship of the Blessed Sacrament reserved in the tabernacle or exposed in a monstrance on the altar.

The International Eucharistic Congress in Philadelphia (August, 1976) is an expression of this faith in Christ's abiding presence in our midst today, no less than he was truly present to his contemporaries in first century Palestine.

Sacrifice of the Mass

At the Last Supper, Christ made it plain to the apostles that what he was there enacting and what he would complete on Calvary was a sacrifice, which he wanted them to continue in his memory. In Judaism bread and wine were familiar sacrificial elements. The words Jesus used at the institution, when he spoke of the New Covenant, of his body that would be given up, of his blood that would be poured out, of doing this in memory of him—all have deep sacrificial implications.

In apostolic times the church had no doubt that, while the sacrifice of the cross was certainly adequate for the redemption of the world, Christ intended to have this sacrifice perpetuated in a ritual manner until the end of time. This was one of the principal themes of the Letter to the Hebrews, which assumed that Christ had offered himself once to God the Father upon the altar of the cross, but went on to affirm that his redemption was an enduring event. Christ's priesthood "remains for ever." It continues "since he is living for ever to inter-cede for all who come to God through him" (Heb. 7:24-25).

Christ's own association of what he did at the Last Supper with what he was to do on Good Friday has been the church's own norm for intimately relating the two. The sacrifice of the altar, then, is no mere empty commemoration of Calvary, but a true and proper act of sacrifice, whereby Christ the high priest by an unbloody immolation offers himself a most acceptable victim to the eternal Father, as he did on the cross. "It is one and the same victim; the same person now offers it by the ministry of his priests, who then offered himself on the cross. Only the manner of offering is different."

The priest is the same, namely, Jesus Christ whose divine person the human minister represents at the altar. "By reason of his ordination, he is made like the high priest and possesses the power of performing actions in virtue of Christ's very person."[7] The victim is also the same, namely, the Savior in his human nature with his true body and blood. Worth stressing is that what makes the Mass a sacrifice is that Christ is a living human being with a human will, still capable of offering (hence priest) and being offered (hence victim), no less truly

---

[6]Ibid., Canon 6, Denzinger, no. 1656.

[7]Pius XII, encyclical *Mediator Dei*, II, 68-69.

today than occurred on the cross.

However, the critical question still remains. Just how is the Mass related to Calvary? It is related in several ways, but mainly as effective application of the merits gained by Christ by his death on the cross. During the period of the Reformation, this was one of the most vexing issues that faced the church whose priests were told they were wrong to claim that Masses were a source of divine grace. The dilemma seemed insoluble: Either Christ died once for all and his death is sufficient for the redemption of humanity or, in spite of his death, Masses must be said to somehow shore up what was presumably inadequate in the passion of the Savior.

The Council of Trent addressed itself to the issue in a memorable statement that summarized fifteen centuries of Catholic belief on the efficacy of the Mass, but an efficacy that depends entirely on Calvary.[8]

What the church teaches is that, while the blessings of salvation were merited for humanity on the cross, they are still to be applied to us, principally through the Mass. Between the two ideas of merit and application stand the towering facts of faith and human freedom: faith to believe that God wants us to use such channels as the Mass, and freedom to humbly unite ourselves in spirit with Christ's self-immolation—he on the cross which he endured, and we on our cross which Christ bade us to carry daily if we wish to be his disciples.

Holy Communion

The Consummation of the eucharistic liturgy is the reception of Holy Communion, in which the body and blood of Christ are received and by which we are intimately united with the incarnate Son of God. Already in apostolic times, the faithful were accustomed to receive the Eucharist every week. Thus in the first century *Teaching of the Twelve Apostles*, the people were admonished that, "having come together on the Lord's Day, you are to break bread and give thanks, after you have confessed your sins, so that your sacrifice might be undefiled. But anyone who is estranged from his friend should not join us, until both have become reconciled, lest your sacrifice be polluted."[9]

From the end of the second century there are indications that many priests and laity received Holy Communion every day. Tertullian mentions that Christians daily extend their hands, according to the prevalent custom, to receive the body of Christ.[10] St. Cyprian states that in Africa "we who are in Christ, daily receive the Eucharist as the food of salvation."[11]

---

[8]Council of Trent, *The Doctrine on the Most Holy Sacrifice of the Mass*, II, Denzinger, no. 1743.

[9]*Didache*, XIV, 1.

[10]Tertullian, *De Idololatria*, 7.

[11]St. Cyprian, *De Dominica Oratione*, 18.

From the beginning of the ninth century we see a notable decline in the frequentation of the sacraments. Instead of improving, however, the situation became worse, until finally in 1215 the Fourth Lateran Council enjoined at least annual Communion at Easter time: "Everyone of the faithful of both sexes, after reaching the age of reason, should in private faithfully confess all his sins at least once a year . . . reverently receiving the Sacrament of the Eucharist at least at Easter time."[12]

Finally in 1551 the Council of Trent passed a decree on the Holy Eucharist, urging "all who bear the Christian name . . . mindful of the boundless love of our Lord Jesus Christ . . . that they may believe and venerate these sacred mysteries of his body and blood, with such constancy and firmness of faith, with such piety and worship, that they may be able to receive frequently that supersubstantial bread." It went on to specify that this meant "at every Mass they attend."[13] These documents placed in the hands of the church's pastors the authority they needed to propagate frequent Communion among the faithful, not only in private correspondence but officially, on as wide a scale as their resources permitted.

As so often happens in the history of the church, there was a strong reaction, with Jansenism presenting the best organized opposition. The Jansenists argued against frequent reception on the score that the Eucharist is rather a reward for virtue already possessed than a source of grace for virtue still to be achieved. The condemnation of Jansenistic rigorism in the seventeenth century did not make an appreciable difference in the general practices of the people, except for putting a check on the extremists. For the next century, Rome kept encouraging bishops and priests to permit more frequent Communion, but the seeds of Jansenism had taken too deep a root in Catholic piety to be eradicated easily. Credit for the final eradication is due to Pius X.

St. Pius X drew on the teachings of the Council of Trent to bring out the fact that the Eucharist is by divine intention the food of which Christ spoke in the Gospel of John and which he instituted at the Last Supper as the sacrament of unity, because its special purpose is to increase the practice of charity:

> The desire of Jesus Christ and of the Church that all the faithful should daily approach the sacred banquet is directed chiefly to this end, that the faithful, being united to God by means of this sacrament, may thence derive strength to resist their sensual passions, to cleanse themselves from the stains of daily faults, and to avoid those graver sins to which human frailty is liable.[14]

-----

[12] Fourth Lateran Council, *The Sacraments*, Denzinger, no. 812.

[13] Council of Trent, *Decree on the Most Holy Sacrament of the Eucharist,* VIII, Denzinger, no. 1649; Council of Trent, *The Doctrine on the Most Holy Sacrifice of the Mass,* VI, Denzinger, no. 1747.

[14] St. Pius X, Decree *Sacra Tridentina Synodus,* Denzinger, no. 3375.

The stress on the Eucharist as a sacred banquet, or in more prosaic terms, *a holy meal*, has been popularized since the Second Vatican Council.[15] Its foundations are biblical and its purpose is precisely that, functional. No less than ordinary food is meant to nourish the body, give it strength, and bring a certain amount of pleasure, so partaking of Christ's body and blood has been given to us as nourishment for the spirit, through the infusion of divine love; as a source of strength to cope with our weakness, especially our proneness to selfishness and greed; and as a cause of our joy in the service of the Lord, by giving us satisfaction in the performance of what human nature (without this grace) would consider burdensome duties.

But the word "banquet" has one more implication today that was not so obvious even in the days of Pius X, namely, the notion of togetherness which our lonely urban civilization makes us realize we so desperately want. It is not too much to say that, in an age when family meals are becoming increasingly rare because family life has been gravely impaired, Holy Communion will obtain the grace for communities everywhere to recover their identity through the reception of him who prayed, "May they all be one, Father, may they be one in us" (Jn. 17:21).

BAPTIST RESPONSE BY ARTHUR B. CRABTREE

I am grateful for this opportunity to respond to Fr. John Hardon's lucid historical presentation of the Eucharist in the Catholic Church. One of the inestimable blessings of God in this ecumenical age is the opportunity to discuss Christian doctrine in candor and love, and one of the happy surprises of such discussion is the discovery of unexpected agreements. My major impression in comparing Fr. Hardon's understanding of the Eucharist with my own is that we have immense areas of complete agreement.

Our agreement includes the following: the real presence of Christ in the Eucharist; the sacrificial nature of the Eucharist as a continuation of Christ's priestly work on the basis of his once-for-all suffering on the cross; the communal nature of the Eucharist as communion with Christ and one another; the communal and commemorative aspects of the Eucharist as a sacred banquet; and the communicative nature of the Eucharist as the communication to us of the benefits of his passion, forgiveness of sins, and newness of life as a sacrament is received in faith.

It is within the context of this comprehensive agreement that I would like to discuss two matters arising from our articles. One is the place of the Eucharist in the liturgy; the other is the doctrine of transubstantiation.

---

[15] Second Vatican Council, *The Church in the Modern World*, I, 38.

Regarding the place of the Eucharist in the liturgy Fr. Hardon writes: "The Holy Eucharist is the center of life and worship in the Catholic Church." This would seem to imply that the Eucharist is central and the liturgy of the Word peripheral. Would it not be better to think of the Word and sacrament as coordinate, like two foci in an ellipse, while recognizing that the Word reaches a certain culmination in the sacrament?

Regarding the relation of the real presence of Christ in the Eucharist and the doctrine of transubstantiation, I rejoice that we are in complete agreement on the doctrine of the presence. The doctrine of transubstantiation is one way of describing this presence, a way which gradually became dominant in the eleventh and twelfth centuries and found expression in the Fourth Lateran Council of 1215. I do not reject it, as the Protestant Reformers did, and as my fellow-Baptist, Eric Rust, still does. I regard it as a legitimate way of describing the mystery of the presence. But I do not regard it as the *only* legitimate way.

The term "transubstantiation" arose, as Father Hardon indicates, during the medieval eucharistic controversies involving Radbertus, Ratramnus, Ianfranc, Berengar, and Gregory VII. The term itself seems to be no older than the twelfth century.[1] That means that for more than a thousand years theologians expressed the mystery of the presence in other ways. During the middle ages other terms were used, such as impanation, consubstantiation, companation, mutation, conversion.[2] Even Thomas Aquinas in his *Summa Theologiae* uses the term "conversion" more often than the term "transubstantiation."[3] Duns Scotus experienced much difficulty with the term "transubstantiation." He had difficulty, as I do, in conceiving how the qualities (*accidents*) of bread and wine can persist after the substance has been changed into the substance of the body and blood of Christ. He accordingly, like Luther, preferred consubstantiation to transubstantiation, and only accepted transubstantiation on the understanding that it is a *transsubstantiatio adductiva*, a transubstantiation, that is, in which the substance of the body of Christ is added to the substance of the bread and the substance of the blood of Christ is added to the wine. This Scotist view seems to me preferable to the Thomist, and deserves, I think, renewed attention by both Catholic and Protestant theologians.

Why should not bread remain bread after consecration and be illumined by the body of Christ, just as a mountain remains a mountain after sunrise and is illumined by the light? Why should not consubstantiation be acceptable as well as transubstantiation? Or why should transubstantiation not be understood Scotistically as *transsubstantiatio adductiva?* Or why should we not, like the Orthodox, be content to speak of a change without defining too narrowly the nature of the change?

---

[1] R. Seeberg, *Lehrbuch der Dogmengeschichte* (Basel: Benno Schwabe, 5th ed., 1953), vol. III, p. 215, footnote 2.

[2] Ibid., pp. 214-218.

[3] *Summa Theologiae*, III, q.75, a.1-4.

In any case, the real saving presence of Christ in the Eucharist and our participation in that saving presence are more important than our doctrine of the precise nature of that presence.

Study and Discussion Questions

1. What eucharistic terminology is used by Baptists and which terminology, if any, is preferred by Crabtree?
2. Trace the interpretation of the Lord's Supper in the Baptist tradition in the eighteenth and nineteenth centuries.
3. In what direction, and because of what influences, has Baptist thinking on the Eucharist moved during the last thirty years? Discuss.
4. Discuss your reaction to Crabtree's eucharistic theology.
5. Crabtree does not discuss the role of the minister in the eucharistic liturgy, while Hardon reiterates the need of a duly ordained minister. Discuss whether you think this difference of approach can be overcome.
6. Crabtree writes, "The real saving presence of Christ in the Eucharist and our participation in that saving presence is more important than our doctrine of the precise nature of that presence." Do you think Hardon would agree with this statement? Do you agree with it?
7. Discuss how the Council of Trent responded to the Reformation controversies about the real presence.
8. Transubstantiation is discussed by both Hardon and Crabtree. Is there any meeting of minds on the meaning and use of this term? Discuss.
9. How does traditional Roman Catholic teaching understand the Mass as sacrifice? From Crabtree's remarks, is this Roman Catholic teaching acceptable?
10. Where do Crabtree and Hardon stand on the question of intercommunion?
11. Do you find any reflection in Hardon's article of contemporary Roman Catholic eucharistic theology? Compare and contrast his article with Osborne's.

JEWISH-CATHOLIC DIALOGUE

Eric Werner—Monika K. Hellwig

PRECIS

Werner provides a linguistic background for an understanding of Eucharist, then discusses an early Jewish reaction to the Christian Eucharist, a sixth-century midrash thought to be based on much earlier sources. The author puts forth the hypothesis that the commentary on the communion verse, "Taste and see that the Lord is good" (Ps. 34:9), subtly suggests that Jesus, like the hyssop, while of lowly estate, was an instrument for God's redemptive purposes.

Hellwig contends that continuing dialogue with Judaism will greatly aid Christian understanding of the Eucharist, because the central criteria of an authentic Eucharist derive from the vision and purpose of Jesus, a Jew. The testimony of the apostolic community, itself closest to this matrix, becomes normative for all later theologizing.

The basic themes of Christian sacramental celebration and the very sense of sacrament derive from Judaism; Jewish table-fellowship and the Passover Seder have been adapted into Christian liturgical use. As in Judaism, so Christian celebration has a triple orientation toward past, present, and future. In the Christian view, the God who acted in Passover acted uniquely in Jesus; this action is encountered anew in the Eucharist. The future orientation is found particularly in the unfinished agenda of the redemption of an uncomprehending world.

The growth of metaphysical speculation tended to obscure the Jewish foundations of Eucharist; Vatican II, in returning to the sources, has happily rediscovered these foundations.

Eric Werner (Jewish) studied at universities and academies in Vienna, Prague, Berlin, Gottingen, and at Strasbourg, where he received a doctorate in classics and musicology. After being named Professor Emeritus of Sacred Music at Hebrew Union College-Jewish Institute of Religion, he inaugurated and headed the Department of Musicology at Tel Aviv University for five years. He has written for dozens of scholarly journals and reference works; his books include *The Sacred Bridge* and *Mendelsohn: A New Image of the Composer and His Age.*

Monika K. Hellwig (Roman Catholic), L.L.B., C.S.Sc., University of Liverpool, M.A., Ph.D., Catholic University of America, is Associate Professor of Theology at Georgetown University, Washington, DC, and spent the 1975-76 academic year at the Ecumenical Institute in Jerusalem. An associate editor of the *Journal of Ecumenical Studies,* her books include *What Are the Theologians Saying? The Meaning of the Sacraments,* and *The Christian Creeds.*

THE EUCHARIST IN HEBREW LITERATURE DURING THE APOSTOLIC AND POST-APOSTOLIC EPOCH

Eric Werner

To discuss the significance of the Eucharist in a Jewish framework is an extremely delicate task if the author, himself a Jew, wishes to respect Christian sensibilities as well as the tenets of critical scholarship. These postulates can be satisfied if the author limits himself to that early period of Christianity that antedates the principles of the "conversion of the gifts" (*conversio donorum*), in short, before the idea of transubstantiation had become accepted doctrine (it became dogma only in 1215 under Pope Innocent III), or, if he can establish so early a Jewish reaction to the idea of *conversio* that it remains untainted by emotions and invectives that later surrounded the Eucharist with associations of violent anti-Semitism, and resulted in furious resentment on the part of the Jews. The author hopes to serve the cause of ecumenism by limiting himself to these two approaches.

I

The term "Eucharist" occurs both in the Greek translations of the Old Testament and in the books of the New Testament and is in many, indeed in most, cases interchangeable with the cognate term *eulogia*, which in turn is the strict translation of the Hebrew *b'rakha*. In secular Greek, *eulogein* means "to praise, to speak well of somebody"; *eucharistein* means to thank, to be grateful. Philo and Josephus prefer *eucharistein* to *eulogein*. In the New Testament no essential difference can be felt between the two expressions, as may be seen in 1 Cor. 14:16-18, or even in the passages of the Last Supper (e.g., Mt. 26:26-27; Mk. 14:22; Lk. 22:17). Quite clearly the term indicates that a *b'rakha* was pronounced (see, e.g., Rom. 1:21–*edoxasan ē ēucharistēsan*; and in 2 Cor. 9:12-14–*eucharistian tō Theō*). "To thank (the Lord)" and "to praise (the Lord)" are so closely connected in the spirit of the Hebrew language that in the Dead Sea Scrolls the word *barukh (eulogētos)* and the word *od'kha (exologoumai soi)* can be exchanged without any difference. The frequent pronouncing of *b'rakot* belonged always to the privileges and duties of a devout man, and the talmudic precept that he should pronounce 100 *berakot* every day is also quite applicable to the Apostle Paul (Eph. 5:4, 20; Phil. 4:6; Col. 1:12, 2:7, 3:15, 17; 1 Thess. 5:17; 1 Tim. 2:1; 2 Cor. 4:15; etc.). For the *berakot* that surround the Jewish meal, Paul always uses the term *eucharistein* (Rom. 14:6; 1 Cor. 10:30; 1 Tim. 4:3; Acts 27:35; etc.).

The pre-Christian grace after the meal (*birkat ha-mazon*) is opened by a kind of invitatorium: "Gentlemen, let us praise (the Lord)!" (Reply: "Let the Name of the Lord be praised forever and ever"–the original Hebrew of *"in saecula saeculorum"*). Exactly these words occur in the Greek liturgies.[1] The thanks-giving element of the term Eucharist is still clearly discernible in the Apology 1:13 of the Christian Justin Martyr (100-165), where it is applied to material goods as well as to the spiritual bounties of God. There the *conversio* of the consecrated Eucharist is already taken for granted, as is implied in the following passage:

> ... and this food is called by us the Eucharist. ... For not as ordin-ary bread and ordinary drink do we receive these, but in like manner as by the word of God Jesus Christ our saviour was made flesh and had both flesh and blood for our salvation, so also the food, which is blessed by the prayer of the Word ... is, we are taught, the flesh and blood of that Jesus who was made flesh.[2]

In this connection, Justin quotes the Gospel's account of Jesus' admonition, "This do in remembrance of me, this is my body" (*eis tēn emēn anamnēsin*; Lk. 22:19; 1 Cor. 11:24-25). This "memorializing," the transition to the central mystery of the Eucharist, bears certain interesting Hebrew overtones. For *anamnēsis* (Hebrew, *zikaron*) not only stands for memory, but also for "to re-present," "to recall" (before God), and the classic passages are to be found in Num. 5:15 (*ki minhat zikaron mizkeret avon*—"for it is a sacrifice of jealousy, a sacrifice of remembrance, to represent the iniquity"), or similarly in 1 Kings 17:18, where Elijah is addressed by the widow in the words, "You have come to me to bring my sin to remembrance." The word *anamnēsis* as used by Jesus has here the significance of "my representation." Pronounced with the third cup of the Seder, the "cup of salvation," it strikes a particularly solemn note.

With Justin we approach the limit, after which the term Eucharist is under-stood as the mysteriously transformed body and blood of Christ. The first clear statement by a Father of the church seems to originate with Irenaeus (130-200), *Adversus haereses*, which I shall quote in Johannes Quasten's translation:

> When, therefore, the mingled cup and the manufactured bread re-ceive the Word of God and the Eucharist becomes the blood and body of Christ ... how can they affirm that the flesh is incapable of receiving the gift of God. ...

and later:

> For as bread from the earth, receiving the invocation of God is no longer common bread but a Eucharist composed of two things, both an earthly and a heavenly one. ...

---

[1]*Liturgies Eastern and Western*, ed. by F. E. Brightman (Oxford: Clarendon Press, [1896] 1965), pp. 64 *et passim*.

[2]Johannes Quasten, *Patrology*, vol. I (Paramus, NJ: Paulist Newman Press, 1950), p. 216.

The fragmentary *Traditio Apostolica* of Hippolytos of Rome (ca. 215) contains similar statements, made in the spirit of his teacher Irenaeus. From here on-wards—after the separation of *Agape* and *Eucharist*—the doctrine of transub-stantiation is inseparably linked to the act as well as to its interpretation of Christian Communion.

II

More than two centuries later we encounter the first—and for many cen-turies the only—Jewish reaction to the idea of *conversio donorum*. It takes the form of a *Midrash* on the psalm verse that in the old Church had accompanied every communion: "Taste and see that the Lord is good" (Ps. 34:9). The text of the Vulgate reads: *Gustate et videte, quoniam suavis est Dominus.* The Jewish-Hellenistic Septuagint has: *Geusasthe kai idete hoti chrēstos ho Kyrios,* where the innocent word *chrēstos*, pronounced "christos," adds a new dimension. The gross application of the verse to the transmuted bread and wine seems to have struck the Jews, and they reacted, however cautiously, in the midrashic litera-ture. The *Midrash, Exodus Rabba*, completed during the sixth century, but containing much older material, gives the following exegesis to Ex. 12:22 ("Take a bunch of hyssop and dip it into the blood which is in the basin, and touch the lintel and the two doorposts with the blood which is in the basin; and none of you shall go out of the house until the morning."). We follow the authentic translation by H. Freedman & Maurice Simon, London:

> 2. Another interpretation of AND YE SHALL TAKE A BUNCH OF HYSSOP. It is written: *As an apple-tree among the trees of the wood, so is my beloved among the sons* (Song of Songs II, 3). Why is God compared to an apple-tree?[3] To teach you that just as the apple though unattractive to the eye yet possesses good taste and flavour, so the Holy One, blessed be He; *His mouth is most sweet; yea, He is altogether lovely* (ib. v, 16). He appeared to the heathens, yet they would not accept the Torah, which was in their eyes a thing of no value. God has taste and fragrance; taste, for it says: *O taste[4] and see that the Lord is good* (Ps. XXXIV, 9); He also contains food, for it says: *My fruit is better than gold; yea, than fine gold* (Prov. VIII, 19). He also has fragrance, for it says: *And the smell of thy garments is like the smell of Lebanon* (S.S. IV, II).[5] Israel said: 'We know the power of the Torah, therefore we will not budge from God and His Torah,' as it says: *Under its shadow I delighted to sit, and its fruit was sweet to my taste* (ib. II, 3). There are many other

---

[3]The Song of Songs was interpreted by the Rabbis as a dialogue between God and Israel.

[4]Lit. translation. E.V. *"consider."*

[5]All these refer not to God but to His Torah.

things which appear lowly, yet with which God commanded many precepts to be performed. The hyssop, for instance, appears to man to be of no worth, yet its power is great in the eyes of God, who put it on a level with cedar in numerous cases,—in the purification of the leper, and the burning of the Red Heifer; and in Egypt too He commanded a precept to be performed with hyssop, as it says: AND YE SHALL TAKE A BUNCH OF HYSSOP. Of Solomon, also, does it say: *And he spoke of trees, from the cedar that is in Lebanon even unto the hyssop that springeth out of the wall* (I Kings V, 13)—to teach you that the small and the great are equal in the sight of God. He performeth miracles with the smallest things, and through the hyssop which is the most lowly of trees, did He redeem Israel. Hence is He like *'An apple-tree among the trees of the wood'*.

Certainly the question will arise concerning the connection of this exegesis with Christianity and Communion. Quite generally it must be understood that the *Midrash* almost always speaks in parables and allegories, also that any open reference to Christianity or its founder is carefully avoided. This understood, we turn to that part of the *Midrash* which directly interprets the scriptural text. The hyssop in general is mentioned in the *Midrash* for three properties:

(a) It is the instrument of purification rites (Lev. 14; Num. 19; Ps. 51:9 metaphorically, etc.), almost like an aspergill; it has to sprinkle blood, water, etc. (of the Paschal Lamb, of the red heifer, etc.) on the impure object. In the crucial passage, Ex. 12:22, the blood on the doorposts of the houses of the Israelites, sprinkled by hyssop, distinguishes them on the night of the Passover. This night of the Exodus—"the redemption of Israel"—was considered an archetypus in Jewish as well as in Christian theology.

(b) Though considered the lowliest of plants, hyssop is occasionally juxtaposed to the majestic cedar, as in 1 Kings 5:13, or in the purification ceremony, Num. 19. Sometimes it represents purification *per se*, as in Ps. 51:9.

(c) The purification of a house suspect of leprosy was to be performed by a sacrifice of burning cedarwood, "scarlet stuff," and hyssop (Lev. 14:49). In the New Testament as well as in the Old, hyssop is the symbol of an act of purification (as in John 19:29), for it does not absorb moisture as does the sponge. The mention of hyssop in Heb. 9:19 is either a scribe's error or refers to another (Hebrew or Greek) text of Exodus, for neither the Massoretic Hebrew nor the Greek Septuagint alludes to hyssop.

The homilist or apologete of the *Midrash* reaches his argument with the thesis: "There are many other things which appear lowly, yet with which God commanded many precepts to be performed. The hyssop . . . Yet through this lowliest of the plants He redeemed Israel." This may hypothetically be seen as a cryptic allusion to Christ, who expected to purify and redeem Israel through his blood. The crucifixion is understood as analogous to the archetypus Exodus, where the sprinkled blood of the lamb (by the hyssop) saved the Israelites. Thus the *Midrash* declares: "It teaches you that the small and the great are equal in the sight of God. He performeth miracles with the smallest things. . . ."

This is, however, not the way the *Midrash* starts. It sets out from the far periphery with a verse from the Song of Songs, but goes into the heart of the argument with the words: "He appeared to the heathens, yet they would not accept the Torah, which in their eyes was a thing of no value. . . ." The *tertium comparationis* is here the lowness of the hyssop—thus the text continues: "God has taste and fragrance, for it says 'O taste and see that the Lord is good. . . .'"

It is hypothetically suggested that the entire *Midrash* reveals an attitude to Christ and Christianity at the same time belittling and respecting it—belittling it by comparing Christ with the blood-sprinkling hyssop, respecting it by considering Christ an instrument to redeem Israel. If one takes into consideration that the Greek version of the Psalm verse *sounded* (not *was*) like "*hoti Christos ho Kyrios*," then the complete identity of Old Testament with New Testament Christology was attained "as was written according to the Scriptures" (*sicut scriptum erat apud scripturas*). The Jew of the second or third century viewed this development benevolently, for—in his opinion—it paved the way to the victory of pure monotheism. It took more than a century, until the first burning of a synagogue under Christian aegis (St. Ambrose identified himself with it) convinced him of his millennial error.

CATHOLIC RESPONSE BY MONIKA K. HELLWIG

In his article, Professor Werner presents two hypotheses of great interest to Christians. The first is, perhaps, the less surprising: that the action of Eucharist is fully comprehensible in Jewish terms under the rubric of a *b'racha* of great solemenity, with the element of *zikaron* or remembrance/representation, in the context of the "cup of salvation" of the Passover *Seder*, and that it was in the earliest Christian generations so understood. Anyone acquainted with the early Christian literature and also with the underlying themes and multidimensional expressions of Jewish worship must surely grant the overwhelming probability of this thesis. Professor Werner, as the Jewish participant in the dialog, discreetly concludes that within that early framework there can be a meaningful discussion of the action between Christians and Jews, but that later developments of the formulae of worship and the theologies built about them offer little if any such scope. It seems to me, as the Christian participant (as indeed already stated in the partner essay), that from the Christian perspective a slightly different conclusion must be drawn. By our own criteria, these earliest understandings have a normative character that makes them the measure of subsequent developments. We have claimed, within Roman Catholic theology, merely to be explicating what was already implicit in the understanding and teaching of the Apostolic community. To remain honest we must bring subsequent developments under the scrutiny of that early understanding and teaching, as scholarly efforts make it progressively more accessible.

In connection with the element of *zikaron*, Joachim Jeremias[1] has a further explanation. He argues that the early community gave to all the meals of Jesus with his disciples overtones of anticipation of the messianic banquet, and that they understood that they were commanded to reconstitute the table-fellowship of Jesus as a kind of messianic sign. He then alludes to the prayer after the Passover meal that was customary at the time of Jesus, that God remember *Messiah* and bring about the great conversion. He interprets the words, "in remembrance of me" as referring not to the disciples' remembrance but to God's being mindful of *Messiah*. That is, he gives these words a strongly eschatological thrust; the Eucharist of the community is a plea to God for the final completion of the messianic task of Jesus.

Even more interesting, and full of practical consequences, is the more controversial hypothesis offered by Prof. Werner concerning the *midrash* on Psalm 34:9, published in the sixth century of the common era but thought to be older: namely, that it contains a second or third century Jewish reflection on the meaning of Jesus for redemption, that he is there seen as positive, and that there is further an argument against Christian eucharistic use of the Psalm verse in a way that was far from its original meaning. On the probability of this hypothesis, the Christian partner in the dialog can not be expected to make a competent judgment, but the implications of the hypothesis, if true, are extremely important for Christians. Prof. Werner infers from it that the Jew of the second or third century was able to think of Jesus as an instrument, though a lowly one, to redeem Israel, and was able to look benignly upon the Christian claims for Jesus inasmuch as they were bringing the nations to the one God.

It must, of course, be said that this was possible not only in the earliest phases of Christianity, but even after long and terrible persecutions—as witnessed by Jehuda Ha-levi in medieval times and by Franz Rosenzweig in the contemporary world. The importance, nevertheless, of the hypothesis concerning the second or third century *midrash* is that it is one more indication that the differentiation of Christianity as "another religion" was far slower and more subtly shaded than Christian theology has acknowledged, and this realization makes certain demands on the way we conduct our research into our sources in those early ages. Moreover, in relation to Eucharist in particular, it implies that we have available a Jewish critique of the interpretation within a generally benevolent attitude to such an assembly and such an action—an attitude that still recognizes the action as having continuity with Jewish worship and thought and therefore being subject to criticism by Jewish criteria. If we do indeed have here such a Jewish critique, Christian theology can scarcely afford to ignore it.

---

[1] Joachim Jeremias, "*Das ist mein Leib.* . . ." (Stuttgart: Calwer Verlag, 1972), pp. 12-13.

THE CHRISTIAN EUCHARIST IN RELATION
TO JEWISH WORSHIP

Monika K. Hellwig

It is generally known and appreciated that the eucharistic action and prayer of Christians have their origin and inspiration from the great liberation theme of the Hebrew Scriptures and from the rich tradition of worship of ancient Israel. Unfortunately, this is as much as most intelligent Christians, even most theologians, have cared to know about the connection. The development of our eucharistic theory and practice has suffered badly from the lack of curiosity in this connection. Recent renewal and reform in the Roman Catholic practice of the Eucharist[1] and the renewed theoretical explorations that have been under way for some time[2] are in no small way due to a return to the Jewish sources by the pathways of New Testament and patristic studies. What is now known to certain specialized scholars about Christian roots in ancient Israel ought certainly to become far more widely known,[3] but the present essay takes this for granted and is concerned with the implications of that knowledge for the present understanding of the Eucharist and with the understanding that may be gained from continuing dialog with Israel.

It may be necessary at the outset to clarify a question concerning authoritative interpretation. Nothing is more central to Christian life and thought than Eucharist; it stands at the center of Christian theologizing. While the Eucharist—the action that is done with the words that are spoken—is already an interpretation of the Christian faith, nevertheless the Eucharist is also a continuing source for theologizing. The proper interpretation of it is a question of the authenticity of the entire Christian endeavor and a question of the survival of a Christian community. Much reflection has therefore been devoted to it in the various Christian traditions, and many formulations have been made, some claiming an almost absolute validity. However, as standard as some of these formulations may have become, they can not claim to be more central or more basic than the vision and purpose of Jesus, as these can be known from the testimony of the

---

[1]This dates from Sacrosanctum Concilium of Vatican II, and has been implemented in stages at the discretion of a central post-conciliar commission whose directives are mandatory for Roman Catholic eucharistic celebrations throughout the world. It has included reform of the text used as the "canon," now offered in four variant formulations; reform of the prescribed actions and gestures and of the relation between the presiding celebrant and the congregation; enlargement of the cycle of biblical readings; a change into the vernacular languages of the congregations; etc.

[2]The literature is vast and multilingual, ranging from historical studies such as those of Josef Jungemann, Jean Daniélou, and Louis Bouyer to new efforts in the systematic theology of the Eucharist such as those of Karl Rahner, Edward Schillebeeckx, J. M. R. Tillard, etc.

[3]E.g., in relation to Eucharist: Frank Gavin, *The Jewish Antecedents of the Christian Eucharist* (New York: KTAV Publishing House, 1969); Joachim Jeremias, *The Eucharistic Words of Jesus* (London: SCM Press, 1966); etc.

apostolic community, and as they must be understood within their own cultural and religious context. This vision and purpose remain forever the central criteria of the authenticity of eucharistic celebration and interpretation. But the vision and purpose are those of a Jew schooled within the experience, the family and community life, the ritual and spirituality, the stories and the symbolism, of his people. It may be expected that, in the course of history, every new return to these criteria—the vision and purpose of Jesus—in the light of continuing research and continuing dialogue with Israel will yield new perspectives on our understanding.

There is no doubt that the drama enacted in the Eucharist is basically that of the Passover Seder, retaining those elements that are more nearly common with the blessings pronounced over every table fellowship.[4] Recent Roman Catholic prescribed eucharistic practice has brought to the fore again the formula that relates to the ordinary (daily) table grace: "Blessed be thou, Lord, God of all creation, because we have this bread to offer, which earth has given and human hands have made . . . ," and likewise the prayer over the cup. This is not a casual reintroduction, but one that focusses attention on the table-fellowship as important in itself. There is deep significance in the assembling of the community of the followers of Jesus in table-fellowship in his name, in response to his invitation. That significance corresponds directly to the significance that the community attaches to the person of Jesus and to his promise and challenge to his followers. There are overtones of anticipating the "heavenly banquet" or fulfillment, of responding now to the final (eschatological) call of God, that is to assemble all God's people from the four corners of the earth in peace.[5]

The gathering of a community that hears the word of God and heightens the awareness of it by the blessing over the bread that is shared and over the cup that is passed around creates a deeper bond and a further commitment to the word that is received and the community that is gathered. Such a gathering is sacramental in the basic sense of that term in Roman Catholic tradition. That means such a gathering provides an experiential happening (visible sign) which makes accessible to experience and observation an otherwise elusive but transforming power (hidden or invisible grace) and which, beyond rendering it accessible to experience, also contributes directly to bringing the hidden reality about (is efficacious). In the very broadest sense, this sacramental quality is to be found in a kiss, a hand shake, and an exchange of glances. In a more specifically religious sense, the sacramental quality is to be found in every blessing, every physically expressed act of worship, and every act of assembling in response to the word of God. In an even narrower sense, the sacramental quality is to be found in those central, solemn, and "highly visible" signs or celebrations which a

---

[4] Argued at some length by Jeremias, *The Eucharistic Words,* chapter 1.

[5] Joachim Jeremias, *"Das ist mein Leib . . ."* (Stuttgart: Calwer Verlag, 1972), chapter 1.

community cultivates and perfects over many generations out of its historical experience and its prayerful reflection thereupon.

It is here respectfully submitted that not only the basic themes of our Christian sacramental celebrations but the very sense of sacrament and of sacramental celebration is a precious heritage that we Christians have from Judaism. The matter must be stated cautiously because well-informed Jews generally reject vigorously the suggestion that there are sacraments in Jewish worship. This may be due to the ever-recurring temptation in Christian experience toward a conveniently non-exigent magical interpretation of the meaning of sacrament, whereby a verbal formula and physical action are seen as adequate to cause a spiritual effect. It may be freely granted that this tendency to magical interpretations is not derived from the religious heritage of Israel, but from that evil inclination that manifests itself in all peoples and tends, among other things, to domesticate the call of the transcendent when it becomes too demanding.[6]

Beyond the table grace or blessings giving a special meaning to the table fellowship and to the meal taken together, the Eucharist of Christians is indebted to the religious heritage of Israel for the Passover Seder theme. In the Passover Seder, the families of Israel from ancient times even to the present participate ritually in the experience of the great liberation from Egypt. That liberation, which we call the Exodus, has long ago become the type or symbol of that full redemption from the consequences of evil deeds which God has promised. In the Eucharist the communities of Christians ritually participate in the experience of the death and resurrection of Jesus. By adopting key elements of the Passover Seder ceremony, Christians are making the claim: for us the true Exodus, the event that anticipates and prefigures that full redemption for which we still hope, is the death and resurrection of Jesus. Christians are saying, in effect: it is this event that we must ritually reenact in order that we may become part of it, and it of us, until we penetrate fully into its significance and it transforms us.

There is an understanding of worship here, an understanding of the relation of humanity to God, and even an understanding of what it is to be human, which are rooted in the experience and reflection of Israel. The act of Eucharist, like the action of the Passover Seder, is an act of communion with God who acts in history—a communion with God by entering into God's wonderful work. In the worship of the gentiles, that is, in those traditions that have not been shaped by the experience and Scriptures of Israel, there may be efforts to commune with the divine by an immersion in nature or by a sublimation in myth, but in history God is not to be encountered and men and women are on their own. The experience and reflection of Israel are other. Israel, like Moses praying on the mountain (Ex. 33:18-23), does not indeed claim to see the face of God, but claims intimate communion with God's purpose and action in history by looking

---

[6]The idea of the "evil *yezer*" is, of course, as common in Jewish thought as the recognition of the "effects of original sin" is pervasive in Christian thought.

at God "from behind," by looking at where God has passed. Looking back in history, Israel can recognize the intervention of God's liberating power in the moment of Exodus, can see it as constituting or creating Israel's very existence, and can identify God by the names of Lordship, graciousness, and compassion.

However, Israel's understanding goes further than this. To constitute a people as God's witness-people among the nations, it is not enough that this realization be received by certain great charismatic figures or by one generation. This realization and understanding must, of course, be widely (even generally) assimilated by the people as a whole, and lived ever anew. The characteristic genius of Israel manifests itself in the festival celebration of Pesach or Passover, where the event is ritually rehearsed so that the present generation may enter into it, become part of it, assimilate its meaning, and be transformed by it. Across the barriers of space and time, in the Passover Seder all Israel becomes part of the event of the great liberation of the Exodus, and in that event comes into communion with God who acts in history.

Characteristically, this understanding of worship does not take the worshippers away from the world, its human history, and the affairs of humanity in order to commune with God, but rather educates them to find God precisely in the world, in history, in the affairs of humanity. It is this understanding that allows for the insertion into the ancient formula of worship of a meditation on the death of Jesus and its implications, although that death was a political matter in the secular hands of the Romans. What makes the celebration of Eucharist by Christians unique is essentially not the understanding of the quality and force of the worshipping ritual, but the understanding of the uniqueness of Jesus in history and of the meaning of his death as the event into which the worshipper enters.

The Christian understanding of the uniqueness of Jesus in history is closely related to a third dimension of worship which the Christian community took over as part of its heritage from Israel—the dimension of the future.[7] In the festival celebration of Israel, there is not only the past event that is made present to and in the community that now becomes participant in it, but also the celebration has its meaning largely from the thrust toward a future yet to be fulfilled—"next year in Jerusalem," or in its older form, "next year in the heavenly Kingdom." The understanding of worship that Christians have from their Jewish heritage does not take them away from involvement in the world and its human history, because it contains this thrust to the future, which always implies the question of what is to be done to meet the promised future. The Christian claim that Jesus is Messiah is not to be seen outside this context. From ancient times we have the formula, "Every time, then, you eat this bread and drink this cup, you proclaim the death of the Lord until he comes"

---

[7]This understanding is variously explained by various authors. The presentation of worship with its three time dimensions in Judaeo-Christian practice as given here is heavily indebted to unpublished lectures on the Eucharist by Godfrey Diekmann, O.S.B.

(1 Cor. 11:26).[8] It is this further "coming" or presence (*parousia*), this complete fulfillment of the mission of Jesus in the future, that is to justify the claims made for him. And the reason for the eucharistic celebration—in which the community becomes present to Jesus in the event of his death and he who invited them to come in all their generations to this encounter is present to them—is that by participating in the experience of the death of Jesus they may read in that death the unfinished agenda of the redemption of the world.

It is from these Christian perspectives which we have from the beginning that a contemporary Roman Catholic theologian, J. B. Metz, is able to make the claim that the whole sense of celebrating Eucharist in the Christian community is that the future may appear "in the memory of suffering," in other words, that we may learn to write history upside down from the point of view of the loser or the vanquished, because it is there that the unfinished agends appears.[9] The underlying insight, of course, is not new but is that of the prophets of Israel, namely, that God speaks in the cry of the poor and the oppressed. The Christian community puts this in a unique perspective focussed on the person of Jesus who appears as the innocent poor man in whom the word of God is most ultimately and decisively spoken. Christians make this claim because from the beginning they heard the words spoken by Jesus and heard the Word that was Jesus, and heard it ringing so true in their understanding and expectation that it seemed to them self-evident. It seemed a self-evident fulfillment of the whole covenant life and longing of their Jewish heritage and of the sensitivity to God so painfully built up over the ages by the merits of their forebearers. Therefore, the death of Jesus by Roman execution in the midst of a bewildered and divided people was the ultimate tragedy to his followers, and the ultimate mystery. When they rallied in the mysterious experience they had of his resurrection, they rallied to the task in history, not to the celebration of the fulfillment. The death of Jesus remains before them always, a stark challenge to enter into the mystery of redemption, to try to understand why the (to them) self-evident word of God is not heard as such even by some who are trained and eager listeners for that word. And the death of Jesus becomes the symbol of the crushing of all the oppressed in whom the self-evident word of God is not heard—even those oppressed by Christian worshippers in their tragic blindness and inconsistency. It becomes the symbol of Auschwitz and of the *barrios* of South America, of *apartheid*, and of the U. S. black city ghetto—the symbol of the stranger in our midst, of the prisoner in our gaols, and of the beggar at our door.

But Christians, like other peoples, find elegant rituals easier to cope with than the tumultuous protests of the oppressed. They also find metaphysical

---

[8]This New Testament quotation, in slightly altered form, has been reintroduced into the Roman Catholic eucharistic celebration as a peoples' acclamation: "When we eat this bread and drink this cup, we proclaim your death, Lord Jesus, until you come in glory."

[9]Johannes Baptist Metz, "The Future in the Memory of Suffering," *Concilium* 8, 6 (June 1972): 9-25.

theologizings easier to contain than the rude demands of their primitive gospel tradition. Christology and eucharistic theology developed relatively little along the lines indicated above, though the authoritative basis for such a development remains to this day in the early documents, in the liturgy, and in the spirituality traditions. The patristic testimony from the earliest centuries gives some very striking hints of the strands of thought that were left undeveloped in later periods. For instance, eucharistic language was used in describing the deaths of martyrs,[10] signalling an understanding of these deaths as contained within the same mystery. Moreover, the reading of the local martyrology was introduced into the structure of the eucharistic celebration. Martyrdom is seen as the moment of purest confrontation between the word of God, expressed in the life and person of the follower of Jesus, and an uncomprehending world. In terms of the cultural boundaries of human consciousness, it would be asking too much of the communities of that time to see that same solidarity with the death of Jesus in every innocent sufferer of human cruelty and rejection. Even today when cultural boundaries have been so constantly challenged, few Christians do in fact see this identification. However, the theme has been acknowledged and preached rather constantly from early times, and the chronicles of the community are spangled with stories of saints who found the moment of truth in such a concrete identification.

Subsequent theology, in contrast to the spirituality teachings, explained the Christian conviction of the uniqueness of Jesus in history and the uniqueness of the experience of God that the community had in its encounter with Jesus, in a metaphysical idiom progressively further away from Jewish modes of thought. The one-time claim that this had universalized the message and translated it into more intelligible terms has been questioned vigorously by the followers of Wycliffe, by the sixteenth-century radical reformers, and by many subsequent groups, including in our day influential Roman Catholic thinkers. Eucharistic theology has parallelled Christology. The tendency to focus more and more on the elements of bread and wine in the celebration and less and less on the community, as well as a tendency to make metaphysical formulations of what is done in terms of substantial change in the bread and wine—these tendencies generated their own opposition from devout persons steeped in the spirituality traditions. There has been, over a span of centuries, a swing of the focus back onto the community and its relation to Jesus and to the unfinished task of Jesus for the redemption of the world. With Vatican II this movement reached revolutionary proportions within the Roman Catholic community throughout the world, though the danger may be that what is officially stated in the order of celebration and contained in the formulations of the prayers is not really the understanding of most of the worshippers.

It may be said that we stand at this point largely because of the scholarly

---

[10]Most obviously in "The Martyrdom of Polycarp," which may be found in English translation in, e.g., *Ancient Christian Writers*, no. 6 (Westminster, MD: Newman, 1948).

pilgrimages that have been made back to ancient Israel. It may also be said that progress from this point into a deeper understanding of what we are about can be aided immensely by a dialogue with contemporary Jewish piety. It is not accidental that the Eucharist is linked with the Lord's prayer, the great eschatological prayer that stands at the heart of Christianity. But that prayer gives us a distillation of the *Amidah* as prayed and understood by Jesus. Israel has prayed that prayer and developed its understanding of that prayer into our own times. Those who have been faithful have endured through centuries of persecution and continued to pray it, and have surely developed their understanding of it by their fidelity. The action of Eucharist can certainly be illumined by the reflection of Jewish piety on the Passover Seder during those same centuries of fidelity, and the "words of institution" certainly take on much greater depth in the context of sober listening to contemporary Passover meditations.

We disagree over the messiahship of Jesus and therefore we must also disagree over the importance of the eucharistic action. This does not preclude helpful dialogue over the dimensions of meaning of messiahship or the dimensions of meaning of the eucharistic action as seen from a Jewish perspective and within its Jewish background of symbolism and celebration. Certainly from the Christian side it is possible to gain a far greater understanding of the Christian Eucharist in relation to Jewish worship.

JEWISH RESPONSE BY ERIC WERNER

According to Harnack, Christianity is a *complexio oppositorum*; Paul would have reason brought into captivity (2 Cor. 10:5); yet the same Apostle proclaimed that Christianity was "a reasonable service of God" (Rom. 12:1, "*logikē latreia*"). This antimony must also be applied to the Eucharist. Between reason and non-reason lies the mystery, and the Eucharist took this place. The apologists defended Christianity as a religion of pure reason, yet from the outset it was accompanied by two rites which no longer can be grasped by pure reason, baptism and Eucharist. They were meant to transcend reason, for they deal with sin, even hereditary sin, with salvation, with death and resurrection. They are sacraments and, by definition, *actions*. As such they are not only symbols, but agents. Dr. Hellwig desires that their action make the Christian aware and mindful of "the crushing of all the oppressed by Christian worshippers in their tragic blindness and inconsistency." This remark might well be applicable to such Christians as Archbishop Capudji or similar characters.

It is true, as Prof. Hellwig observes, that "some striking hints of the strands of thought (remained) undeveloped in later periods." Thus she reminds us that the "Reading of the local martyrology was introduced into the structure of the eucharistic celebration." Such associations were, to be sure, intentional in the ordines; yet, if memory serves me, the anniversaries of martyrs were, at least up to the fifth and sixth centuries, celebrated as joyous festivals. I trust she is right in stating that "there has been, over a span of centuries, a swing of the focus back onto the community and its relation to Jesus and to the unfinished task of Jesus for the redemption of the world."

Seen in retrospect, the millennial history of synagogue and church comprises various stages: the dialogue, the dispute, the confrontation, and the "neutral" coexistence. Yet it is hard, not to say impossible, for a thinking Jew not to be reminded, by every eucharistic formula of each Mass, of the Holocaust and Christianity's silence. And, although thousands of Christian priests condemned that silence, the voice of Judaism, the voice of Rachel weeping for her children, will rise "over a span of centuries," and declare that a fraternal dialogue between synagogue and church can take place only when the church—*qua ecclesia* has confessed its monumental guilt before the world.

Distinguishing between the church and its servants is, especially in this instance, a moral postulate, and we do not wish to argue over events for which one generation of ecclesiastic servants may be held partly responsible. Yet the symbol of the Eucharist—*"sacramenta continent gratiam"*—is millennial and stands for the entire body of the church. A symbol does not bear guilt, nor does a sacrament. Its *actio* or *interpretatio* states its existential function. The Jewish position in this fundamental matter has authoritatively been established by Hermann Cohen in his *Die Religion der Vernunft aus den Quellen des Judentums* (Leipzig, 1919), pp. 377, 494 ff.

Prof. Hellwig's idealistic, humane, and truly Christian thoughts, and especially her emphasis upon the social doctrine of the Eucharist, are most welcome to a modern—or a "traditional"—Jew. For she has entered common ground. The prophets saw the greatest danger for society and state in the sharp difference between poor and rich, between the oppressed and the oppressors. The prophets do not view the tragedy of the human condition in death, for them a natural phenomenon without "its mystical attributes" (H. Cohen). Yet they allow themselves a messianic panorama—one may call it fantasy—and this vision corresponds in many details with the Christian hope for the *parousia*. It is here on prophetic grounds where our hopes, our ideals, also our sufferings—according to the Jewish tradition "the birthpangs of the Messiah"—coincide.

Study and Discussion Questions

1. Discuss the meaning of the words *eucharistein, eulogein,* and *b'rakha.*
2. Discuss the meaning of the words *anamnesis* and *zikaron.*
3. Werner offers an example of midrashic literature. What is midrash in general, and how is midrash to be interpreted?
4. How is hyssop interpreted in the midrash, *Exodus Rabba?*
5. Werner offers the midrash as a hypothetical reference to Christ. Discuss Hellwig's observations about this midrash and Werner's interpretation.
6. Hellwig suggests that many Christians do not realize the Hebrew sources of their eucharistic worship. Do you agree? Discuss.

7. "The vision and purpose of Jesus, as these can be known from the testimony of the apostolic community" are considered by Hellwig to be normative to an understanding of the Eucharist. Discuss.

8. What does Hellwig mean that "the very sense of sacrament and of sacramental celebration is a precious heritage . . . Christians have from Judaism"? Do you think Jews would generally agree with this statement? Do you agree?

9. In what way is there a parallel between the Jewish understanding of Passover Seder and Christian understanding of Eucharist? In what way is there a difference? Discuss.

10. Hellwig emphasizes the connection between Eucharist and the ongoing redemption of the world. Discuss whether you think this social aspect of Eucharist is well understood in today's congregations.

EUCHARIST IN ECUMENICAL PERSPECTIVE

Leonard Swidler

PRECIS

Before Vatican II Roman Catholics were forbidden to have public religious discussions with non-Catholics, let alone participate in their worship services. The Second Vatican Council, however, reached an ecumenical high-water-mark when it encouraged joint worship, including the Eucharist occasionally. But in the implementation of this Decree the Vatican countermanded the Council Fathers and forbade shared Eucharist for the fostering of unity.

However, many of the official bi-lateral consultations set up after Vatican II focused on the Eucharist and attained such extraordinary doctrinal agreement that there is every reason to encourage the authorities in the Roman Catholic Church to carry out the Vatican II mandate for shared Eucharist. Examples of moves in this direction by Episcopal Conferences, individual bishops, and parishes are cited.

Leonard Swidler (Roman Catholic), B.A., St. Norbert's College, M.A., Marquette University, S.T.L., Tübingen, Ph.D., University of Wisconsin, is Professor of Catholic Thought and Ecumenism in the Religion Department at Temple University, Philadelphia, and editor of the *Journal of Ecumenical Studies*. His publications include *The Ecumenical Vanguard*, *Freedom in the Church*, and *Bishops and People*.

THE EUCHARIST IN ECUMENICAL PERSPECTIVE

Leonard Swidler

For the Roman Catholic Church the ecumenical concern with the Eucharist came into focus with the "Decree on Ecumenism" of the Second Vatican Council. Before then, any Catholic involvement with ecumenism was almost totally excluded.[1] The "ecumenical" aspect of the Eucharist was the teaching that the Eucharist of the "schismatics" (Orthodox) was authentic, but normally illegal for Catholics to receive; the Eucharist of "heretics" (Protestants) was not authentic—Protestants only thought they were receiving Holy Communion, but they really were not. There was no discussion at all about Catholics even possibly taking part in that illusion.

But Vatican II changed all that. Instead of being generally forbidden to take part in religious discussions with non-Catholics,[2] all Catholics—not just clergy—were charged with the responsibility of participating in the work of ecumenism as vigorously as they could;[3] indeed, they are urged to take the initiative in

---

[1]For example, see the June 5, 1948, *Monitum* of the Vatican's Holy Office, as found in the *Acta apostolicae sedis* 40 (1948): 257: "The Supreme Sacred Congregation of the Holy Office: A Warning. Since it has been learned that, contrary to the prescriptions of the Sacred Canons and without the previous authorization of the Holy See, mixed gatherings of non-Catholics and Catholics in which matters of faith were treated have occurred in various places, everyone is reminded that according to canon 1325, 3 any manner of involvement in these gatherings, without the above-mentioned authorization, whether by laity or clergy, both secular and religious, is to be prohibited. How much less, however, is it licit for Catholics to call and institute such gatherings. Therefore, Ordinaries are to urge that these regulations be adhered to precisely by all.

"By how much greater right must they be observed when it concerns gatherings which are called 'ecumenical,' in which Catholics, both lay and clerical, without the previous authorization of the Holy See, can in no manner take part.

"Since in fact, whether in the above mentioned gatherings or outside of them, even acts of a mixed cult (*mixti cultus*) occur not infrequently, everyone must again be warned that according to canons 1258 and 731, 2 any kind of common worship (*sacris communicationem*) is to be totally prohibited.

"Given at Rome from the building of the Holy Office, the fifth day of June, 1948.
Petrus Vigorita Notarius"

[2]See canon 1325, 3: "Catholics should take care not to have any disputations or conferences, especially public, with non-Catholics, without the authorization of the Holy See, or if the case is urgent, of the local Ordinary." One authoritative commentator commented: "The S. Congregation has often expressly forbidden them [disputations and conferences] on the ground that they do more harm than good, since false eloquence may cause error seemingly to triumph over truth. Religious superiors are urged to forbid such public disputations and conferences to their missionaries. This rule in our opinion also effects public disputations with Socialists, because their tenets often contain heresies." P. Charles Augustine, *A Commentary On The New Code of Canon Law*, 8 vols. (St. Louis: B. Herder, 1921-22), vol. VI, p. 336.

[3]"The Sacred Council exhorts, therefore, all the Catholic faithful to recognize the signs of the times and to take an active and intelligent part in the work of ecumenism. . . . The concern for restoring unity involves the whole Church, faithful and clergy alike. It extends to everyone." "Decree On Ecumenism," sections 4, 5.

working toward Christian unity.[4] Rather than avoiding prayer with non-Catholics as occasions of sin and public scandal, as required by the current canon law,[5] Catholics were told by the highest authority of Catholicism that it was a good and holy thing to pray publicly with non-Catholics.[6]

But the most radical statement in this direction dealt with the heart of the Christian prayer life—the Eucharist. The Council Fathers noted that the Eucharist had two main functions: on the one hand it was to signify the unity a group of Christians had in faith; on the other, it was to serve as a means of grace to foster this unity in faith among Christians: "There are two main principles upon which the practice of such common worship (*communicatio in sacris*) depends: first, that of the unity of the Church which ought to be expressed; and second, that of the sharing in the means of grace. The expression of unity very generally forbids common worship. Grace to be obtained sometimes commends it."[7] Clearly this statement meant that participation in the Eucharist was no longer always to be restricted only to members of the same church—otherwise, why bother to make the distinction?[8] This intention was reinforced when the Fathers wrote: "Yet worship in common (*communicatio in sacris*) is not to be considered a means to be used indiscriminately for the restoration of unity among Christians."[9] If the Eucharist was not to be shared ecumenically in an indiscriminate fashion, then logically it was to be ecumenically shared in a discriminate fashion—"for the restoration of unity among Christians."

This was a Roman Catholic high-water mark in ecumenism. From this vigorous conciliar affirmation of ecumenical participation in the Eucharist as a vital means of fostering Christian unity, the Vatican officials of the Catholic Church drew back. The Council Fathers had made provision for the detailed working out

---

[4]"In ecumenical work, Catholics must assuredly be concerned for their separated brethren . . . making the first approaches toward them." Ibid., section 4.

[5]Canon 1258, 1: "It is not licit for faithful in any fashion to assist actively or take part in the worship (*sacris*) of non-Catholics." Canon 731, 2: "It is forbidden to administer the Sacraments of the Church to heretics or schismatics, even to those who err in good faith or those who request them, unless they first reject their errors and become reconciled to the Church."

[6]"It is allowable, indeed desirable, that Catholics should join in prayer with their separated brethren." "Decree On Ecumenism," section 8.

[7]Ibid.

[8]Lest an argument be made that the second principle, i.e., ecumenical *communicatio in sacris* was not thought to be for the sake of grace of fostering Christian unity, but simply to obtain grace for the individual, it should be recalled that this statement is within the context of a Decree focusing entirely on fostering Christian unity, that the chapter inside of which it falls is on "The Practice of *Ecumenism*," and that its subsection deals "with public and private prayer for the unity of Christians." Furthermore, in the immediately preceding paragraph, when speaking of ecumenical prayer services "for unity," the Decree parallels the two principles for ecumenical *communicatio in sacris* and there expressly speaks of petitioning for the grace of unity, making it perfectly clear that that also is what is intended in the next, parallel, paragraph: "Such prayers in common are certainly a very effective means of petitioning for the grace of unity, and they are a genuine expression of the ties which still bind Catholics to the separated brethren."

[9]"Decree On Ecumenism," section 8.

and supervision of those circumstances when Catholics could participate in ecumenically-shared Eucharist in a discriminate fashion. They stated: "The concrete
course to be adopted ... is left to the prudent decision of the local episcopal
authority, unless the bishops' conference according to its own statutes, or the
Holy See, has determined otherwise."[10] Rome determined otherwise.

When the Secretariat for Christian Unity issued its Directory,[11] where it
mattered most for the vast majority of Roman Catholics—that is, in relation to
Anglicans and Protestants—there was no provision whatsoever for the ecumenically-shared Eucharist as a means of fostering Christian unity.[12] Only in cases of
very special urgency for individuals was an ecumenically-shared Eucharist to be
allowed. This was clearly a reversal of both the letter and spirit of an Ecumenical
Council Decree. Was it to be explained as a return to conservatism by the
bishops as they returned from the euphoria of the Vatican Council to their home
dioceses? Possibly, to some extent. Was it a return to conservative Roman cen-
tralism after the bishops were once again dispersed after the Council? Quite
likely, judging from other conservative trends stemming from Rome.

The ecumenical reversal of the Council cannot be explained simply by suggesting that the working out of the theological problems naturally involved in an
ecumenically-shared Eucharist proved much more intractable and drawn-out
than anticipated, for almost the exact opposite proved to be the case: extraordinary advances have been made in the theological area in a relatively short
time. But these far-reaching theological advances have remained almost totally
unreflected in Roman directives concerning ecumenically-shared Eucharists as a
means of fostering Christian unity.

Does this mean that the Vatican II notion of an ecumenically-shared Eucharist should be put aside until Rome decides once again to move on it? If the
notion has any value, that would hardly be a course calculated to foster its
realization. Empirically we know that no centralized bureaucracy ignites by
spontaneous combustion; the spark, tinder, and draught (*spiritus*) needed to fan
it must come from the outside. To follow the metaphor, the initial spark was

---

[10]Ibid.

[11]*Directory Concerning Ecumenical Matters: Part One*, May 14, 1967. Latin text in
Acta apostolicae sedis 59 (1967): 574-592. The English translation can be found in Austin
Flannery, ed., *Vatican Council II* (Collegeville, MN: The Liturgical Press, 1975), pp.
483-507.

[12]It is perhaps ironic that where the Directory, following the "Decree On Ecumenism,"
allows and even encourages eucharistic sharing with Eastern Orthodox Churches, the move
was turned back by the Orthodox Churches. The Directory quoted the Decree, "Therefore
some sharing in liturgical worship (*communicatio in sacris*) ... is not merely possible but is
encouraged" (nr. 39), and went on to specify that "this offers ecclesiological and sacramental grounds for allowing and even encouraging some sharing in liturgical worship—even
eucharistic—with these churches" (nr. 40). In the bi-lateral consultation between Orthodox
and Roman Catholics in the U.S. it was stated that eucharistic sharing was not possible at
present because of "serious differences ... in our understanding of the Church, eucharistic
discipline and pastoral practice." "An Agreed Statement on the Eucharist," *Diakonia*, 5
(1970): 72.

provided by the Council, but it has been so dampened that still more combustible material and blowings of the Spirit are needed to fan it into flames: "Veni Sancte *Spiritus*, reple tuorum corda fidelium et tui amoris in eis *ignem* accende."[13] But it is not sufficient to pray, in quietist fashion, for the coming of the Spirit. Concerned Catholics, lay and clerical, must also act. But how? The first thing that must be done is to inform oneself quite precisely about what the theological advances in the area of the Eucharist have been: "We must become familiar with the outlook of our separated brethren. Study is absolutely required for this."[14]

Bi-lateral Consultations

For Catholics ecumenical contacts have been taking place since Vatican II on every level, theological and otherwise. In the theological area the ecumenical influences have been manifold, ranging from the reading of non-Catholic theology, local informal and formal theological discussions, and joint study of all kinds, to common theological institutional undertakings such as the exchange of professors or students, collaborative teaching and training of laity and clergy, and mutual research and publication projects. But in a very important way, all this ecumenical theological effort has come to focus, as far as the Eucharist and other previously theologically diverse issues are concerned, in the official bilateral consultations which have taken place since 1965. These consultations have been held on both national and international levels, sometimes once a year for a limited number of years, sometimes twice a year in ongoing fashion.[15] In surveying the reports and publications of the bi-laterals, one is immediately struck by the fact that a very large number of them spontaneously decided to deal with the questions of both ministry and Eucharist.

For Catholics the Eucharist obviously occupies a key place. Hence it is

---

[13]Pentecost Alleluia versicle in the traditional Roman liturgy.

[14]"Decree On Ecumenism," section 9.

[15]The following is a list of the bi-laterals dealing with the Eucharist that have involved Roman Catholics, and their major publications:

(1) Anglican-Roman Catholic (A-RC). Windsor, September, 1971, "Agreed Statement on Eucharistic Doctrine," *Documents on Anglican/Roman Catholic Relations* (Washington, DC: United States Catholic Conference, 1972), abbreviated as *ARC-DOC*.

(2) Anglican-Roman Catholic/Scotland (A-RC/sct). *The Ecclesial Nature of the Eucharist*, 1974. Order from J. S. Burns & Sons, 25 Finlas Street, Glasgow G22 5DS, Scotland.

(3) Anglican-Roman Catholic/USA (A-RC/usa). In *ARC-DOC*.

(4) Christian Church (Disciples)-Roman Catholic/USA (CC-RC/usa). St. Louis, April-May, 1968, "Responsible Theology for Eucharistic Communion in a Divided Church: Summary Memorandum," *Mid-Stream*, VII, 2 (1967-68): 90 f.

(5) Lutheran-Roman Catholic (L-RC). Malta, 1971, Final Report, "The Gospel and the Church," *Lutheran World*, XIX, 3 (1972): 270 ff.

(6) Lutheran-Roman Catholic/Philippines (L-RC/phil). "Progress Report to the Respective Churches on the Current LCP-RCCP Dialogue on the Holy Eucharist," 1972.

especially important for them to attempt to reach some accord on it with their ecumenical partners. But in turn a key element of the question about the authenticity of the Eucharist is the validity of the minister presiding at the Eucharist. Only a *yes* to the latter could provide a basis for a *yes* to the former, which in turn is a prerequisite to recommending a shared Eucharist, i.e., inter-communion.

An overview of the bi-lateral consultations reveals a quite startling general agreement in these neuralgic questions of ministry and Eucharist. The Consultation between the Disciples of Christ and Catholics expressed the situation simply: "We have discovered that our understandings of the Lord's Supper are more similar than we had expected."[16] The Lutheran-Catholic Consultation noted that, concerning the Eucharist as sacrifice and the real presence of Christ in the sacrament, two issues which have been "especially divisive in the past," they could agree that "we are no longer able to regard ourselves as divided in the one, holy, catholic, and apostolic faith on these two points."[17] The international Anglican-Roman Catholic Consultation expressed rather blandly a near total theological congruence: "We believe that we have reached substantial agreement on the doctrine of the Eucharist. . . . This doctrine will no longer constitute an obstacle to the unity we seek."[18]

In the more than a dozen bi-lateral consultations throughout the world that Catholic theologians have been engaged in since Vatican II and that have dealt with the Eucharist, the major topic areas are four: recognition of ministry, Eucharist as sacrifice, the real presence, and intercommunion. We will treat each of them very briefly.

---

(7) Lutheran-Roman Catholic/USA (L-RC/usa). *Lutherans and Catholics in Dialogue* (Washington, DC: United States Catholic Conference, 1967, 1970), vols. III and IV.

(8) Methodist-Roman Catholic (M-RC). "Report of the Joint Commission between the Roman Catholic Church and the World Methodist Council, 1967-1970," *Book of Proceedings of the Twelfth World Methodist Conference* (Nashville: The Methodist Publishing House, 1972).

(9) Old Catholic-Roman Catholic (OC-RC). "Protokolle der bisherigen Sitzungen der römisch-Katholische/altkatholischen Gesprächskommission in Deutschland," *Internationale Kirchliche Zeitschrift*, 61, 2 (1971): 75-78.

(10) Orthodox-Roman Catholic/USA (O-RC/usa). Worcester, MA: December, 1969, "An Agreed Statement on the Holy Eucharist," *Diakonia* 5 (1970): 72.

(11) Reformed-Roman Catholic (R-RC). Woudschoten/Zeist, February 1974, "Common Report."

(12) Roman Catholic-Presbyterian/Reformed in USA (RC-P/R/usa). "Ministry in the Church," *Journal of Ecumenical Studies* IX, 3 (Summer, 1972): 589-612.

(13) Reformed/Lutheran-Roman Catholic (R/L-RC). Les Dombes, France, September, 1971. "Accord doctrinal entre catholiques et protestantes sur l'Eucharistie," *Documentation catholique*, nr. 1606 (April 2, 1972), pp. 334-338.

From now on references to the above works will be by way of the parenthetical abbreviations above.

[16] CC-RC/usa.

[17] L-RC/usa, vol. III, p. 198.

[18] A-RC, "Windsor Statement," p. 50.

Recognition of Ministry

Bi-lateral consultations with three of the major church families of the Reformation dealt with the question of the ordained ministry. The Anglican-Roman Catholic Consultation USA stated that, after having studied the ordained ministry and its relationship to the common priesthood and the role of the laity, "there was no basic difference of understanding on these topics and that whatever minor differences of understanding did exist, they did not *in themselves* constitute the barrier to the two Churches celebrating and receiving communion together."[19] The consultors, including bishops on both sides, clearly were convinced of the authenticity of each other's ordained ministry and propriety of mutual recognition and then spoke of devising an effective means of moving the two churches to that action: "we now feel our next step in ARC should be to move on toward mutual recognition of ministry in a statement that we can forward to our respective church authorities for action."[20] That next step is still in the offing.

The second consultation treating the ordained ministry was the Roman Catholic-Presbyterian/Reformed Consultation in the U.S.A. The consultation was early concerned about eucharistic sharing and came thereby to realize that it could never solve that problem unless it first resolved the question of the recognition of the eucharistic minister. That matter was resolved when the consultation stated that, although it avoided the terms "validity" and "mutual recognition of orders" because they often connoted a mutual qualifying of ministers for official ministry in each other's church (to which the consultors did not want to commit themselves), they came "to the realization that Christ is operative, however differently, in the ministries of both churches, and further ask that this realization be publicly recognized. . . . We recommend . . . that proper steps be taken to have the appropriate organs of our respective churches at the highest level officially affirm in some appropriate way that Christ is present and at work in the ministries and Eucharist of each of our traditions."[21]

The Lutheran-Roman Catholic Consultation was the third bi-lateral that took up the question of the authenticity or validity of the eucharistic minister. The Lutherans had been concerned about what they saw as a vitiating separation of word and sacrament in the Roman tradition, but in the wake of Vatican II reforms found that concern met. Consequently they wrote, "We recommend to those who have appointed us that through appropriate channels the participating Lutheran churches be urged to declare formally their judgment that the ordained Ministers of the Roman Catholic church are engaged in a valid ministry."[22] The

---

[19] A-RC/usa, p. 11, issued in 1969.

[20] Ibid., p. 16.

[21] RC-P/R/usa, pp. 609, 911.

[22] L-RC/usa, vol. IV, p. 22.

Catholics noted that "in the history of the church there are instances of priests (i.e., presbyters) ordaining other priests, and there is evidence that the church accepted and recognized the ministry of priests so ordained."[23] They also wrote that because, "in the first two centuries of Christianity apostolic succession in doctrine (fidelity to the gospel) was considered more important than simple succession in office or orders . . . despite the lack of episcopal succession, the Lutheran church by its devotion to gospel, creed, and sacrament has preserved a form of doctrinal apostolicity."[24] In the end, the Catholic consultors insisted that "in our study we have found serious defects in the arguments customarily used against the validity of the eucharistic Ministry of the Lutheran churches. In fact, we see no persuasive reason to deny the possibility of the Roman Catholic church recognizing the validity of this Ministry. Accordingly, we ask the authorities of the Roman Catholic church whether the ecumenical urgency flowing from Christ's will for unity may not dictate that the Roman Catholic church recognize the validity of the Lutheran ministry."[25] Here there was no hesitation about either using the term validity or urging the mutual recognition of the validity of ministry.

Eucharist as Sacrifice

The notion of the Eucharist as a sacrifice has in the past been a very divisive point, especially between Catholics and Protestants. But again the dispute appears to have been resolved, and on an even broader scale than the matter of the recognition of ministries. The various participants of the several bi-laterals used much the same language to make similar points, namely, (1) the sacrifice of Christ is adequate and unrepeatable; (2) this sacrifice of Christ's extends not only to his death, but to the whole of his life; (3) though that sacrifice is unrepeatable, the Eucharist is the Church's celebration of Christ's sacrifice, making it present and sharable now; (4) that re-presenting is explained largely by the notions of sign and "memorial" (*anamnesis*).

(1) "Lutherans and Roman Catholics alike acknowledge that in the Lord's supper Christ is present as the Crucified who died for our sins and who rose again for our justification, as the once-for-all sacrifice for the sins of the world who gives himself to the faithful."[26] (Greatly broadening the breadth of agreement, the Lutheran-Catholic Consultation USA here quoted from the nine-church COCU statement,[27] which was later also adopted in the multi-lateral

---

[23]Ibid., p. 25.

[24]Ibid., pp. 26 f.

[25]Ibid., p. 32.

[26]Ibid., vol. III, p. 188.

[27]*Consultation on Church Union: Principles* (Cincinnati: Forward Movement Press, 1967), p. 50.

statement of the National Council of Churches.)[28]

(2) The Anglican-Roman Catholic Consultation wrote: "The sacrifice of the Holy Eucharist is not just the sacrifice of the Cross, but the sacrifice of Christ's whole life of obedience to the Father, which culminated in His death on the Cross and His glorious Resurrection."[29] A similar thought was expressed by the Roman Catholic-Presbyterian/Reformed Consultation: "The Eucharist . . . is the effective sign of Christ's gift of himself as the Bread of Life through his offering of his life and death and through his resurrection."[30]

(3) The World Methodist-Roman Catholic Consultation stated: "The Eucharist is the celebration of Christ's full, perfect and sufficient sacrifice, offered once and for all, for the whole world."[31] The Roman Catholic-Presbyterian/Reformed language was similar: "In the Eucharist the church celebrates the unrepeatable sacrifice of Christ and shares in its saving power."[32]

(4a) "The term 'sign,' once suspect, is again recognized as a positive term for speaking of Christ's presence in the sacrament. For, though symbols and symbolic action are used, the Lord's supper is an effective sign: it communicates what it promises."[33] "Communion with Christ in the Eucharist presupposes his true presence, effectually signified by the bread and wine which, in the mystery, become the Body and Blood."[34] "Bread and wine. . . . Within the Eucharistic celebration they become the sign *par excellence* of Christ's redeeming presence to His people. . . . They are therefore efficacious signs of the Body and Blood of Christ."[35]

(4b) "The Holy Eucharist is the memorial of the history of salvation, especially, the life, death, resurrection and glorification of Jesus Christ."[36] "Christ instituted the Eucharist as the memorial (*anamnesis*) of his whole life, especially his death and resurrection. . . . It is not merely a mental or spiritual recollection of a past event or its significance, but the proclamation-making-present the whole of God's great work in Christ Jesus, enabling the church through its fellowship with Christ to share in that reality."[37]

---

[28]"The Eucharist in the Life of the Church: An Ecumenical Consensus," *The Ecumenist* 8, 6 (September-October, 1970): 90-93.

[29]A-RC/usa, "ARC IV Statement on the Eucharist," May 29, 1967, p. 4.

[30]RC-P/R/usa, "The Unity We Seek. A Statement by the Roman Catholic Presbyterian Reformed Consultation," Washington, DC, May 24, 1975. P. 58 of ms.

[31]M-RC, nr. 84.

[32]RC-P/R/usa, "The Unity We Seek," p. 59 of ms.

[33]L-RC/usa, vol. III, pp. 192 f.

[34]A-RC/usa, nr. 6.

[35]M-RC, nr. 83. Cf. also the quotation for note 30, above.

[36]O-RC/usa, p. 72.

[37]RC-P/R/usa, "The Unity We Seek," p. 59 of ms. This wording was taken almost verbatim from the agreement composed by a group of Reformed, Lutheran, and Roman Catholic theologians meeting at the Trappist monastery in Les Dombes, France. See above, R-L-RC.

The illustrative quotations could be multiplied from the same and other consultations. What is striking is not only the number of different statements attesting to shared doctrines, but the constant repetition of almost the very same language, suggesting that in this key area of doctrine—previously so disputed— the shared understanding is not only broad, but also extraordinarily deep.

The Real Presence

In the past the presence of Christ in the Eucharist was also often a point of deep division. It is clear from the multiple bi-lateral consultations that this likewise is no longer the case.[38] All the consultation participants affirm a belief in the real presence of the risen Christ in the Eucharist: "We Catholics and Lutherans affirmed our agreement on the real presence and on the sacrificial character of the Lord's supper. . . . We affirm that in the sacrament of the Lord's supper Jesus Christ, true God and true man, is present wholly and entirely, in his body and blood, under the signs of bread and wine."[39] The international Anglican-Roman Catholic Consultation stated: "The elements are not mere signs; Christ's body and blood become really present and are really given."[40] "We [Presbyterians, Reformed, Catholics] profess, therefore, the real, living, active presence of Christ in this sacrament. . . . We are united in affirming in faith the mystery of Christ's real presence in the Lord's supper."[41]

One of the problems Protestants have perceived on the Catholic side was the apparent insistence on the doctrine of transubstantiation to explain the Real Presence. The Anglican-Roman Catholic Windsor statement settled the problem by stating, "The word transubstantiation . . . should be seen as affirming the *fact* of Christ's presence and of the mysterious and radical change which takes place. In contemporary Roman Catholic theology it is not understood as explaining *how* the change took place."[42] The Lutheran-Catholic Consultation had earlier utilized similar language when, after careful analysis, it concluded, "It can thus be seen that there is agreement on the 'that,' the full reality of Christ's presence. . . . Today when Lutheran theologians read contemporary Catholic expositions (Rahner and Schillebeeckx documented as examples), it becomes clear to them that the dogma of transubstantiation intends to affirm the fact of Christ's presence, and of the change which takes place, and is not an attempt to explain how Christ becomes present."[43]

One of the traditional concerns Catholics had with some Protestants was

---

[38] L-RC/usa, vol. IV, p. 27.

[39] Ibid., vol. III, p. 192.

[40] A-RC, p. 50.

[41] RC-P/R/usa, "The Unity We Seek," pp. 60 f.

[42] A-RC, p. 50.

[43] L-RC/usa, vol. III, p. 196.

that they seemed to make Christ's presence dependent on the faith of the
believers. That concern was met thus: "The presence of Christ does not come
about through the faith of the believer, or through any human power, but by the
power of the Holy Spirit through the word."[44] "The real presence of Christ in
the Eucharist, however, does not depend upon the belief of each individual but
on the power of Christ's word."[45]

Again, illustrative quotations on the eucharistic presence could be easily
multiplied. Let these suffice to indicate that agreement here is broad, deep, and
pervasive.

Intercommunion

Quite naturally many of the consultations came to discuss the possibility of
shared Eucharist, or intercommunion, but not all did. As mentioned above, the
Roman Catholic relationship with the Orthodox is a sort of inversion of its
relationship with the other Christian traditions. Here the Catholics recommend
shared Eucharist, but the Orthodox reject it for a variety of reasons. In Western
Christianity the Windsor statement on the Eucharist expressed basic Anglican-
Roman Catholic agreement, but left the question for a later time. The American
A-RC V (January, 1968) "concluded that there was no basic difference of understanding on these topics [doctrine of the Eucharist and role of the ordained
priesthood] and that whatever minor differences of understanding did exist,
they did not *in themselves* constitute the barrier to the two Churches celebrating
and receiving communion together."[46] However, after that the two chairpersons
(bishops) agreed that there were other barriers to intercommunion and that
"precipitous action by this group at this time would not be to the advantage of
the whole Church."[47] Almost two years later in A-RC VII the consultation
listed a range of non-eucharistic topics wherein agreement would have to be
reached before even partial eucharistic communion could be considered.[48]

The American Lutheran-Catholic Consultation also took a conservative
stand on intercommunion: "We have not discussed the implications that a recognition of valid Ministry would have for intercommunion or eucharistic sharing.
Obviously recognition of valid Ministry and sharing the eucharistic table are
intimately related, but we are not in a position to affirm that the one must or
should lead to the other."[49] They did not subsequently take up the subject.

However, a number of the consultations treated the question of intercom-

---

[44] Ibid., p. 193.

[45] RC-P/R/usa, "The Unity We Seek," p. 60.

[46] A-RC/usa, p. 11.

[47] *One In Christ* IV, 3 (1968): 299 f.

[48] A-RC/usa, p. 17.

[49] L-RC/usa, vol. IV, p. 33.

munion affirmatively. The Disciples of Christ-Catholic consultation stated that "we have found sufficient theological justification in *principle* for some eucharistic sharing . . . [to] make some eucharistic sharing desirable";[50] to date, however, they have not progressed further on the matter. The international Lutheran-Catholic Consultation carried the position of the above-discussed American Lutheran-Catholic statement considerably further by stating that, "At the present it should already be recommended that the Church authorities, on the basis of what is already shared in faith and sacrament and as a sign and anticipation of the promised and hoped for unity, make possible occasional acts of intercommunion as, for example, during ecumenical events or in the pastoral care of those involved in mixed marriages."[51] The Roman Catholic-Presbyterian/ Reformed Consultation made a like recommendation: "Serious divisions remain between Roman Catholics and Reformed Christians, divisions serious enough to preclude *general* eucharistic sharing for the present. Nevertheless . . . we therefore recommend to the ecclesiastical authorities to whom we are responsible the implementation of such *limited eucharistic sharing*."[52] The same consultation four years later, in 1976, reiterated that recommendation, insisting that in their judgment this request is grounded "on the basis that the Eucharist is a source of unifying grace for the divided pilgrim church on its journey toward oneness in Christ."[53] They also went on to chide Rome mildly for not living up to that principle enunciated in the "Decree on Ecumenism" of Vatican II: "Remarkable is the fact that Roman Catholic documents avoid, though they do not deny, application of the principle that the Eucharist is the cause of the grace which unites the church as well as the expression of that grace of unity."[54]

Thus it is apparent that, with the exception of the Orthodox, there is a general willingness on the part of the non-Catholic partners to move forward on the matter of shared Eucharist; even most of the Catholic participants seem similarly oriented. The resistance apparently comes from Rome.

Conclusion

Although *de facto* intercommunion has been taking place on a broad scale for years,[55] it is not something that can be advocated as a solution to the problem. In the end, the church laws will have to be changed. Otherwise, after the enthusiasm of the time passes, future Christians will continue to suffer from the old divisions. It is clear that on the level of national bishops' conferences,

---

[50] CC-RC/usa, p. 90.

[51] L-RC, nr. 73.

[52] RC-P/R/usa, p. 610.

[53] RC-P/R/usa, "The Unity We Seek," p. 67.

[54] Ibid., pp. 81 f.

[55] See RC-P/R/usa, p. 609, for an extensive bibliography dealing with *de facto* intercommunion.

strong actions could be taken, both on their own and vis-à-vis Rome. The Swiss Bishop's Conference provided one example of such action in a 1975 instruction which noted that if in following one's conscience a Catholic receives the Eucharist from a Protestant minister without a "valid" sacrament of orders, "this step should not be interpreted as necessarily implying a rupture with his own church, even though common sharing of the Eucharist remains problematical as long as the separation of the churches continues."[56] Even bolder, the Committee for Christian Unity of the French bishops issued a document in 1975 which accepts the possibility of limited intercommunion with Protestants and notes that it is the responsibility of the local bishop to exercise discretion in particular cases.[57]

The other bishops' conferences need to be encouraged, petitioned, and challenged also to act vigorously. Ecumenical groups could effectively approach them; so could bodies of theologians, such as the Catholic Theological Society of America, the College Theology Society, ad hoc groups such as the Ecumenical Conference of the Eucharistic Congress, special committees of the American Academy of Religion, joint committees of university theology departments, research institutes, and the like. These same bodies might also consider simultaneously approaching the Vatican, local bishops, pastoral councils, etc.

The example of Bishop Elchinger of Strasbourg might suggest similar actions that other individual Catholic bishops could contemplate: as of late 1972, under specific conditions, couples of mixed marriages in his diocese were permitted occasional reciprocal sharing in each other's Eucharists.[58] It should be noted that in December, 1973, the regional Lutheran church reciprocated Bishop Elchinger's action, and that Rome has not repudiated the action. Furthermore, Bishop Schmitt of Metz, as of July 10, 1973, permitted certain Catholics of his diocese to share the Protestant Eucharists "under the conditions anticipated in the Directives of the Bishop of Strasbourg, Msgr. Elchinger."[59] Again, local bishops should be encouraged and petitioned to act by the above-mentioned and other groups, such as parishes, and also by individuals.

On the congregational level the spread of covenanting parishes between Roman Catholic congregations on the one hand and Episcopalian or Lutheran congregations on the other has given a vivid example of what might be done. On the basis of thorough study of the supportive documents of the pertinent bilateral consultations, their extensive institutional and other collaborations, and joint prayer life, at least one set of Episcopalian-Roman Catholic and one of Lutheran-Roman Catholic covenanting parishes formally petitioned their local bishops and Rome for permission for shared Eucharist.[60] They were turned

---

[56]*Documentation catholique*, nr. 1677 (1975), pp. 529-531.

[57]Ibid., nr. 1669 (1975), pp. 126-129.

[58]Cf. "Reports and Documentation," *Lutheran World* 22 (1975): 151.

[59]*One In Christ* 9, 4 (1973): 371-387. See above, Avery Dulles' essay for further discussion of the matter.

[60]Write to the Bishops Committee on Ecumenical and Interreligious Affairs, 1312 Massachusetts Ave., Washington, DC 20005, for documents on covenanting parishes.

down, but if this sort of serious, responsible parochial action were sufficiently multiplied, it certainly would have a profound, concrete effect. Even fewer than a hundred such serious petitions would certainly precipitate action.

A limited eucharistic sharing will be only a step on the way to full Christian unity, but it is a necessary step, and the next one.

Study and Discussion Questions

1. How does the officially mandated attitude of Roman Catholics toward *communicatio in sacris* with non-Catholics before Vatican II compare with that after the Council?
2. Compare the official Catholic position on shared Eucharist with Orthodox Christians and with Protestants. Why the difference? What has been the response to both?
3. Why does the author think the bi-lateral consultations are so important?
4. What sorts of agreements have been reached on the sacrificial nature of the Eucharist, the Real Presence, and intercommunion? With whom?
5. In what areas of eucharistic teaching and practice are further study and discussion still needed? Are they of primary or secondary importance?
6. What implication does the fact that some Lutheran, Episcopal, and Reformed churches have intercommunion with each other have for the question of intercommunion between them and the Roman Catholic Church?
7. Where does the author think the source of the non-implementation of the Vatican II Decree on shared Eucharist lies? Do you agree?
8. What are the practical steps the author suggests on the various levels? Are they feasible?
9. What are the specific concrete steps YOU are going to take now?